Modern Theatre in Russia

Related Titles

Russian Theatre in Practice: The Director's Guide
Edited by Amy Skinner
9781474284417

The Sixth Sense of the Avant-Garde: Dance, Kinaesthesia and the Arts in Revolutionary Russia
Irina Sirotkina and Roger Smith
9781350087408

The Great European Stage Directors Set 1: Volumes 1–4: Pre-1950
Edited by Simon Shepherd
9781474254113

The Great European Stage Directors Set 2: Volumes 5–8: Post-1950
Edited by Simon Shepherd
9781474254168

Modern Theatre in Russia

Tradition Building and Transmission Processes

Stefan Aquilina

methuen | drama
LONDON • NEW YORK • OXFORD • NEW DELHI • SYDNEY

METHUEN DRAMA
Bloomsbury Publishing Plc
50 Bedford Square, London, WC1B 3DP, UK
1385 Broadway, New York, NY 10018, USA
29 Earlsfort Terrace, Dublin 2, Ireland

BLOOMSBURY, METHUEN DRAMA and the Methuen Drama logo
are trademarks of Bloomsbury Publishing Plc

First published in Great Britain 2020
This paperback edition published in 2022

Copyright © Stefan Aquilina, 2020

Stefan Aquilina has asserted his right under the Copyright, Designs
and Patents Act, 1988, to be identified as the author of this work.

For legal purposes the Acknowledgements on pp. viii-ix constitute
an extension of this copyright page.

Cover design by Louise Dugdale
Cover images © iStock / Shutterstock

All rights reserved. No part of this publication may be reproduced or transmitted
in any form or by any means, electronic or mechanical, including photocopying,
recording, or any information storage or retrieval system, without
prior permission in writing from the publishers.

Bloomsbury Publishing Plc does not have any control over, or responsibility for,
any third-party websites referred to or in this book. All internet addresses given
in this book were correct at the time of going to press. The author and publisher
regret any inconvenience caused if addresses have changed or sites have
ceased to exist, but can accept no responsibility for any such changes.

A catalogue record for this book is available from the British Library.

A catalog record for this book is available from the Library of Congress.

ISBN: HB: 978-1-3500-6608-3
       PB: 978-1-3502-4667-6
     ePDF: 978-1-3500-6610-6
    eBook: 978-1-3500-6609-0

Typeset by Integra Software Service Pvt. Ltd.

To find out more about our authors and books visit www.bloomsbury.com
and sign up for our newsletters.

Contents

List of illustrations	vii
Acknowledgements	viii
Translation credits and a note on transliteration	x

1 Introduction — 1
- Modern theatre and the problem of continuity — 1
- Lines of continuity in the Russian theatre tradition — 5
- Implications to tradition building — 14
  - Milestone, stagnation and renewal — 14
  - A concerted effort — 16
- Cultural transmission — 17
- Chapter summaries — 21
- Suggestions for practice — 25
  - Note on the practical exercises — 25
  - Transmission exercise and belts — 25

2 Stanislavsky: Renewing tradition through transmission — 29
- Renewing theatre traditions — 29
- Scenic Transmission: The case of Ludwig Barnay — 34
- The First Studio: An example of Democratic Levelling — 41
- Rehearsal Transmission: Stanislavsky's work on *Artists and Admirers* — 47
- The international dimension of the Stanislavsky acting tradition — 53
- Conclusion — 61
- Suggestions for practice — 61
  - The Gorky Method — 61

3 Misinterpretation of theatre practice: Stanislavsky-Smyshlaev — 63
- Why cultural transmission? — 63
- Smyshlaev's diary: January–December 1917 — 66
- Theatre references in Smyshlaev's diary — 70
- The Stanislavsky-Smyshlaev rift: Collective creation — 74
- The use of improvisation — 80
- Work processes in *The Technique to Process Stage Performance* — 83

	Conclusion	88
	Suggestions for practice	89
	From individual to group work	89
4	**Amateur and proletarian theatre in post-revolutionary Russia**	**97**
	Aesthetics and theatricality on the amateur stage	97
	Historiographical difficulties	105
	Transmission point 1: Critical processing	113
	Transmission point 2: Collective creation and independent action – from the studio to everyday life	118
	Insurrection as an example of proletarian theatre	125
	Conclusion	130
	Suggestions for practice	132
	Amateur aesthetics and collective practices	132
	Political scenarios and improvisation	134
5	**Meyerhold: Bias in transmission processes**	**135**
	Researching Meyerhold: From bias to myth-making	135
	Recurrence and difference in Meyerhold's work	139
	Meyerhold's rediscovery of past traditions	143
	The Borodin Studio as an instance of Practice as Research	148
	The Meyerhold Theatre's foreign tour of 1930	154
	Meyerhold's internationalism discerned from Western newspapers	160
	Suggestions for practice	167
	Introducing Meyerhold's theatricality	167
	'Expressing thoughts spatially'	169
6	**Lesser-known names: Rediscovering female voices**	**171**
	The status of women in early Soviet Russia	171
	Contributions of female artists	174
	The case of Asja Lācis	180
	Conclusion	190
	Axioms about modern theatre in Russia	190
	Organizational principles when running transmission workshops	192
Notes		194
References		209
Index		222

List of illustrations

1	Meyerhold with his actors after a performance of Ostrovsky's *The Forest* (1924).	13
2	Konstantin Stanislavsky in the 1920s.	30
3	Ludwig Barnay playing the title role in *Uriel Acosta*.	37
4	Vasily Kachalov in the role of Narokov, in the Moscow Art Theatre's production of Ostrovsky's *Artists and Admirers*, 1933.	48
5	Valentin Smyshlaev.	65
6	I. V. Lazarev in the role of Boss, in the First Studio production of *The Wreck of the Ship 'Hope'*, 1913.	72
7	A poster of the Blue Blouse.	101
8	Cover image of the journal *Rabochii i teatr* (*Worker and Theatre*).	131
9	Meyerhold with composer Sergey Prokofiev and painter and set designer Alexander Tyshler, during a rehearsal of Prokofiev's opera *Semyon Kotko*, 1939.	137
10	Meyerhold's actors training in the 1920s.	146
11	Vsevolod Meyerhold working with Zinaida Raikh during the rehearsals of *The Government Inspector*, 1926.	162
12	A scene from *The Magnanimous Cuckold*, directed by Vsevolod Meyerhold, set by Lyubov Popova, 1922.	180

Acknowledgements

This book has been in gestation for about three years. Many have contributed in their own way to the project, offering advice and encouragement. Gratitude needs to be extended to the various institutions who have hosted my work in the last few years. First among these is the Department of Theatre Studies of the School of Performing Arts (University of Malta) where I work, and which I now call my second home. At this school I am fortunate to work with a fantastic group of colleagues, especially Vicki Ann Cremona, Frank Camilleri, Mario Frendo, Marco Galea and Lucía Piquero, whom I would like to thank for their support. The University of Malta has also supported this research by granting me sabbatical leave and by means of the various research grants it offers through its Research Grant Committee. I would also like to thank students in Malta with whom many of the exercises given here were attempted. Their feedback was valuable to fine-tune the exercises.

Other institutions that hosted my research were the School of Performance and Cultural Industries (University of Leeds), the Department of Music, Theatre and Performing Arts (University of Otago), through its Williams Evans Fellowship, The Oxford Research in the Humanities (University of Oxford), and the Moore Institute (National University of Ireland, Galway), through the Ros Dixon Fellowship. At these institutions Maria Kapsali, George Rodosthenous, Joslin McKinney, Susan Little, Stuart Young, Hilary Halba, Philip Bullock, Julie Curtis and Elizabeth Tilley have been particularly generous with their time and feedback. I remain particularly indebted to Jonathan Pitches, of the University of Leeds, and Paul Fryer, of the Stanislavsky Research Centre, for their continued support and friendship. I would also like to thank the team at Methuen Drama, especially Mark Dudgeon and Susan Furber, who immediately saw value in the project, and Lara Bateman for her meticulous work during production. I would also like to thank James Moffett, Franklyn Cauchi, Sergei Tcherkasski and Victoria Ysotskaya, for their various contributions to the project.

My thanks are also extended to Laurence Senelick, who delivered the keynote speech at the fourth edition of The S Word Stanislavsky Symposium held in Malta in April 2019. The symposium was co-convened by myself and Paul Fryer. Prof. Senelick was very generous in sharing several of the pictures printed here. For this and more, I thank him wholeheartedly.

Finally, this project would not have been possible without the love and support which my family unconditionally give me on a daily basis. This book is dedicated to them: to my wife Yulia, and our two boys, Matthew and Daniel.

Every effort has been made to trace copyright holders of all copyright material in this book. Any omissions brought to my attention will be rectified in future editions.

Translation credits and a note on transliteration

Avatar Ltd.
Anrusenko, S. (2004; sections of); Kerzhentsev (1918a), (1918b), (1918c), (1918d), (1919a) (1919b), (1919c); Lunacharsky (1919); Pletnev (1919), (1924); Gorky (1955; sections of); Vinogradskaia (2000; sections of), (2003; sections of).

Maria Kabanova
Smyshlaev (1918), (1919); Stanislavskii (1958; sections of), (1959; sections of).

Natalia Fedorova
Picon-Vallin (1992); Smyshliaev (1922; sections of); Ilinsky (1962; sections of).

Larissa Dold
Barnay (1913; sections of); Lācis (1971; sections of).

All other translations, from Russian, Italian and French, are the author's. I would also like to thank Yulia Belozerova for her assistance in checking some translation details.

Names have been translated in ways that are easily apprehended by an English-speaking reader. Therefore, the spelling of names already familiar in English (e.g. Stanislavsky, Meyerhold, Chekhov) has been retained. Laurence Senelick's volume *Stanislavsky – A Life in Letters* (2014) was a useful source for transliterating names.

1

Introduction

Modern theatre and the problem of continuity

In a 1912 essay titled 'Russian Dramatists', theatre director Vsevolod Meyerhold spoke about the central role which the repertoire plays in the creation of a theatre tradition. Using Spanish and French theatres as examples, he argued that a tradition of playwriting is formed when a large number of exponents, beyond, in these cases, the canonical names of Lope de Vega, Calderón and Molière, congregate together on shared aesthetical and ethical grounds:

> We know the French theatre of the seventeenth century because it bequeathed us a splendid collection of texts by Molière.
> This is not simply a matter of the talented abilities of the masters of drama I have cited [and reproduced above].
> The repertory came into being as an individual entity, an aggregation of plays united by a *common intellectual schema* and *common technical devices*. (in Senelick 1981: 200; emphasis added)

Meyerhold opens further on what these intellectual schemas and technical devices are, invoking in turn the performance pillars of content and form. In the case of Spain, for example, the content or 'ideological plane' was informed by nationalism, while its 'technical plane' displayed 'one task: to concentrate the rapidly unfolding action into *intrigue*' (201; emphasis in original). French theatre exhibited its own form and content, but beyond such contextual specificities, it is the evidence of recurrent elements in practices authored by different practitioners that Meyerhold signals as the first condition for tradition building.

That in this essay Meyerhold focused on tradition building should come as no surprise, considering how Russian theatre at the turn of the twentieth century was questioning the relative merits of theatre traditions in general and of its Russian manifestation in particular. My aim is to unpick some of these questions and to use the modern critique of the Russian theatre tradition, of which Meyerhold was an integral part, to discuss how theatre traditions are established. Different to Meyerhold's 1912 emphasis on the repertoire, however, my focus will be on transmission approaches, i.e. the processes (including training, rehearsal, performance, documentation, diaries and newspaper reports) through which theatre and performance practices get transformed when they move between individuals and communities of theatre makers. The point that I will return to with some consistency is that there is a tight connection between tradition building and transmission processes because it is also through the latter that theatre traditions are formed and consolidated.

My focus therefore will be on Russian theatre during the first decades of the twentieth century, a period which is often referred to as an example of 'modern theatre' or 'modernism in the theatre'. This is a period when theatre practitioners were particularly aware of their position vis-à-vis past theatre traditions, in relation to which they articulated a position of either continuity or detachment and criticism. However, before I go any further, I would like to expand on what constitutes 'modern theatre' as this is a major through line that binds together the various case studies in the book. Issues of what 'modern' is and of 'modernism' remain, as Jane Milling and Graham Ley assert, 'critically fraught topics' (Milling and Ley 2001: vii), a result perhaps of an unfortunate whitewashing together of related but not analogous terms like 'modernism' itself, 'modernist' or even 'modernity'. Consequently, though practitioners and theoreticians like Meyerhold, Konstantin Stanislavsky, Antonin Artaud, Adolphe Appia, Rudolph Laban, Jacques Copeau and Bertolt Brecht are readily associated with turn-of-the-twentieth-century modernism, what modernism is remains problematic. Symptomatic of this confusion is the way that 'modern theatre' has entered non-specialized discourse to refer to the contemporary theatre scene; see, for example, how Robert Leach uses it to refer to 'the theatre of today' (Leach 2004: 1). A similar straightforward use is also evident in Robert Russell and Andrew Barratt's introduction to their edited volume on *Russian Theatre in the Age of Modernism* (1990), where 'modern' and 'modernist' are adopted as direct variations of 'modernism'. The book's use of 'the *Age* of Modernism' (emphasis added) in the title seems to give a temporal definition to modernism (the years between 1900 and 1940), and the term is then modified in the narrative to 'modern Russian theatre' and 'Russian modernist theatre' (Russell and Barratt 1990: vii and ix).

While nuanced definitions of modern and modernism are probably counterproductive to Russell and Barratt's multi-authored perspective and, therefore, possibly unnecessary, the terms 'modernity', 'modern' and 'modernism' are here central to underscore the role of *continuity* in tradition building.

Processes of continuity are startlingly present in modernity. Punctuated by the massive social, political, technological and philosophical upheavals associated with the end of feudalism, the Enlightenment and the Industrial Revolution, modernity indicates the protracted 'process of transformation [...] which refers to a long historical process of becoming "modern"' (Wallace 2011: 16). The term goes beyond culture and the arts to embrace the widest spectrum of human activities possible. Modernism, on the other hand, is more restrictive in its remit and collates the contributions made by the arts towards this process of becoming modern. It is a section or part of modernity (Jeff Wallace refers to it as an 'episode'), one which can be located with some surety between the Romantic period and the Second World War and its aftermath.

Rather than focusing on the identification of precise start and end points, an alternative way to define modernism is by identifying recurrent characteristics across a wide tapestry of practices at the turn of the twentieth century. Many writers underline experimentation and anti-conservatism as defining features of modern art, with Bert Cardullo describing modernism as 'a period of dramatic innovation [...] when the sense of a fundamental break with inherited means of representation and expression became acute' (Cardullo 2013: 3).[1] Experimentation in both form and content of performance is certainly not unique to the early 1900s, but modernism indicates that the performing arts at the turn of the twentieth century were particularly experimental in nature. In underlining this experimental attitude modernism is invariably brought in conflict with an alternative but equally common way of articulating early twentieth-century theatre, that of the 'avant-garde'. This is the appellation which Robert C. Williams (1977) uses to group together experimental Russian theatre of the 1905–1925 time frame. The material which Williams covers includes Meyerhold, Vladimir Mayakovsky, Sergei Eisenstein, Kazimir Malevich and Vladimir Tatlin, artists which he frames around a definition of the avant-garde as a 'conjunction of artistic innovation and revolutionary involvement' (Williams 1977: 3). Notwithstanding his centrality to the scene, Stanislavsky's name is absent from Williams's study, hinting that his name is synonymous with modernism and modern theatre but not with the avant-garde.[2] In fact, while artistic innovation was clearly a driving force in Stanislavsky's work (see Chapter 2), his revolutionary, read political, involvement remained, at best, peripheral. As will be made evident in the pages that follow, Stanislavsky's role in the transmission of the Russian theatre tradition in the early twentieth century and beyond was a central one, and I therefore use the terms 'modern theatre' and 'modernism' over 'avant-garde' to weave Stanislavsky into this study.

The use of 'modernism' and 'modern' over 'avant-garde' also helps me to start untangling my central theme of continuity. While Cardullo's words above speak of modernism as a fundamental break with the past, the fact remains that modern theatre in Russia developed on what I refer to as strong 'lines of continuity'. These lines connect the late 1920s to the years between the revolutions of 1905 and 1917 (also known as the Silver Age of Russian Theatre). They also hark back to the practices which started to develop, roughly speaking, during the mid-nineteenth century, an era in Russian theatre and the arts known as the Golden Age. This continuity contrasts with the supposed discontinuity postulated after the revolution by the most extreme voices of the avant-garde. Among those who proclaimed independence from past artistic practices were the Proletkult – a non-government organization formed on the eve of the October Revolution which tasked itself with the creation of proletarian culture (see Chapter 4) and the 'leftists', artists loyal to the revolution who placed faith in theatre's potential to rebuild everyday life on scientific and technological principles. Both boldly 'declared earlier art to be dead' (Kleberg 1993: 4). These extreme statements were, however, carefully articulated as radical declarations to provoke and garner attention. Writing in a very direct tone, avant-garde artists employed the rhetoric of short manifestos or newspaper articles that barred the development of reasoned argumentation.[3] Their extreme voices for rupture with the past were, however, countered by a set of equally strong calls demanding continuity, made by individuals who in the artistic practices of the previous generations found much that was useful. Instead of consigning practices to the past, these voices – who included strong political leaders like Alexander Bogdanov[4] and Vladimir Lenin – arbitrated for a process of transmission, i.e. the displacement of past theatre techniques and their assimilation within modern milieus. Strongest among these voices was Anatoly Lunacharsky, the first Soviet People's Commissar of Education who, in a direct criticism of the Proletkult, asserted the need for continuity with the past:

> In the area of art, we must never, under any circumstance, let the proletariat be ignorant of all the wonderful products of human genius.
>
> [But,] [t]here are people who believe that any distribution of 'old' science and 'old' art is an indulgence of bourgeois tastes, a cultural curse, and the contamination of the young socialist organism with the blood of rotting junk.
>
> There are relatively few radical representatives of this delusion. However, the harm which they bring could be great. [...] No, I repeat for the thousandth time that the proletariat must be *armed with the entirety of human education*. The proletariat is a historical class. It must go forward because of its past.

To discard the science and art of the past because of their bourgeois roots is as absurd as dropping machines in the factories or railways because of the same reason. (Lunacharsky 1919: 2; emphasis in original)

In other words, voices of discontinuity were part of the modern scene without, however, defining it. They would ultimately be crushed, but this tug of war between continuity and discontinuity does point towards a crucial characteristic of modern theatre in Russia, namely that it defined its position in relation to the Russian theatre tradition and that it did so through the lines of continuity which I will discuss below. This is one of a tripartite of characteristics – the other two being the time frame (from 1898 to about 1932-4) and experimentation – that qualify modern theatre in Russia as understood here.

Lines of continuity in the Russian theatre tradition

Strictly speaking, my story starts with the opening of the Moscow Art Theatre (MAT) and develops over the first three decades of the twentieth century. However, it is necessary to go beyond these time frames, at least in this Introduction, because modern theatre in Russia must be viewed against the backdrop of important trends that had been developing in Russia from the mid-nineteenth century onwards. Names such as Nikolai Gogol, Alexander Ostrovsky and Mikhail Shchepkin far from disappeared from theatre consciousness, and modern practitioners like Stanislavsky and, perhaps surprisingly, even Meyerhold, Yevgeny Vakhtangov, Alexander Tairov, Fyodor (Theodore) Komissarzhevsky and others, appraised them in challenging and fresh ways. The lines of continuity, of perhaps different thicknesses and visibilities, which cut across the Russian theatre tradition, can be articulated as follows:

- dates and artists living across different historical eras;
- a moral dimension to theatre;
- a debate surrounding realism;
- the concept of authorship;
- modern staging of nineteenth-century texts.

On the simplest of levels, a degree of continuity emerges from a quick survey of the dates. A lot is sometimes made of the fact, for example, that Stanislavsky was born in the same year that Shchepkin died (1863).[5] Stanislavsky's connection to Shchepkin is easy to discern, and it is on this connection that one link between the nineteenth and the twentieth centuries rests. Stanislavsky himself articulated on several occasions his position vis-à-vis Shchepkin's heritage, especially during various MAT anniversaries (e.g. see Whyman 2008: 30). Beyond the polite statements characteristic of such celebrations, Stanislavsky made Shchepkin's tenet of living rather than representing the role the foundation of his System.[6] In his correspondence with P. V. Annenkov, Shchepkin voraciously emphasized the need to back up one's intuition and natural talent with study and hard work (in Schumacher 1998: 195–6). It is this balance that Stanislavsky strove to achieve through his 'from the conscious to the unconscious' dictum. Less known but equally compelling are the positive appraisals of modern practitioners who, though far removed from Shchepkin's aesthetics, still felt the need to go back to his teachings and treat these as the basics. For example, Laurence Senelick says that Vakhtangov 'prescribed Shchepkin's habits of working on a role to his students' (Senelick 1984: 251). Little acknowledged is Fyodor Komissarzhevsky's debt to Shchepkin. This he himself articulated in a 1913 essay in which he asserted the similarity between his approaches and Stanislavsky's, both of which 'are to a greater or lesser extent derived from Mikhail Shchepkin' (Komissarzhevsky quoted in Borovsky 2001: 277). Meyerhold, on his part, drew a line from his production of *The Government Inspector* (1926) back to Shchepkin's work, adding that he consciously followed the path suggested by the great actor (Malcovati 1977: 263). Gogol proved another reference point, and *The Government Inspector* kept its position as a key performance text.[7] Ultimately, the government made direct links with the past a matter of ideological importance, through its 'Return to Ostrovsky' policy (1923), which encouraged theatre artists to adopt the playwright's critical disposition towards social realities (Rudnitsky 1988: 116–18).[8] Against the background of such political appropriation, Meyerhold's statement linking his work to Shchepkin and Gogol was laden with artistic significance but also transformed into a political defence mechanism.

A further level of continuity is provided by a number of practitioners who lived long enough to experience different historical eras and who remembered, for example, the coronation of Tsar Nicholas II (1896). They often juxtaposed that era to the war with Japan, the revolution of 1905, the First World War, the February and October Revolutions, the Civil War years, the NEP years, and the late 1920s and early 1930s. Stanislavsky described these decades as a transition from serfdom to Bolshevism and Communism (Stanislavski 2008a: 3). Vladimir Nemirovich-Danchenko similarly juxtaposed the two eras of pre- and post-revolutionary Russia and underwrites, by accident more than by design, how such transitional moments exhibit a tension between structure and repetition on one side and improvisation and change on the other. Taking Maxim Gorky's *The Lower Depths* as an example, he argues that

> [i]n the same theatre, between the same walls, the same play would be played; even the majority of the actors would be the same [...] while the decorations and the *mise en scène* would also remain the same, untouched by the quarter-of-a century evolution of theatrical art; in a word, the performance would not show the slightest change. Only the audience would change – unrecognizably. It would become wholly new. (Nemirovich-Danchenko 1936: 244)

Other prominent practitioners who bridged the two eras included Meyerhold, who needed little persuasion to update his practices with a new, industrial terminology, and symbolists like Vyacheslav Ivanov and Andrei Bely, who also 'sought to place their [pre-1917] theories at the service of the revolution' (Worrall 2008: 8). A further example is that of Nikolai Evreinov, who did emigrate to the West in 1925 but not before building on his earlier experiments in retrospectivism and monodrama by staging in 1920 the mass spectacle *The Storming of the Winter Palace*.[9] More than discarding their pre-revolutionary findings, these practitioners sought to adapt to a different context, a different audience and, in many cases, different collaborators coming from the young generation spawned by the revolution.

A recurrent concern for a moral dimension to theatre provided a strong line of continuity within the Russian theatre tradition. As Lars Kleberg says (1993: 4), the idea of art for art's sake never had any real footing in Russia, as practitioners and theoreticians consistently underlined the enriching and developmental potential of theatre. Sure, what 'enriching' and 'developmental' meant changed from generation to generation and even from one individual to the next, but it is clear that theatre in Russia was consistently treated not only as a form of amusement and entertainment but also as an influential means of education. Victor Borovsky refers to the developmental role of theatre as 'a ceaseless effort to enlighten [...] audiences' (Borovsky in Leach and Borovsky 1999: 10), while Nick Worrall refers to theatre as a 'high-minded, moral and educative cultural form' (Worrall 2008: 1). Jean Benedetti, on his part, described the Russian stage as 'a moral instrument, whose function is to civilise, to increase sensitivity, to heighten perception' (Benedetti 1989: 11). Theatre practice in Russia, therefore, was not a frivolous activity, meaning that all-too-clear business ventures that aimed at profit-making were consistently seen with suspicion. To people like Gogol, Ostrovsky and Shchepkin, but also Ivanov, Meyerhold, Stanislavsky, Lunacharsky, Platon Kerzhentsev and the Proletkultists, theatre was a serious art form that needed to be treated with the required attention, in the writing of its plays, the acting and production processes developed, the theories composed, and also in the audience's reception.

What the moral dimension of theatre amounted to was intimately linked with the surrounding sociopolitical context. The political upheavals of the nineteenth century – which included the Napoleonic Wars, the lost Crimean War in 1856, the 1861 emancipation of the serfs and the 1881 assassination of Alexander II – led to a considerable amount of inward-looking examination by the Russian intelligentsia, who became preoccupied with Russia's roots and its contemporary moral fibre, what Cynthia Marsh refers to as 'Russianness'. Consequently, nineteenth-century authors like Aleksei Potekhin, Aleksei Pisemsky and Lev Tolstoy were concerned with 'an examination of Russian society, her history, her customs, and her people' (Marsh in Borovsky and Leach 1999: 146; see also 148). Senelick uses the word *narodnost'*, a term coined as early as the late eighteenth century by the critic Pyotr Plavilshchikov to refer to a sense of 'national quality' to which 'all serious Russian writing about drama addresses itself in one way or another throughout the nineteenth century' (Senelick 1981: xvii).

The emphasis on 'what it means to be Russian' is also evident in Murray Frame's analysis of nineteenth-century society and theatre. Frame identifies the rise of civil societies – formal but independent institutions like learned societies, theatres and printing circles set up to provide opportunities for cultural growth – as an important catalyst in the 'efforts to define and assert Russian national identity as a means of binding society together' (Frame 2006: 6). Parallel to the national line, however, Frame also notices a more 'individualist' articulation of theatre's moral dimension, one which drew from the rise of a strong middle class and the value it placed not on birth but on personal achievement. Instead of focusing on general and all-encompassing issues of Russianness, this line focused more on the question of 'what it means to be an individual human being'. It is within such questioning that Anton Chekhov can, for example, be situated. Incorporated within this second line of moral theatre is a person's intricate relationships with the world and people around him.

A concern with how human beings relate to each other and the world around them lends a strong ethical undercurrent to theatre practice, especially when one treats ethics as *communal ethics*, i.e. 'how we organise the ways in which we live with one another' (Ridout 2009: 12). This 'communal organisation' took a more mystical tone during the Silver Age, when the developmental potential of theatre was seen an opportunity to put 'the audience of nonartists in touch with the higher realm' (Senelick 1981: xl). Ivanov was the main theorist for this theatre. His conception of a communal theatre that brings performers and spectators together in ecstatic involvement proved to be infectious both to the Symbolists of the Silver Age and to the communal fervour sparked by the revolution, effectively creating a continuous link between the two periods. As mentioned above, Ivanov's theories were not immediately forgotten. He went on to work at the TEO (theatre) section of the Narkompros (Commissariat of Education; see Fischer-Lichte 2005: 99). Meyerhold himself spoke positively in 1920 of Ivanov's condemnation of the proscenium (Malcovati 1977: 192), while even Lunacharsky addressed favourably his theories (Senelick 1981: xl).[10]

It has always been tempting to treat the first post-revolutionary decade or so as a homogenous block, fuelled by the totalitarianism that would become synonymous with Soviet Russia and the well-documented attempts by the party 'to expand Communist control over economy, education, and culture [with the aim of] [...] recasting the entire society' (Brovkin 1998: 21). Cultural recasting after the revolution, especially during the more open and eclectic 1920s, was, however, far from a homogenous process. This allowed the scene to diversify itself. The developmental potential of theatre after 1917 was reasserted. It took a more political underpinning to extol the revolutionary spirit of the working classes. However, it was also diversified, as 'the avant-gardists, the Proletkult activists, and the few Bolsheviks interested in art were in reality associated with different cultural contexts which automatically guaranteed various decodings of their sometimes almost identical phraseology' (Kleberg 1993: ix). Cultural nuance gave rise to different readings of the theatre's role. These included advancing the Bolshevik Party's 'right' to lead the class struggle, bringing classic literature to a wider audience, providing opportunities of theatre production to the workers as a means of class emancipation, the exemplification of correct everyday behaviour (e.g. hygiene) and instilling belief in the victorious denouement of the revolution. The instructive potential of theatre was, however, upheld as a continued characteristic of the Russian theatre tradition.

In Russian theatre the moral and developmental use of theatre forms part of a broader discussion about the relative merits of realism. The debate surrounding realism fuelled further the continuity of the Russian theatre tradition because despite the modernist critique, realism's position was ultimately consolidated in the politically reworked approach of socialist realism. Realism's foregrounding of 'authorship' and the role of the 'author' also cuts through the phases in question. The term 'author' is conventionally linked to the exercise of authority; etymologically, 'author' shares the same root as 'authority' and 'authoritarian' (Partridge 1966: 178–9). Realism in Russian theatre, however, appraised positively the processes associated with the figure of the author, by distancing the term from issues of authority and bringing it closer to the skills associated with the construction or composition of an artefact. This knowledge is reflected in the 'how' one carries his or her endeavours, invoking in turn issues of professional specialization.

Such a compositional accent relates to the selection and organization of artistic material, and it is at the heart of realism in a way that differentiates it from naturalism. While Stanislavsky's first historical productions at the MAT underscored naturalism's resolve to create the externals of daily life, in retrospect he was particularly careful to articulate his position within the tradition of realism's selective and organizational processes, as Benedetti makes clear:

> It is important to define what Stanislavski understood by the term Realism and to distinguish it from Naturalism, a word which he normally employed in a purely pejorative sense. Naturalism, for him, implied the indiscriminate reproduction of the surface of life. Realism, on the other hand, while taking its material from the real world and from direct observation, selected only those elements which revealed the relations and tendencies lying under the surface. The rest was discarded. (Benedetti 1989: 11–12)

This penchant for selection is evident in the criticism given to a production of the play *A Bitter Fate* (1863), written in 1859 by Aleksei Pisemsky. Mikhail Saltykov-Shchedrin, the critic in question, admonished Pisemsky over his full depiction of peasant life, including the reproduction of the coarse language associated with that class. Realism, the critic argued, 'should always carry a notion of the ideal, should indicate a healthy *authorial* point of view, and [recalling the discourse on the moral dimension of theatre] should serve to "remind man of its humanity"' (Marsh in Leach and Borovsky 1999: 150; emphasis added).[11] The artist, therefore, must 'make' his own work, even in those cases when he derives his material from history or from the observation of life. In selecting material for representation he invariably organizes and constructs his work so that what develops is an artistic piece and not a straight copy of an existing phenomenon. Gogol also underlined how processes of selection are characteristic of realism and strongly refuted claims that he was only an imitator of life. He argued that a dramatic work loses significance when the author 'is a mere describer of the scenes that pass before him, without arranging them in proof of something that must be said to the world' (Gogol quoted in Senelick 1981: xxv–xxvi).

Authorial realism transcended playwriting to also impact on acting and directorial processes. The understanding that the actor is an author who composes his roles can be traced back to Shchepkin himself who, dissatisfied with the limiting range of character types or emploi that he inherited, injected a healthier dose of personal interpretation into his stage personas. Borovsky says that the actors of Shchepkin's generation 'assumed the role of co-author, creating characters and producing ideas that went far beyond the limits of the written text' (Borovsky in Leach and Borovsky 1999: 19). Modern theatre, in Russia and abroad, similarly advanced the figure of the director as the author of productions, especially through the establishment of the mise-en-scène as the specialized process that leads to the staging of a play. The contributions made in this field by Stanislavsky, Tairov, Vakhtangov and Meyerhold are of course paramount, and together they became responsible for the rise of the figure of the director-auteur who arranges the stage materials from his own point of view by creating montages of visual and sound elements, acting, text work and other elements.

If anything, modernism further foregrounded authorial processes by proudly proclaiming these are performance material and by shifting them from the rehearsal or workshop spaces to the stage. Wallace identifies the staging of work processes, what he calls '[a]esthetic self-consciousness or reflexivity' (2011: 15), as a characteristic feature of modernism, one that finds manifestation, for example, in Meyerhold's creation of a peephole in *DE* (1924) to show off Erast Garin's skill in costume change and character transformation (Braun 1998: 196) or in Vakhtangov's actors during *Turandot* festively dressing on the stage, after which they were 'introduced to the audience as *actors about to perform the play*' (Malaev-Babel 2013: 222; emphasis in original). Instead of hiding it, the actor's compositional transformation into the role is something to behold, as Meyerhold explains in the following extract:

> [In] this production [*DE*] we have given each actor the interpretation of more than one role. We did this not because the Theatre has fewer actors than the number of roles but because our aim in this production is the principle of transformation. Transformation in the theatre has seldom been used before: for the first time, we make use of it in large quantities. The director usually resorted to transformation as a means to diminish the number of interpreters. Moreover, he often sought to hide this practice from the audience. On the contrary, we inform the spectator of this practice from the posters. We invite the spectator to come and watch the actor's talent in his skilled transformations. (Malcovati 1977: 204)

The bridge between the practices of Meyerhold and Vakhtangov in the 1920s and the nineteenth-century concept of authorship is the Silver Age practice of *uslovnost'*, variously translated as stylization, theatricality or conventionalism (see Chapter 5). This practice had in Valery Bryusov one of its main spokesperson and theoretician. In 1902 Bryusov had already called for alternative forms to realism in his seminal essay 'The Unnecessary Truth'. He emphasized the actor's primary position within theatre production, calling him 'a creator (read *poet*) in the theater, whose raw material consists of voice, pantomime, gesture and physical being as well as the words, action, characters and ideas in the drama performed' (Senelick 1981: xlvii; emphasis in original). The theatrical school also believed in the spectator's imagination to concretize the details suggested by a mise-en-scène. Starting from the premise that the recreation of reality on stage is impossible, stylized theatre postulated minimalism or the use of only those objects that are strictly necessary by the stage action. The action is fleshed further by what the actor does with these objects; for example, see Meyerhold's creation of a garden in *The Magnanimous Cuckold* (1922) through the way that one actor handled a single flower (Gorchakov 1957: 200). It is on purpose that I make reference to Meyerhold's *The Magnanimous Cuckold* when discussing turn of the twentieth-century theatricality, to underline further the continuity between the practices of the Silver Age and those of the early post-revolutionary epoch.

A final sense of continuity is discerned from the productions staged after the revolution of nineteenth-century texts. These texts were processed using inherently modern techniques. Meyerhold's productions of Ostrovsky's *The Forest* (1924) and Gogol's *The Government Inspector* (1926) were two typical examples. In the former Meyerhold was also responding to the aforementioned 'Return to Ostrovsky' policy, though he made sure that this return was as forward looking as possible. Thus, instead of following the Act/Scenes composition, he divided the play into thirty-three episodes[12] and rearranged the text 'according to the principles of cinematic montage' (Braun 1998: 209). He can be seen to have created a startling realism-modernism hybrid, by updating the content for the twentieth century and encapsulating it in a sharp theatrical form. In the process he created a tight union between the two, where the form itself spoke about the content and the other way round.

The way that Meyerhold updated *The Forest* to the twentieth century emerges from a juxtaposition of two speeches which he delivered about the production, one in February 1924 when it had just opened and the other marking the production's tenth anniversary in January 1934. In the former speech Meyerhold spoke about the mise-en-scène and its aesthetics and explained that as a director he had searched his models in the Spanish Siglo d'Oro. This explained the playing of the guitar, the singing, the presence of techniques associated with the Spanish type of the *gracioso*, and the shifts

Figure 1 Meyerhold with his actors after a performance of Ostrovsky's *The Forest* (1924). The play became a veritable battleground between the modernists and the traditionalists. Courtesy Sputnik Images.

between the comic and the dramatic, which he also saw in Shakespeare (Malcovati 1977: 201–2). At a time when artistic experimentation in Russia was reaching its apex, Meyerhold advised against a literal interpretation of Ostrovsky or of any other classic text because while the playwright 'had been imprisoned by the stage technique of his time, we have developed this markedly' (201). Continuity with past theatre tradition is, on the other hand, much more foregrounded in the 1934 speech. In this speech Meyerhold reflected back on the 1924 version of the production and argued that he had then followed Lenin's words that a proletarian culture could only be created on the knowledge and elaboration of the culture of the past. He argued further that the production had re-elaborated a masterpiece of the past without obliterating its political, class-oriented content. In his eyes it had actually provided a sharper revelation of this content:

> We left the main roots of the work intact, but strengthened their expression. […]
>
> We only underlined the political element in Ostrovsky, something which he could not do, even though he was aware that the spectator

would have received a certain message from the stage. In the text there already is a juxtaposition between two classes, and all we did was to further evidence it.

[...]

Through a rereading of the roles and their characteristics, the social motive of this comedy has acquired a more consistent relief. (Malcovati 1977: 202–3)

These were necessary concessions from Meyerhold, seeing how by the mid-1930s his theatre had come under a barrage of political attacks. Emphasizing his continuity with the practices of the Russian theatre tradition had therefore become one of Meyerhold most important defence mechanisms. It is against this background, therefore, that his statement about how his approach to characterization had always been realistic needs to be understood (Braun 1998: 290).

Implications to tradition building

Milestone, stagnation and renewal

What does a study of Russian theatre as it developed across the Golden Age, Silver Age and modernism tell us about how theatre traditions are formed? One suggestion made is that the three stages of milestone, stagnation and renewal are a helpful framework to study tradition building. In this process peak moments see the establishment of canonical names whose practices and outputs become synonymous with the tradition in question. These moments are often followed by a period of crises or indecision, where creativity is seen to dwindle. This is the phase typified by imitation rather than development. More than bringing a sense of closure, however, this second stage of stagnation instigates the experimentation of the third stage, that of renewal.

The pattern of milestone, stagnation and renewal is clear in the Russian theatre tradition. The paradigm shifts of Gogol, Ostrovsky, Shchepkin and their Golden Age counterparts did not immediately generate a line of successors that could build on their achievements. In fact, experimentation and independent creativity were subdued, and instead of socially relevant plays, European boulevard drama, what the writer Oliver M. Sayler referred to as 'made-over plays from the French' (Sayler 1920: 132), dominated the scene. These dramas became synonymous with a phase of stagnation in Russian theatre history, a 'torpid inertia', as Senelick described it (1981: xxxviii), which characterized the latter decades of the nineteenth century.

Worrall's review raises similar points. The Imperial Theatres' repertoires were mostly conservative, as evidenced by the relative failure in the 1896 production of Chekhov's *The Seagull* at the Alexandrinsky Theatre. Rehearsals were perfunctory affairs, run by the star of the companies at the expense of both the play and the ensemble. Stock sets were used. The commercial theatres of the provinces were run by independent entrepreneurs, who staged classics but again relied on an extensive diet of melodramas and farces (Worrall 2008: 1–2). This stagnation is evident not only to our twenty-first-century eyes, who in retrospect can compare these practices to the achievements of both earlier and later years, but also to contemporary writers who commented on Worrall's lines. These included Nemirovich-Danchenko (1936: 31 and 68), Chekhov himself (quoted by Hohman in White 2014: 30) and Nikolai Gorchakov (1957: 3–19). Stanislavsky's articulation of this stagnation called on the inner-outer dynamics which he consistently used to frame the actor's work. In Prov Sadovsky, the main actor at the Maly after Shchepkin's death, Stanislavsky could see that the tradition of emotive experiencing had developed into a pale, outer imitation of Shchepkin's practices. Actorial clichés took the place of the inner 'spiritual essence' (Stanislavsky in Senelick 1984: 250).

This stagnation was still felt as late as 1908 when a collection of essays titled *The Crises of the Russian Theatre* was published (Russell 1988: 1–2). It is, however, in reaction to this crises that the theatre and performance examples discussed in this book were directed, nurturing in turn the third phase of renewal or the modernism of both the Silver Age and the 1920s. The renewal of the Silver Age can be summarized in the debate between realism and symbolism that developed, the rise of the director, an increased experimentation in the aesthetics of performance, a tug of war between the star performer and the ensemble, an increased visibility of the actress as an artistic figure and an intensification of theoretical writing. An argument can be made that in entering the cultural arena in the 1920s, and more forcefully in the 1930s, the Bolshevik Party brought this process of renewal to an abrupt end. In fact, the setting up of the Union of Soviet Writers in 1932 and its 1934 endorsement of socialist realism aimed at bringing different artistic factions together under one ideological programme. Modernism revelled in diversity, but this multiplicity was crushed when experimentation was pushed to the periphery as a type of 'conflictless' drama and production developed (see Carnicke 2009: 199). However, an alternative argument can be made that in playing a cultural role the party guaranteed the Russian theatre tradition a degree of continuity into the twentieth century. In other words, it sustained the tradition's unrelenting existence, albeit in a form which Gogol, Shchepkin and Ostrovsky might not have recognized.

A concerted effort

Rather than a few names whose practices were considered exceptional, the Russian theatre tradition showed a concerted effort by many individuals and forces who, though disparate in some ways (particularly, in the aesthetic choices they made), still shared enough common grounds and recurrent elements to allow their grouping together under one encapsulating movement. It is this line that A. D. P. Briggs takes in his analysis of Russian theatre in the first half of the nineteenth century. Taking as a typical example a play entitled *Oedipus in Athens*, written by Vladislav Ozerov and staged in St Petersburg as early as 1804, Briggs argues that the verse productions of the time were 'instantly successful, though ultimately insubstantial' (Briggs in Leach and Borovsky 1999: 87). The plays are today seen as mediocre and therefore transient rather than exerting a continued hold on the imagination of theatre makers and audiences; testament to this is their lack of revival. These verse productions in Russia did not form an extended tradition because 'from an outgrowth of largely inglorious entertainment, three or four plays [...] broke the rules of the day and in doing so established themselves as indisputable masterpieces' (88). In this case, that particular theatre scene did not have the necessary range to develop into a tradition.

A theatre scene is, on the other hand, elevated into a tradition through the diversity of its players. The players of the Russian theatre tradition included actors and actresses, directors, playwrights, designers, teachers, musical contributors and theoreticians, many of whom went on to become household names in their respective fields. Its spaces were equally diverse, from the Imperial and grand theatres of the capitals, to the private institutions like the MAT, the Korsh Theatre and Suvorin's Society of Literature and Art Theatre; the theatres in the provinces and satellite states; the smaller spaces and forms like the Interlude House, the Distorting Mirror Theatre and the Players' Rest; and, after the revolution, the workers' clubs and the streets themselves. While their production processes differed, these theatres were brought together by their commitment to a serious theatre, and even the seemingly light nature of popular and show-booth theatres did not stand in the way of their practitioners taking their audiences and artistic work seriously (Golub in Leach and Borovsky 1999: 288).[13]

The more extreme forms of modernism contributed to the consolidation of the Russian theatre tradition even during those moments when its criticism was at its most robust. Russian modernism is at times restricted to a series of outwardly unresolvable tensions, between realism and conventionalism for example, or tradition and avant-garde, avant-garde and socialist realism. As Amy Skinner says, however, these are only 'perceived' binaries (Skinner 2016: 259).[14] Binary oppositions might have been critiqued by postmodernism, but their hold on how human endeavours are organized has not relinquished. The organization of modern theatre in Russia as a set of binary opposites seems, in other words, to be a characteristic example of the human mind's predisposition to organize phenomena dualistically. A more helpful organizational framework is the contextual approach developed by Thomas Postlewait, where particular theatre events and realities are both seen drawing from but also reacting to their surrounding world(s), agents, reception and artistic heritage (Postlewait 2009: 11–18). Disparate theatre phenomena are therefore not only seen to exist alongside each other but also to enliven and enrich one another. In this way realism and modernism in the Russian theatre tradition are seen as offshoots of one another which cannot exist independently. Available literature seems to imply such a correlation. Cardullo, for instance, says that avant-garde theatre was 'provoked' by conventional forms of performance (Cardullo 2013: 2), while Russell and Barratt specifically underline the Moscow Art Theatre's 'role as a catalyst for the many anti-naturalistic experiments which followed in its wake' (Russell and Barratt 1990: vii). Marsh calls modernism the 'antithesis' (Marsh in Leach and Borovsky 1999: 163) of realism, implying an opposite viewpoint to an opening idea or theory which, in a Hegelian sense, facilitates a synthesis of ideas.

Cultural transmission

My focus in this book will not be an all-encompassing one. Instead of giving a survey of the scene, I will, a little like stylization, be rather selective of the material that I will expound upon. Tradition building is, as should be clear by now, one of the frames around which I organize my material. The other is that of cultural transmission and the movement of theatre and performance knowledge: acting techniques, training approaches, performance practices, work attitudes and objectives, documentation, etc. Within this context of modern theatre in Russia, how did theatre knowledge move? How was it transmitted? In the process of transmission, how did theatre knowledge change and become appropriated? The second term that warrants some introduction therefore is that of transmission. In this brief exposition I will focus on a sub-category of transmission practice, namely that of 'cultural transmission', first because of the existence of a corpus of literature which in the last decade or so has started to theorize on the movement of knowledge between cultures, and second because theatre and performance are increasingly being treated through cultural lenses (see, e.g., Balme and

Davis 2017). Ideas about culture, especially after the revolution under the guise of 'proletarian culture', were also tightly embedded into the scene (see Chapter 4).

The application of cultural transmission to the study of theatre practice still remains a relatively underused area of investigation.[15] This might be explained by the fact that the study of cultural transmission (not cultural transmission per se, of course) is a twenty-first-century phenomenon and, therefore, still in its infancy. Cultural theorist Ute Schönpflug notes the lack of common terminology and comprehensive theory that covers the field (Schönpflug 2009: 465). Broadly speaking, cultural transmission is concerned with the exchange, sharing and transfer (i.e. transmission) of cultural practices and artefacts. As Schönpflug and Ludwig Bilz assert, 'cultural transmission indicates the transmission of cultural elements that are widely distributed, such as social orientations, knowledge, skills, and behaviors (e.g., rituals)' (Schönpflug and Bilz in Schönpflug 2009: 212; emphasis in original). Such a definition is, however, one sided in its weight. It predicates content and culture as a formed product, an emphasis which George Oswell critiques when he distances himself from the understanding that culture comes into being only when a process of change stabilizes into a form.

Cultural transmission avoids the dialectical opposition between content and process, allowing us 'to think not just of the stuff that is carried [i.e. the content] but also all that goes on in the carrying [i.e. the process]' (Oswell 2006: 3). In other words, instead of focusing on the transmitter of information or the receiver it engages our attention on a third field, namely that space in between the two and what happens there. Both content and process are captured in the following succinct definition, in which cultural transmission is described as 'a transfer process carrying cultural information from one generation to the next, and from one group to the next' (Schönpflug 2009: 1). The cross-generational composition of Russian theatre in the early decades of the twentieth century is a strong case of such cultural transmission. While the transference of acting skills was certainly not a twentieth-century development – see, for example, the family-based erudition of *commedia dell'arte* troupes or Charles le Brun's early eighteenth-century drawings of human passions – Russian practices of the modernist period drew from the then contemporary cultural trait of consistent human renewal, what Toby Clark described as an 'all-round development of mental and physical capacities' (Clark 1993: 33), to generate a marked proliferation of laboratorial and studio spaces as well as trainers and pedagogues.

The cultural categories or contents suggested above by Schönpflug and Bilz – social orientations, knowledge, skills and behaviours – can be grouped in two, with social orientations and behaviours on one side and knowledge and skills on the other. Social orientations and behaviours find their logical home in everyday life, which manifests the ways in which particular cultural groups carry themselves in public, dress, cook, build houses and so on. Michael Gardiner refers to these orientations and behaviours as 'the pragmatic activities of social agents within particular social settings' (Gardiner 2000: 7). Ordinary practitioners of everyday life become capable of performing these pragmatic activities through combinations of routine and familiarity. Knowledge and skill, on the other hand, imply expertise and are valued precisely because not everyone is equally competent in their application and performance. More explicit and thought-out training scenarios are needed to transmit skilled knowledge, necessitating professionals (like teachers and mentors) who typically demand payment for their services. Theatre and performance training falls within this skilled category, but without rescinding the behaviours – what educational theorist Robert M. Gagné (1977) calls 'attitudes' (e.g. confidence, attention to detail, discipline) – which also travel when skills such as the investigation of a role, dissection of a text and the creation of a score are imparted (Aquilina 2017: 20–2; see also Chapter 4).

A concern with the processes of cultural transmission foregrounds the channels used to mobilize cultural knowledge. In the language of cultural transmission these channels are referred to as 'transmission belts' (Schönpflug 2009: 5–6). The aforementioned juxtaposition between everyday life as a channel to learn daily modes of behaviours and the more skill-oriented contexts like technical schools elucidates two examples of these transmission belts, but the issue involves much more than the creation of a list. Different transmission belts do not operate in isolation from one another but, crucially, they can actually reinforce one another. The dissemination of tacit knowledge is a clear example of how different transmission belts coalesce in a supportive manner. Tacit knowledge contrasts with 'codified knowledge', which can be pinned down with a certain surety because of the material form that it takes. User manuals describing how to operate a machine are typical examples. Tacit knowledge is, on the other, 'invisible, intangible, inchoate, and elusive' (Holden in Harorimana 2010: xvii) and necessitates a more experiential form of transmission based on human interaction and through practical-doing. Examples of tacit knowledge include leadership, intuition and language. The experiential transmission of tacit knowledge, however, does not exclude a fruitful combination with codified forms of knowledge, even if theatre practice tells us that such a combination is always problematic: see, for example, how much Stanislavsky laboured on his acting manuals, in the awareness that the translation of a tacit 'system' into a 'grammar' runs the risk of transforming a practice that revels in the here-and-now interaction between transmitter and receiver into a set of fixed instructions and rules. What is clear, however, is that transmission processes are not homogenous affairs because they are intimately tied to the unique contexts (artistic, economic, political, cultural, etc.) that nourish them, making the combined applications of a diverse range of transmission belts particularly welcome to negotiate particularized transmission scenarios. In the case of theatre, these transmission belts normally include training spaces, production examples and documentary sources (see Pitches 2012: 3), though this study asks if this list can be extended.

Apart from drawing our attention to content and process, Schönpflug's definition of cultural transmission also highlights human agency as a defining characteristic of cultural transmission. In other words, it is people who are brought together to partake in transmission activity. While humans and animals do share genetic transmission, '[w]hat may be unique to mankind is the capacity to transmit knowledge explicitly to other individuals in space and time by means of such devices as deliberate teaching through shaping the behavior of other individuals' (Schönpflug 2009: 2). Cultural transmission brings people together as transmitters and receivers, even though actual transmission practices again show that such a duality is too clean and limiting. The roles of transmitter and receiver are interchanged when knowledge transfer takes the form of knowledge exchange, i.e. when different sets of knowledge of equal or comparable value are brought to the table and interchanged in a barter of sorts. Theatre practice similarly critiques tight definitions, with workshop leaders often remarking that transmission activity gives them the chance to rethink and reposition their own practice. Moreover, the roles of both transmitter and receiver are marked by a strong agency to make transmission processes a two-way interaction rather than a unilateral transfer of knowledge. The transmitter naturally imprints on the ways that a receiver will receive the knowledge, especially through the transmission belts that he chooses and his relative skill in their application. The receiver is, on the other hand, never an impartial entity but contributes to the transmission activity through 'a potent selective filter' (Schönpflug 2009: 5). In the parlance of cultural transmission this selective filter is known as transmission bias, which in the course of the discussion in this book will serve as a crucial theoretical and analytical tool, especially in Chapters 3 and 5.

That cultural transmission negotiates relationships between people lends its activities a decidedly political dimension. The use here of the term 'politics' carries none of the implications associated with governance, with how the 'higher realms' (Lefebvre 2008b: 45) of political institutions are run. It rather ties with the activities of any group of related people that involve forms of influence, control, the exercise of power or authority. This is a more 'everyday' reading that situates politics in daily contexts such as the workplace, the classroom, at home and between human relationships. Control in cultural transmission raises questions such as these: which knowledge is chosen for transmission? How are the transmitters and/or receivers chosen? How is the transmission activity carried out? Why is a person engaging in transmission activity? Who gauges the success or failure of a transmission act, and how? These questions imply notions of selectivity and inclusion/exclusion, underlining how cultural transmission is never a neutral activity as there are social, economic and utilitarian rewards to be made. In theatre and performance terms, especially those relevant to modern theatre in Russia, these notions of selectivity and inclusion/exclusion created clusters of practitioners that revolved around shared manifestos, styles or methodologies, evidenced by nomenclatures such as realism, symbolism, conventionalism, constructivism, but also System, biomechanics or synthetic theatre, and their setting against a sociopolitical scenario where the initial promise of democratic freedoms quickly transformed into an ever-more repressive and authoritarian regime. The distinctive nature in the application of cultural transmission in this study, perhaps, rests on the ways in which modern theatre in Russia gravitated between these 'everyday' and 'higher realms' readings of politics.

Chapter summaries

In this Introduction (Chapter 1) I sketched a scenario where the Russian theatre tradition of the nineteenth century was seen developing into the modernism of the early twentieth-century stage. Lines of continuity (the moral dimension of theatre, realism, authorship and the modern productions of nineteenth-century texts) substantiate this development. My intention with this Introduction was also to review relevant literature, hence my predominant use of secondary sources. As I move on in my exposition my use of sources will bring into the fold primary texts from the Russian theatre makers, with an emphasis on what Stanislavsky, Meyerhold, Smyshlaev, the Proletkultists and others had to say on tradition and transmission. Attention will be given to sources which might not have been given much attention in Western scholarship, particularly those texts which have yet to see a translation into English. These include a collection of Stanislavsky's post-revolutionary speeches found in his *Collected Works*, Smyshlaev's book about acting theory, Kerzhentsev's books *Theatre and Revolution* and *The Creative Theatre*, and the Proletkult's 1924 compilation about artistic work at the workers' clubs.

It remains, then, only to introduce formally the contents of the book and to indicate the key stages in its development. Chapter 2 tackles Stanislavsky's work within the Russian theatre tradition. Based on the fact that Stanislavsky's strongest statements about the value of tradition were made when he himself was going through major moments of transition, the chapter argues that traditions can only survive if they are open to change and transformation. Two newly articulated terms are presented. The first is 'Scenic Transmission', which refers to a common practice among modernists, when they looked at visual and photographic material of each other's performances in order to get staging ideas. The relationship between Stanislavsky and German actor Ludwig Barnay, who specifically asked for pictures of productions such as *Uriel Acosta*, will serve as a case study. The second term is 'Rehearsal Transmission', which postulates the use of rehearsal time not only as an endeavour to stage a particular performance, but also as a channel to transmit acting techniques. The aim of Rehearsal Transmission is to provide techniques which performers could detach from the rehearsal to then apply them to diverse performance situations. The term is supported by the notes of Stanislavsky's rehearsals for the 1933 production of Ostrovsky's *Artists and Admirers*, which in itself is a little-known chapter in his career. Moreover, the rehearsal notes explicate ways in which Stanislavsky carried out the shift from the small rehearsal space to the bigger stage of the theatre. The chapter also tackles the First Studio as an instance of democratic levelling, i.e. as a space that used improvisation to dissolve hierarchies between actors, directors and playwrights, and ends with a short section about the international migration of Stanislavsky's practices beyond the Russian border. It makes a case, therefore, for the international dimension of the Russian theatre tradition.

In Chapter 3 I will tackle the idea of 'misinterpreting theatre practice'. As its case study the chapter will call onto the aforementioned work of Valentin Smyshlaev, the one-time member of the Moscow Art Theatre and its First Studio whose 1921/2 acting manual *Theory to Process Stage Performance* proved of considerable popularity. The manual was based on Stanislavsky's ideas, who however found little value in it and underlined that the text was full of outdated and misinterpreted concepts and ideas. I will argue that more than misunderstanding Stanislavsky's ideas, Smyshlaev's acting and performance theories show an inclination towards hybridity where a number of his mentor's techniques were realigned within a context that made collective work its political and artistic driving force. A second important source used in this chapter is Smyshlaev's diary, which not only paints a vivid picture of the artist's reaction to the revolution but also sheds light on the life experienced on a provincial tour during the last months of Russia's involvement in the First World War. Smyshlaev's work is certainly part of the Russian theatre tradition but it is very little known outside of Russia. Therefore, the chapter will contribute much to introduce his name to a new audience.

Chapter 4 discusses the theatrical underbelly spawned by the Russian Revolution, that of the amateur theatre of the workers. Of interest to any scholar engaged in historical study is the opening part where a number of historiographical issues are raised, namely the naming of theatre phenomena, the reliability of sources and periodization. The chapter then tackles transmission issues that emerge directly from the study of amateur and proletarian theatre in post-revolutionary Russia. First, concrete examples of amateur theatre often show practitioners from different backgrounds coming together to create a unique professional-amateur combination. For instance, Smyshlaev's production of Émile Verhaeren's poem *Insurrection* at the Moscow Proletkult (1918) relied on the compositional expertise of the professional director but left the actors free to contribute their own revolutionary material to the production. Second, taking as a key text the obscure essay titled 'A Unified Studio of the Arts' (1924), the chapter subsequently argues that the transmission of acting skills envisaged at the workers' theatre circles not only aimed at developing a capable proletarian actor, but also served as a vehicle where those same skills (physical ability, practical use of words, working collectively) could spill into the everyday life of the worker.

A reappraisal of the concept of transmission bias, first introduced in the third chapter, frames much of the exposition about Meyerhold in Chapter 5. Transmission bias is the necessary background, both experiential and technical, which a receiver brings when participating in transmission activity. It serves as a potent sifting device through which receivers select useful techniques while discarding others. The grotesque will be identified as the transmission bias deployed by Meyerhold to read past theatre traditions. Rather than attempting a reconstruction of the past, he could be seen scrutinizing the 'truly theatrical traditions' for material to transmit into his own modern experiments. The methods which he used to study past theatre traditions are also described, with particular reference to the Borodin Studio and how this laboratory shared much with twenty-first-century Practice as Research (PaR). The final two sections of the chapter discuss the reception of the Russian theatre tradition abroad by expounding on the international reach of Meyerhold's work. First, Meyerhold's only European tour is discussed, with particular reference to the artistic and political contexts in which it ended up being entangled, both at home and also abroad (especially in Paris). Sections from Igor Ilinsky's autobiography which cover this tour provide a helpful reference point. Second, an exploration of newspapers published in the West shows a plethora of references to Meyerhold and his work, underscoring the fact that he was a theatre maker with quite an international reputation and who was therefore worth reporting on. These references in American, Canadian and English newspapers are a veritable transmission channel in their own right, which occasionally even open up new research avenues.

Chapter 6 gives voice to some individuals who are on the fringes of our knowledge of Russian modernism. In line with current studies that shed light on the role of women in turn of the twentieth-century social history and art, attention will be given to female artists whose gender might have stopped the 'natural' transmission of their practices and techniques. Particular attention will be given to Asja Lācis, a Latvian-born actress and director primarily known for her work with children, but whose other work, in Riga for example, relied on cunning ploys to elude the vigilant eye of the authorities. In tackling Lācis a door is also opened on modern theatre outside the main cities of Moscow and St Petersburg.[16] The chapter and book in general end with some concluding axioms about tradition building and transmission processes arising from the Russian case study. It also offers some general guidelines to those readers who might wish to organize transmission workshops.

In summary, the narrative that follows about modern theatre in Russia offers several unique features, which can be listed as follows:

- It broadens our understanding of Russian modernism by focusing on issues of tradition in tandem with transmission.
- It backs its argumentation by using primary sources that have seldom featured in English scholarship, while also uncovering instances of practices from more canonical names, like Stanislavsky and Meyerhold, which we have tended to sideline.
- It challenges conventional historiographical approaches by providing a distinctive analytic frame derived from the field of cultural transmission.
- It offers a model against which other theatre traditions outside of Russian modernism can be analysed.
- It suggests practical and workshop exercises for contemporary use, derived from the historical practices and events discussed (see below).

Suggestions for practice

Note on the practical exercises

The exercises provided here are a result of my own personal reflection on modern theatre in Russia. They reveal my own attempts at translating some of the historical and theoretical ideas into practical material that is of use in a classroom or rehearsal situation. No prior experience is necessary to carry out the exercises, as the emphasis is not on proficiency or skill, though you are certainly encouraged to use any of these activities to hone your acting and performance skills. On the other hand, my aim with these exercises is to suggest practical means through which to develop a more experiential understanding of the performance realities involved. Following from this, it should also be clarified that I am not looking at reconstructing or compiling the actual training approaches developed by Stanislavsky, Meyerhold, M. Chekhov, Smyshlaev, Eisenstein and others, and readers looking for such material are encouraged to look at sources such as Gordon (1988), Pitches (2003), Merlin (2003) and Hodge (2010). Finally, each exercise here comes with a series of questions and points for consideration. These questions are included to help practitioners reflect on the processes they are experiencing and can be used both individually and privately as well as a stimulus for class discussion.

Transmission exercise and belts[17]

1. Identify a photographic image of a modern theatre production from the Russian context. Rudnitsky (1988) is a particularly rich photographic source. Feel free to choose any image that attracts your attention and which seems to speak to you. The only point to keep in mind is that the image needs to feature a variety of human figures.
    - What characteristics can be inferred from the image that make the production typical (or not) of modern theatre in Russia?

2. Identify and recreate 8–10 physical positions from this image. If need be, use more than one image. Aim at clear and well-defined positions. These could be realistic (e.g. sitting down on a chair), abstract or combinations of both.

3. Compose a physical piece by joining together these positions into a routine. The routine will probably be short, perhaps less than a minute. Give attention to (i) having a clear beginning and end (ii) the 'in-betweens', or the connections and transitions between the positions and (iii) the use of different levels.

- How do you transit from one position to the other?
- In staccato (i.e. where each position is sharply detached or disjointed from the others)?
- In legato (i.e. where there is a sense of flow between the positions)?
- A combination of both staccato and legato?
- Do you need to create other positions to help you in these transitions?

4. Describe the routine in writing; i.e. translate it from a physical practice into a written form.
   - You will use this written form to teach, i.e. transmit, the physical routine. What facilitates the transmission, a longer description (e.g. in paragraphs) or shorter statements (e.g. a bullet list)? Why? Therefore, think of the best way of translating the physical routine into writing.

5. Create a video recording of the routine.
   - What are the implications of committing the routine to video?

6. Give a name to the routine.
   - What are the implications of naming the routine?
   - What does naming facilitate? What does it hamper? Always think in terms of 'positive' and 'negative' implications.

7. Set up a 'transmission group' with three other participants. Each participant is given one transmission belt from (i) the direct, one-to-one, live transmission (ii) the written document and (iii) the recorded video. Each participant is to use their transmission belt to 'recreate' the source routine. Allow this some time and then compare and contrast the resulting pieces.
   - Discuss the implications arising from each transmission process (embodied, documented, videoed).
   - Note the changes between the four versions. What prompted these changes and transformations? Physical limitations? Lack of clarity in the written description? One focal point in the video version?
   - In the transmitted versions, can the original positions still be discerned with clarity? Remember that these were the starting point in creating the routine. Have these starting points changed?
   - Give attention to the 'in-betweens'. How did the rhythms change, if at all?
   - Has the practice of 'essentialisation' or 'reductionism' featured in any of the three transmitted versions? Are the transmitted versions shorter? If yes, what remained?
   - Did the source routine tell a story or narrative of sorts? If yes, did this change?

- What is lost in the transmitted versions? What is gained or added?
- Identify a technical aim or objective for your version of the routine. If you were to use this version as part of your daily training, what would its aim and objective be? Why would you use it? Which practical skills does it develop? Try to be specific, and formulate more detailed aims than 'as a physical routine or exercise'. Compare the four aims.
- Is the name given to the source technique appropriate to the transmitted versions? Why?

2

Stanislavsky: Renewing tradition through transmission

Renewing theatre traditions

For a theatre maker with an unrelenting drive for self-improvement like Konstantin Stanislavsky, tradition building was not necessarily a positive thing. In fact, he juxtaposed 'tradition and routine' or 'false tradition' with what the Czech writer Jaroslav Kvapil termed, in relation to the Moscow Art Theatre's productions of the 1906 European tour, 'tradition and innovation' (Kvapil in Stanislavski 1963: 163). Tradition building, in other words, needed an important qualification, namely continued innovation or continued renewal, which Stanislavsky deemed as essential as the creation of milestone names, plays, techniques and theatrical events. He described the need for constant renewal as follows:

> [T]o guard traditions is to give them development, because genius requires movement, not academic immobility. [...] Unfortunately, the zealots of past traditions did not understand this, precisely because they were too jealous of all that was old. Adherents of the past renounced, once and for all, all that is young in art, and stubbornly froze in one place, not wanting to move away from it.
>
> These zealots fell in love with traditions, not with their genius but their own habits. They fell in love with the form, without knowing its soul, which even now patiently waits for its expression. (Stanislavskii 1958: 494)

Stanislavsky was and still is considered a defining figure of the Russian theatre tradition and of modern acting in general. However, the strong transmission culture that developed around his name and his System produced a kind of 'tradition within a tradition'. This refers to the Stanislavsky acting tradition, which not only links Stanislavsky to other Russian practitioners

Figure 2 Konstantin Stanislavsky in the 1920s. Courtesy Laurence Senelick Collection.

like Vsevolod Meyerhold, Nikolai Demidov, Valentin Smyshlaev, Mikhail Chekhov, Richard Boleslavsky and Anatoly Vasiliev, but also looks outwards, beyond Russia, to other theatre realities which in Stanislavsky found not only a kindred spirit with whom they shared similar concerns, but also a paradigm for theatre modernization and renewal. Stanislavsky-informed processes of transmission partake strongly in Ute Schönpflug's definition (Chapter 1) that cultural transmission invokes both cultural content and processes, and an underlining consideration of this chapter is that Stanislavsky studies expand markedly the remit covered by these two markers. The transmission content in the Stanislavsky acting tradition includes production processes and the use in performance of those elements which comprise a mise-en-scène (costuming, lighting, use of props, groupings of actors, use of gestures, etc.); embodied training material and acting techniques; and acting theories. The transmission spaces in which Stanislavskian ideas migrated are equally diverse. These create a startlingly modern mix between, on the one hand, contexts that are defined by close proximity (i.e. the Moscow Art Theatre and its satellite studios) and, on the other, more international and cross-cultural, in this case European rather than American, realities. The latter include studios that were opened on Stanislavskian models (e.g. the actress Stanislawa Wysocka's recreation of the First Studio project in her native Poland) or practitioners who wittingly or not displaced elements of the System from the source context and applied them to their own work.[1]

When did Stanislavsky speak about tradition building? A contextualization of Stanislavsky's statements highlights that he made his most forceful assertions about tradition building when he himself was going through major moments of transition. This emerges when comparing two key texts on tradition building, an 1897 letter to French playwright and drama critic Lucien Besnard, and a series of post-revolutionary texts and speeches found in Volume 6 of his *Collected Works* (1954–61; Stanislavskii 1959). The former is a relatively well-known text. Sections of it have appeared in a 1963 collection of texts by and on Stanislavsky (Stanislavski 1963: 231–5). It has also been reproduced more fully in the collection of letters edited by Laurence Senelick (2014: 77–82). At the time of writing this letter to Besnard Stanislavsky had already garnered some twenty years of theatre experience, during which he had made a name for himself as an actor and director of real originality. Privately, however, he was still licking his wounds from what had been a relative failure in his portrayal of Othello. Crucially, this letter, which Stanislavsky had put off from writing for more than a year, was dated 20 July 1987 and therefore written just four weeks after he had met Vladimir Nemirovich-Danchenko and set in motion concrete plans to open the Moscow Art Theatre. This was a clear moment of transition for Stanislavsky, and a crucial one at that, when he was inevitably contemplating his own future as a professional theatre maker and his place in relation to the stage masters of the previous centuries. In front of him he identified two paths. One led to 'obsolete tradition and [the] routine [...] of art', as displayed by the actors playing Molière at the Comédie Française. The other would take him to the 'greater scope [of] imagination and creativity', as demanded by Shakespeare's texts and encapsulated in Hamlet's speech to the actors (Senelick 2014: 81).

While Stanislavsky's allegiance to the latter goes without saying, it is curious to note the tight link that he fostered in this letter between acting traditions and playwriting. In fact, in Stanislavsky's scheme at the time of writing to Besnard, acting traditions were defined by playwrights, in this case Molière and Shakespeare, accentuating the heavily text-based theatre culture that he inherited and in which he operated. Here, Stanislavsky identified the world of playwriting as a model for theatre making. Literature served as a model because of the standards which it reached first in the depiction of the depths of human life and which theatre practitioners were then compelled to strive for. The late nineteenth century which, as I have argued in Chapter 1, was seen as a stagnating time in Russian theatre, found actors who were not meeting the challenge set by Molière and Shakespeare. Stanislavsky even affirmed that the actors of the Comédie Française were simply regurgitating stereotyped conventions from performance to performance without even considering adding anything new. Such an evaluation is, of course, highly individualized and contentious, and it reflects the broader tension between the French acting tradition, rooted in technical composition, and the emotional identification and experiential dimension of the Russian school.[2] It does, however, signal Stanislavsky's desire to search for models – foreign actors, Russian actors of the previous generations, prominent contemporaries, achievers in other fields – against which to evaluate his own practices and findings.

In the letter to Besnard Stanislavsky recognized that it was transmission processes that had failed the development of the French acting tradition. The example he gave is that of the lineage between Francois-Joseph Talma, a popular tragedian of the turn of the nineteenth century, and Jean-Sully Mounet, an actor of Stanislavsky's time. Instead of focusing on the quality of Talma's stage creations, Mounet concentrated and imitated the former tragedian's grand gestures and expanded vocal gymnastics. This he did by 'blow[ing] himself up and shout[ing] as loud as he can to affect his own nerves and the nerves of his audience' (Stanislavski 1963: 231). In this process Mounet failed to understand that these gestures and vocal inflexions were by-products and not end products of Talma's acting processes. A transmission of knowledge unwittingly took place from Talma to Mounet, which allowed the latter – either voluntarily or through deficiency, or probably via a combination of both – to appropriate work elements which Stanislavsky considered of secondary importance. More broadly, what Stanislavsky put into motion here is a matrix to evaluate transmission processes, one which was based on artistic criteria (as formulated by Shakespeare in Hamlet's speech), a standard or model (the cultural memory of Talma's performances), and what chimed best with his own idea of theatre (a disdain for 'the theatre in the theatre').

The second source in which Stanislavsky spoke about tradition building, i.e. the series of post-revolutionary speeches and texts contained in Volume 6 of this first *Collected Works*, appears at an equally transitional moment.³ These speeches are set again against the backdrop of yet another failed role, this time that of Colonel Rostanev in Dostoevsky's *The Village of Stepanchikovo* (1917). The repercussions of this failure were shattering: devastated by his failure in bringing the role to life, and by Nemirovich-Danchenko's decision to pull him out of the production, Stanislavsky never attempted again the creation of a new role (Benedetti 1999: 231). This decision impacted directly on his research, as Stanislavsky lost one of the most important testing grounds for his System – his own experience as an actor and creator of new roles. This lack of personal experience was further compounded when a heart attack in 1928 cut short his acting career. In any case, these post-revolutionary speeches find Stanislavsky in a combative mood as he asserts his desire to play an active part in the developing post-revolutionary theatre scene:

> Russian theatrical art is dying, and we must save it, this is our common responsibility. There is only one way to save it: keep the best that has been created so far by us and our predecessors, and with great energy take up the new work [...]. At this moment the Moscow Art Theatre has to play a very critical role. Among the devastated Russian theatre, it is almost the sole repository of the true traditions of Russian theatrical art. [...]. (Stanislavskii 1959: 34)

> It is impossible to defer the art of theatre, hang the locks on its studio, and suspend its existence. Art cannot be put to sleep to be then awakened when we wish. If it goes to sleep, then it dies. Once stopped, it dies. To pause art means to destroy it. (Stanislavskii 1959: 118)

These statements were collated from two interventions made by Stanislavsky, one during the General Meeting of the MAT Board (May 1918), the other during a meeting of the Workers of Theatre Arts (December 1919). Both took place during one of the most liminal times in Russian, or even world, history. Events after the February and October Revolutions followed each other in quick succession. The humbling treaty of Brest-Litovsky with Germany took place in early March 1918, at a time when the revolution was also quickly morphing into the Civil War. The position of the new government was, therefore, far from secure. The conditions in Moscow during the first years of Bolshevik rule were a 'living hell' (Komisarjevsky 1929: 2), with food, clothing, transport, fuel and other daily needs in short supply. On the

Moscow Art Theatre's front, Stanislavsky's call to save the Theatre was not metaphorical: the Theatre's three-week closure in November–December 1917 was certainly still a fresh memory on everyone's mind, as was Stanislavsky's own brief arrest in August 1918 (Benedetti 1999: 251–2). Instead of playing it safe, Stanislavsky compelled the theatre arts to analyse past achievements, not to replicate them, but as a means to move forward. His approach in 1918 to tradition building and renewal had changed from the days of the letter to Besnard, and it can be articulated as follows: instead of advocating a clear model, sourced from the world of playwriting, he called on his more recent experience of opening and working in studio contexts, in turn predicating the uncertain process of transmission and research over the reaching of a concrete and pre-defined milestone.

In this chapter I will discuss several proposals which Stanislavsky made at different points in his career in relation to *how* theatre traditions can be developed and not left to deteriorate. Through his proposals Stanislavsky can be seen to have encouraged the seemingly paradoxical stance of preserving theatre traditions by developing them further. Within this context of tradition building, I will provide three case studies of transmission activity. These case studies have been selected not only because they present material in Stanislavsky's biography which might have escaped our attention, but also because they allow me to broaden the study of transmission processes in theatre and performance studies. This broadening is achieved by framing the exposition around a set of newly articulated terms, namely:

- Scenic Transmission, through a sharing of production photographs between Stanislavsky and German actor Ludwig Barnay;
- Democratic Levelling, where the actor, director and playwright contribute together to create stage material;
- Rehearsal Transmission, by opening on Stanislavsky's 1932–3 rehearsal work for the Moscow Art Theatre production of Alexander Ostrovsky's *Artists and Admirers*.

The chapter concludes with an exposition on the international reach of the Stanislavsky acting tradition.

Scenic Transmission: The case of Ludwig Barnay

One of the markers of modern theatre is that practitioners saw themselves in an increasingly international and globalized way, as a result of touring, cross-border communication, sharing of ideas and so on.[4] I have already made reference to the international dimension of modernism and how theatre at the turn of the twentieth century was looking at itself in an increasingly international and globalized way. Modern theatre practitioners internationalized their endeavours through the cross-cultural movement of theatre knowledge in which they partook, and one way in which this movement of ideas took place was through the transmission belt which I will refer to here as 'Scenic Transmission'. Contrary to embodied transmission, which predicates the migration of body-based training practices like the System and Biomechanics through the direct and live encounter between master and student, Scenic Transmission facilitates the movement of staging and production ideas and practices, of less tacit knowledge such as costume patters, light designs, scenic arrangements, groupings of actors, gestural and vocal patterns. These are the more visual (Stanislavsky would call them 'outer') aspects of performance that are contained in a mise-en-scène.

The publication of whole mises-en-scène facilitated but also inflexibly pinned down the movement of these visual and auditory elements from one context to the other. At the turn of the twentieth century, the movement of production ideas gained further momentum as a result of the increased availability and technical improvements of photography. The use of photography in the modern period signals the practitioners' willingness to record and document their work and to have elements of it available for posterity. In such cases photography was allied to other forms of documentation (theoretical writings, diary entries, sketches, interviews, newspaper reports and published mises-en-scène) to counter the ephemeral nature of theatre performance. It is no coincidence that the post-mortem analysis of performance increased at the turn of the twentieth century, as practitioners found themselves with more reflective material at their disposal – see, for example, Stanislavsky contemplating his acting processes during his 1906 holiday in Finland by looking at his diaries and performance logbooks. Photographing stage productions, however, served more than documentary purposes. Through Scenic Transmission it connected practitioners together. Like other transmission channels, the potential of photography increases when Scenic Transmission is applied not in isolation but in conjunction with other means of transmission (see Introduction). In fact, the emphasis which Scenic Transmission puts on the outer side of production directs attention away from the inner side of the actor's work. This is a crucial criticism, considering that Stanislavsky was constantly preoccupied with performances running the risk of becoming 'ruled by objects, props, the externals of daily life' (Stanislavski 2008a: 228). This danger can be kept in check by studying Scenic Transmission alongside testaments from the actors, for example, which on the contrary tend to relate the personal and subjective processes performers experience.

Still, the capacity of Scenic Transmission to transfer theatrical knowledge is not to be downplayed. Several examples can be cited from Stanislavsky's biography which indicate the transmission of photographic and other visual material. For instance, in July 1897 Stanislavsky was in Berlin to watch *Hannele*, *Much Ado about Nothing*, *Coriolanus* and *The Sunken Bell*, when he 'filled a whole notebook, sketched a whole album' (Stanislavsky in Senelick 2014: 81). He had already produced the first two plays in 1986, which provided a comparison, while the following January he would go on to stage *The Sunken Bell*. In another case, this time in 1910, the Belgian Symbolist writer Maurice Maeterlinck thanked Stanislavsky for his generous permission to copy the sets of *The Blue Bird* (Stanislavski 1963: 167). From his 1914 trip the English director and critic Harley Granville Barker brought back ninety photos and eight programmes of the MAT's productions (Morgan 1961: 311; see below). André Antoine, on his part, stated that his library 'was long enriched by albums that were full of the scenic accomplishments of the Art Theatre' (Stanislavski 1963: 175). Photographs of the MAT productions produced between 1924 and 1928 were also inserted in American newspapers (Senelick 2014: 497), possibly for promotional reasons in preparation for a possible MAT tour in the late 1920s. These details might appear as incidental, but they do indicate the cross-cultural migration of theatre ideas between German, Russian, English and French practitioners, and Stanislavsky's early reach beyond Moscow. In a way, these instances of Scenic Transmission can be considered as having paved the way for the more embodied transmission that would take place when Stanislavsky's ex-students or collaborators visited these and other countries and opened their own studios.

An extended example of how photographic dissemination and Scenic Transmission informed particular instances of modern theatre is provided by the case study of Ludwig Barnay (1842–1924), a German actor, touring star and eventual manager of his own theatre in Berlin and Wiesbaden. Barnay was already a prominent figure in the German theatre of the 1870s. He guested with many companies, most notably the Meinengen, with whom he appeared as a regular guest and, from 1874 onwards, as an honorary member (Osborne 1988: 66). He seems to have been at odds with a number of the Meinengen's practices, however, initially seeing the Duke's over-zealous approach as a waste of time (Koller 1984: 129). He is also recorded to have taken a bow, in a clear violation of verisimilitude, during a performance in London of Shakespeare's *Julius Caesar* (Osborne 1988: 110). Barnay would, however, later come to appreciate the Duke's acting techniques, such as the use of costume to reveal character, and the director's ingenuity to use spectacular effects to arrive to the heart of a dramatic text

Figure 3 Ludwig Barnay playing the title role in *Uriel Acosta*. His correspondence with Stanislavsky shows a strong interest in the visual and photographic documentation of performance. Courtesy Laurence Senelick Collection.

(Koller 1984: 85). Barnay's reputation culminated in 1906 as the principal director of the Royal Theatre in Berlin, a position which he followed in 1908 with the directorship of the Royal Theatre in Hannover (Grange 2006: 14). He excelled in portraying tragic parts, played in the romantic mould, with roles that included Othello, King Lear, Kean, William Tell and, crucially, Uriel Acosta. These roles were included in the repertoires that he took on his American tours of 1883 and 1888 (*The New York Times*, 22 December 1882; 3 and 8 March 1888: 8).

Over the years Barnay became well acquainted with Stanislavsky. They seem to have met first in May 1896, when Stanislavsky's house at Red Gate was hired by the German Embassy as their base to attend the coronation of Tsar Nicholas II. An evening programme featuring Barnay was staged by the embassy at Red Gate. Barnay and Stanislavsky seem to have discussed the mounting and dismantling of the stage, but more importantly they also looked at the photographic album of *Uriel Acosta*. This was a production which Stanislavsky had directed the previous year for the Society of Arts and Literature and in which he also played the title role. Barnay and the rest of the German entourage expressed their admiration for this production, though Stanislavsky had at the time doubted their sincerity. Barnay also asked Stanislavsky to see pictures of *Othello* (Vinogradskaia Vol. 1 2003: 180, 183, 184). The Russian director was interested enough in Barnay's work to attend the opening night of his Moscow tour in 1896. He always gave significant importance to such visits, seeing them as potentially valuable lessons.[5] The two seemed to have been brought together not only by their inclination to portray tragic roles, but also by their shared defiance of tradition and stereotype. Similarly to Stanislavsky, Barnay was not afraid of confounding expectations. A rather conservative American critic, for instance, described his portrayal of Hamlet in the following words:

> The charms of Ludwig Barnay's Hamlet are numberless. It is a perfectly consistent and harmonious piece of acting. [...] [But] [t]here are things in the portrayal that we do not like, that no student of the English drama can accept without dispute. But an admiration is compelled by the facility of the actor, by the aptness and east of his byplay, even where his manner does not conform to our ideas. We do not like this use of the dagger in the soliloquy on immortality. Hamlet has not got so close to the idea of self-slaughter as that device implies. Barnay's treatment of the soliloquy, indeed, seems fussy and undignified. (*New York Times*, 6 April 1888: 5)

Common grounds between the two were strong enough so that plans were devised for Barnay to guest in the Society's production of *Othello*. These appearances were scheduled for late 1896. The intention was for Barnay to play the title role, while Stanislavsky would star as Iago (Stanislavskii 1960: 660). Stanislavsky had also considered having Barnay guest in *Uriel Acosta*, possibly as a draw to improve the Society's dire financial situation. In a very business-like letter written in November 1896 to Vladimir Schulz, an agent who specialized in arranging tours for foreign actors, Stanislavsky remarked that performances with Barnay would be 'very desirable for us', i.e. for the Society (Stanislavskii 1960: 101). A month later Barnay watched the Society's *The Polish Jew*, after which he wrote to Stanislavsky saying that 'you surprised me with your truly excellent and creditable accomplishments as a dramatic performer and a first-class stage director. I may tell you frankly that the performance of *The Polish Jew*, which I saw in your theatre, delighted me' (in Stanislavski 1963: 158). Stanislavsky seems to be have liked Barnay, describing him in the appendices of *My Life in Art* as a 'handsome man with a poetic soul' (Stanislavskii 1954: 420).

A later reference to Barnay is found in a letter which Stanislavsky wrote to his brother Vladimir in February or March 1906. This letter was written from Berlin while the MAT was on tour. Stanislavsky wrote that 'the constant visitor to our performance is Barnay. He has already watched all the plays twice, and gave us wreaths with the inscriptions "To the Best Theatre"' (Stanislavskii 1960: 335–6). However, it is their encounters in 1895–6 that seem to have left the strongest mark. Most revealing to a discussion on Scenic Transmission is how Barnay described the impact of *The Polish Jew*, underlining for example 'the picturesque scenes in the second act' (in Stanislavski 1963: 158). It is the visual dimension of this performance which therefore caught Barnay's eyes, which should come as no surprise considering that Stanislavsky had chosen that particular text not for its inherent dramatic value, which he found lacking, but for what the play allowed him to create in terms of spectacular effects (Stanislavski 2008a: 131–5). Barnay particularly praised the mass scenes in the second act, 'which looked so vital and truthful' (Stanislavskii 1960: 661). The mass scenes of *Uriel Acosta* made a similarly strong impression. These were vividly recalled by Barnay as late as December 1906, when he wrote to Stanislavsky urging him to send as quickly as possible 'portraits of the performers and pictures of the groups'. Stanislavsky obliged soon after (in Vinogradskaia Vol. 2 2003: 52 and 54).

Crowd scene seems to have been lacking in the production of *Acosta* which Barnay took on his American tour in 1888. Barnay was certainly familiar with the organization of crowd scenes, and this knowledge hints that their absence in the *Acosta* of 1888 was a deliberate choice and not a result of some artistic deficiency. He had been, after all, exposed to crowd scene while guesting with the Meinengen, even though not uncritically: he, for example, seems to have bemoaned the noisy crowd which silenced him at the start of Marc Anthony's famous speech at Caesar's funeral (in Osborne 1988: 109–10). A brief newspaper entry on his own production of *Julius Caesar* further evidences his knowledge of the organization of crowd scenes. This production was also included in the 1888 tour, and in New York 'the mob was composed of two hundred amateurs from the best-gebred-highest-geborn families of the German aristocracy in the city' (*New York Amusement Gazette*, 19 March 1888: 9). No reference to mass scenes is however made in a review of *Uriel Acosta*, performed in New York on 24 March 1888. This suggests that mass scenes were at the very least significantly downplayed in this production, as the reviewer cannot be expected to have missed commenting on a practice which Laurence Senelick would single out, even as late as 1923–4, as being 'what distinguished the effect of the Art Theatre from that of tours of earlier foreign stars' (Senelick 2008: xvii). What the reviewer opted to write about, on the other hand, was the work and range of particular actors. In this analysis, Barnay came off as 'more rounded and consistent, less flawed by weak spots' (*The New York Times*, 24 March 1888: 4). Most revealing is the following part:

> 'Uriel Acosta' seems a play more enjoyable to read than to see in action. The troubles of a Jewish freethinker, who brings the curse of his co-religionists not only on himself but on his mother, on the girl he loves and on her father, are fitter for a novel than a play. Yet the tragedy has several fine situations, though it revolves on a narrow pivot and has little variety of incident or change of scene. As a piece of literary work it is as good as an excellent style, purity of diction and sober, reserved statement, rising occasionally into fine passages, can make it. (*The New York Times*, 24 March 1888: 4)

Barnay therefore seemed to have staged a rather static and verbose version of the play, one which heightened the tragic pathos arising from a beautified delivery of the language rather than concrete and visible human action.

The emphasis on the literary merits of Barnay's production clearly contrasts with the action-packed mise-en-scène of Stanislavsky's version. In order to hide the shortcomings of several of the amateur actors, but also in the belief that stage movement was a potent sign-carrier, Stanislavsky added a barrage of choreographed action to his version. These included the infuriated mob attacking the main character, the carefully planned entries and exists of actors, elaborate bows, use of fans, hand gestures and so on.[6] After this production of *Acosta*, the Society in fact seems to 'have acquired the patent for crowd scenes' (Stanislavski 2008a: 130). In specifically asking Stanislavsky for pictures of the mass scenes, Barnay was receiving material through which to construct action and mob scenes. This is substantiated from a brief reference in Barnay's autobiography, where he praised the mass crowd during *Acosta*'s garden scene which he had seen in Moscow on the Society's stage (Barnay 1913: 65). The garden scene is vividly described by Stanislavsky in *My Life in Art* (2008: 129), pictures which Barnay would have seen either in 1896 or when the two corresponded again in 1906. It is these images that would have impacted on Barnay's staging of *Uriel Acosta* in Berlin, evidencing how the German director received knowledge of production processes through the visual dimension of Scenic Transmission.

The First Studio: An example of Democratic Levelling

While Scenic Transmission allows the movement of theatre ideas to take place at a distance, embodied live transmission necessitates a close connection between transmitter and receiver, who actively choose to come together in a sharing of time and space. This typically takes place in studio environments, such as the Moscow Art Theatre's First Studio. Opened in 1912, the First Studio's contribution to Stanislavsky's experimentation in acting technique and the development of the System was pivotal, especially in its earlier years.[7] Rather than discussing this contribution to acting processes, I opt to direct my attention to how a transmission space like a studio was used by Stanislavsky to question received theatre traditions, in this case the hierarchies between the actor, director and playwright. In contrast to hierarchical organizations, Stanislavsky suggested a more equal relationship, what I will refer to as 'a democratic levelling' between the three.[8] It is this democratic levelling between the actor, director and playwright that underlines Stanislavsky's conception of studio culture, at least within the early experiments of the First Studio.

Stanislavsky's fraught relationship with Nemirovich-Danchenko is often roped in to exemplify the broader tensions between text- and actor-centred approaches to theatre within the Russian tradition. The part which the director plays as the connecting tissue between the actor and the playwright is also invoked. In the case of Stanislavsky and Nemirovich-Danchenko, the veto system which they pinned down during their historical meeting in 1897 – 'The literary veto goes to Nemirovich-Danchenko, the artistic to Stanislavski' – soon transpired to be too clumsy and rigid to serve as a long-term working method. Nemirovich-Danchenko even noted soon after the meeting that the veto would make for a volatile relationship between the two (in Vinogradskaia Vol. 1 2003: 200). Hence, Jean Benedetti is particularly dualistic in his description of their relationship, highlighting in turn the theatre hierarchies which the two co-founders upheld, at least initially:

> Later correspondence, when the two men were no longer on good terms, reveals what Nemirovich meant by 'collaboration'. As a writer he believed in the absolute supremacy of the dramatist. Theatre consisted in the translation of the author's intentions into stage terms. [...] He did [...] possess an outstanding ability to analyse a play and reveal its hidden meanings. [...] Stanislavski, on his side, possessed the directorial flair Nemirovich lacked. He had demonstrated his skill in creating vivid theatrical images, in selecting significant detail. (Benedetti 1999: 60)

This tug of war between performance processes (acting and directing) and text was not restricted to Stanislavsky and Nemirovich-Danchenko. It was rather the context which they inherited.[9] Even as late as 1912, an essay by Yury Aikhenvald titled 'The Denial of Theatre' postulated the inferiority of theatre in relation to literature: 'Stage performance [Aikhenvald argued] was not only parasitical and dependent on written texts for life's blood but also limited in light of its ability to arrive at literature's intricate creations of meaning' (Rzhevsky 2016: 8–9). Aikhenvald believed that stage materiality dampens the imagination of the spectator, a criticism which Meyerhold also levelled to naturalism (Braun 1969: 25–6). Typical of the multifarious and vociferous nature of modernism, the essay proved highly controversial and was challenged by Nemirovich-Danchenko, Fyodor Komissarzhevsky and Nikolai Evreinov.

Our twenty-first-century understandings of theatre might read modernism's struggles with text-driven hierarchies as a necessary and transitory step towards the 'progress' of post-dramatic theatre and devised production processes, but to early twentieth-century practitioners it posed a real problem: are received theatre hierarchies stifling theatre experimentation? How can these hierarchies be destabilized? Are there contemporary, more 'modern' and democratic ways of articulating the relationship between the actor-director-playwright? Instead of hierarchies, can the actor, director and playwright enter into a democratic and more equal relationship? Stanislavsky tackled these questions at the First Studio when he used improvisation to democratize a space between acting processes, directorial intervention and dramatic composition. Seeing the First Studio only in terms of acting research is, therefore, restrictive, and the literature of the time corroborates this. For example, the press announcement for the opening of the First Studio stated that one of its main purposes was 'to research and test new foundations for plays' (Vinogradskaia Vol. 2 2003: 343). Similarly, in his *Notes about the*

Studio, Sulerzhitsky paraphrases one of Stanislavsky's intentions for the First Studio as to 'give new experience in the collective creation between authors, actors, and directors in creating a play' (in Vinogradskaia Vol. 2 2003: 344). This experience was, of course, placed side by side with the clear and focused experimentation in the System and its key acting techniques within a three-pronged programme of work which Pavel Markov articulated as follows: '1. Cultivation of the psychology of the actor's creativity 2. elaborating the way the actor feels physically 3. bringing the actor close to the author' (in Gauss 1999: 40).

The improvisations carried out at the First Studio saw the actors improvise on outlines provided by a playwright. The latter's role did not stop with these outlines, however. The playwright was subsequently expected to polish the material arising from the actors into more developed dramatic compositions. In this work the outline (what Alexander Blok referred to as 'canvas' and 'plot') was the playwright's, while the 'words were provided by the actors' (Blok in Vinogradskaia Vol. 2 2003: 349). In a report about the First Studio's work dated 6 April 1913, the actors' improvisation on a playwright's outline was described in the following way:

> The essence of this experiment, in its most general and schematic form, is as follows: a play is created together by an author and the actors. It is a result of their common work. The author gives the first push. He can be likened to the throwing of the grain in the actors' soil. The actors then develop this grain through their own experiences, feelings, and talents. Subsequently, the author collects the harvest and gives it back to the actors. (in Vinogradskaia Vol. 2 2003: 381)[10]

This approach became known as Gorky's Method, who was the first to suggest the practice; he certainly sent Stanislavsky some scenarios for the actors to work on in September 1912 (Gorkii 1955: 259–69). One scenario revolved around the way members of a family treat a rich relative who is tried over some crime. Another scenario depicted student-actors before and after the examination to enter the Moscow Art Theatre School.[11] A substantial part of the letter is given to a long description of a comedy, involving, among others, a lazy and good-for-nothing son, his doting mother, his cheerful wife, a disgraced engineer, a petty bourgeois working in the foreign office who is forever worried about an attack by the Chinese, and a conductor of an orchestra who has a dislocated right hand. This outline was also to serve as material for improvisation (Gorkii 1955: 264–9). Gorky handed the actors significant responsibility in this process, even relinquishing, if possible, the playwright's role in perfecting the dialogue and style of the emerging play. Even the theme and characters, he argued, could be changed beyond recognition in the process of development given by the actors (Gorkii 1955: 269).

In his correspondence Gorky also delineated the type of actors best suited for this improvisatory approach. They need to be daring actors, ready to transcend one of the most ingrained of acting habits, that of using someone else's written words to give expression to their thoughts. The actors are therefore treated as actor-dramaturges, creative people who 'can give unique forms to [their] ideas' (Gorkii 1955: 259). Gorky argued that the potential to manifest thoughts and ideas in subjective and personally authored forms is a characteristic feature of human nature, one which however was not fulfilled because

> [w]hen a person wants to give a clear and precise form to his life experience, he uses for this purpose readymade forms – words, images, pictures of other people. He follows the prevailing, generally accepted points of view, and forms his personal opinion like someone else's. (Gorkii 1955: 259–60)

To offset this inclination towards imitating someone else's expressive forms, Gorky suggested that actors should look at everyday life for possible material to adapt and organize into stage images. This observation of everyday life, specifically of people (e.g. cabmen, shopkeepers, mothers, other actors) going through their daily business, supports the actors in their improvisations. A character is composed – it is revealing to underline that in this letter Gorky argued that dramatic plots emerge from clearly delineated and contrasting characters and not the other way round[12] – by choosing and putting together fragments of behaviour sourced from different people in their everyday life. This composition helps the actors 'to form in his or her own way, the type of person' needed (Gorkii 1955: 260). Ultimately, Gorky expressed regret that the first experiments in collective creation of the plays would go on without his personal involvement and asked Stanislavsky to join him in summer in Capri with the First Studio participants so as to try and create together 'a dramatic comedy, a drama, a melodrama of a new type' (Vinogradskaia Vol. 2 2003: 348).

Seeing the difficulty which Stanislavsky and the MAT had in fulfilling their early promise to stage contemporary work, the First Studio experiments in actor-playwright composition reads as a broader attempt to revitalize the Theatre's repertoire, which by 1912 was still missing a man of letters who could take Anton Chekhov's position as a kind of house playwright. The number of new productions based on the works of contemporary playwrights was at the time seriously dwindling. Apart from Gorky, Stanislavsky similarly wanted to collaborate with the writer Aleksei Tolstoy, who in February 1913 had also shown interest in Stanislavsky's experiments. Even Nemirovich-Danchenko, who was no big fan of Gorky, seems to have found value in the project and provided a scenario that revolved around actors living together in rented apartments (in Vinogradskaia Vol. 2 2003: 373 and 349). As the leader of the First Studio, Sulerzhitsky also contributed with some scenarios of his own, including one titled at the 'workshop of the tailors'. He saw this particular session as the closest attempt to achieve what Gorky and Stanislavsky had discussed together:

> Sometimes when I had no more imagination for a theme, I took a story, or an episode from a story, and the students acted out such theme in their own words. But then again we took the theme rather than the images. [...] What the scenes had to be like was not discussed in advance. At the end, however, we agreed on the organisation of the scenes so that we do not interfere with each other's work. (Sulerzhitsky in Vinogradskaia Vol. 2 2003: 374)

Sulerzhitsky's particular contribution was his suggestion to improvise on themes which were also technical in nature and reflective of the first version of the System. These included concentration, temper and ability to communicate with a partner.

The April 1913 report mentioned above described this method of dramatic composition as 'a revival and a new variation of the old Commedia dell'Arte' (Vinogradskaia Vol. 2 2003: 382). This generated a rebuke from Meyerhold, who at the time was himself experimenting with *commedia dell'arte* techniques (see Chapter 5). Meyerhold's focus was on the acting techniques that he could appropriate from *commedia*, such as the composition of character types, the use of props and objects, and the application of gesture as a medium for signification. In a letter to the writer S. S. Ignatov he expressed pessimism on the First Studio's experiments in improvisation, saying that Stanislavsky will be never prepared for *commedia*.[13] Stanislavsky's experiments in improvisation as a tool for dramatic composition seem, at least in this letter, to have escaped Meyerhold: rather than reconstruction or even research in *commedia dell'arte* per se, it was the creation of a repertoire through 'the process of mutual artistic exchange between an actor and an author' (Stanislavsky in Vinogradskaia Vol. 2 2003: 407) that interested Stanislavsky.

It is in broadening his research focuses at the First Studio that Stanislavsky brought a democratic levelling between the actor, playwright and director within the processes of performance transmission and creation. Both

Stanislavsky and Sulerzhitsky formally directed several full productions for the First Studio, but within these improvisations the role of the director was transformed. The director's role as the over-arching organizer of performance events was relinquished, for that of a facilitator to emerge. The director is not negated but his role transformed. Gorky articulated the director's role within these improvisations in rhythmic terms. He is to accelerate the development of the action when it is too slow or reduce the range of material when it is too broad (Gorkii 1955: 262). In leading such improvisations, the director-facilitator has to walk a very fine line: his inputs need to keep the action moving forwards, while ensuring that the actors remain within the set thematic or technical parameters. At the same time he needs to give particular attention not to impose his own point of arrival on the improvisation. This is a balance which permeates the configuration of theatre as an ensemble of artists, of actors, directors, playwrights, but also composers, designers, painters, musicians and even the more humble ushers and attendants working together in concert and towards a common aim: '[All those] working in the theatre [...] are the servants of the basic goal of art and totally subordinate to it. Everyone, without exception, is a co-creator of the performance' (Stanislavski 2008b: 570). While the Stanislavsky acting tradition is defined by practitioners that seek to adopt and apply the System, Stanislavsky's leaning towards ensemble formations – in the production process, on the stage and at the First Studio – proved an equally influential pull on the modernization of other theatre realities, broadening significantly the scope of his influence.[14] It is one which Smyshlaev would then put at the centre of his interpretation of Stanislavsky (Chapter 3) and which resurfaces when the amateur theatre of the workers took collective creation as a working method.

In the short term, Stanislavsky experiments with dramatic improvisation at the First Studio must have been seen as a failure. No play was created and staged using this method, at either the First Studio itself or the main house. A new repertoire was not created. The long-term impact of these experiments on Stanislavsky's trajectory, however, is not to be downplayed. Through these experiments Stanislavsky acquired crucial experience in how to run improvisatory sessions, experience which he returned to when placing improvisation at the heart of his final work on Active Analysis.[15] Two features of Active Analysis are worth highlighting here. First, in the early rehearsals actors were barred from memorizing the text. Only knowledge of a plot's outline was needed for the actors to improvise on, but as subsequent improvisations move closer to the text, the words become easier to learn. This, in fact, is one of the main benefits which Bella Merlin today sees in Active Analysis (in White 2014: 327 and 339). Second, Stanislavsky's final experiments in improvisations revolved around placing the actor in the

Given Circumstances of the play, which is facilitated by using the actor's own everyday physical actions with which he is most familiar.[16] Symptoms of both practices can be found at the First Studio. At one point student-actors had improvised on a text by Molière, 'without knowing the words but by a detailed description of the characters and situations. The actors fill up the pauses with their own words' (Blok in Vinogradskaia Vol. 2 2003: 349). Similar to Active Analysis, these improvisations at the First Studio were intended as a way to get the actors close to the text. Improvisations on everyday situations and in everyday spaces also recurred in both phases of work, highlighting Stanislavsky's tendency to revisit and adapt rather than drop previous approaches.

Rehearsal Transmission: Stanislavsky's work on *Artists and Admirers*

One chapter in Stanislavsky's career that scholarship has tended to sideline is that of the 1932–3 work that led to the production of Alexander Ostrovsky's *Artists and Admirers*. This might be explained by the fact that the rehearsal notes we have of the production, reproduced in I. Vinogradskaia's edited collection *Stanislavski Repetiruiet*, seem at face value to only repeat many of the points raised by Vasili Osipovich Toporkov in his own, more popular account of Stanislavsky's final work. Both sources, for instance, underline Stanislavsky's shift towards action that characterized his last ten years of work.[17] A closer look to the notes of *Artists and Admirers*, however, produces several new contributions to Stanislavsky studies, readings which I have already presented elsewhere (Aquilina 2012b, 2013, 2016). Here, I will contribute a further discussion on these rehearsal notes. First, the rehearsal approaches which Stanislavsky used will be elaborated on. These approaches will be treated as instances of practice with a reach that went beyond the performance being prepared. In other words, the rehearsals served as transmission activities through which acting techniques were distilled, in view of their further application in other performance situations. Second, ways in which Stanislavsky negotiated the shift from a small rehearsal studio, typically that of his own private apartment, to the big stage of the MAT, will also be discussed. This shift will again be treated as an act of transmission.

Ostrovsky's play, written in 1881, tells the story of a provincial actress called Negina and her various admirers. Negina is passionate about the theatre, and the play revolves around her love for Pyotr Meluzov, a young and idealistic university graduate, whom she however renounces to live with Ivan Velikatov, a rich land and factory owner who could offer her a much better chance of

Figure 4 Vasily Kachalov in the role of Narokov, in the Moscow Art Theatre's production of Ostrovsky's *Artists and Admirers*, 1933. Director – Nina Litovtseva, artistic supervisor – Konstantin Stanislavsky. Courtesy Laurence Senelick Collection.

success in the theatre. The actors started rehearsing the play in March 1932 under the direction of N. N. Litovtseva. Stanislavsky became involved in the production in December, and the play opened on 23 September 1933. The rehearsal notes, variously collected by actress Alla Tarasova[18] and stage director G. V. Kristi, give details of eighteen sessions with Stanislavsky. Notes of two dress rehearsals, recorded by the director and actor of the Leningrad Young People's Theatre B. V. Zon, are also included. The notes show evidence of a substantial range of acting material tackled in the rehearsals, including the use of action to arrive at feeling, the construction of the through-line, the difference between nuanced performance and grotesque acting, rhythm, improvisation, the laws governing speech and the use of inner images.

What kind of rehearsal approaches did Stanislavsky use in these rehearsals, and how do they become transmission activities? The notes show a Stanislavsky wearing two hats, that of the director and that of the teacher-researcher or, in other words, the transmitter of acting tenets. The rehearsal notes themselves are framed by Vinogradskaia as instances of *both* direction and research: 'It is impossible in Konstantin Stanislavsky's practice to separate questions related to the science of creativity from the construction of performance and interpretation of the characters' (Vinogradskaia 2000: 207). Thus, while certainly working to prepare his actors for performance, Stanislavsky was also extrapolating over-arching and transferable acting techniques, making the rehearsals not only a space to construct performance but also an environment where acting techniques could be articulated. The rehearsal notes constantly show him moving from working on a particular scene, where he tackled narrow solutions to specific acting tasks, to the formulation of broader acting tenets that could be reapplied across a range of performance circumstances. A typical example can be found when the actors were rehearsing the scene of Negina's departure with Velikatov. In order to give different inflexions to the scene, Stanislavsky asked the group to find different ways of mocking Meluzov (cheerfully, ironically, admirably, enthusiastically, shockingly, etc.). He wanted to create a variegated rather than one-dimensional crowd. From this example Stanislavsky then transmitted the following acting tenet or advice of a more applicable and general nature: '*The most powerful colour is the contrasting one, when admiration is expressed by despair, anger by happiness, etc.*' (emphasis in the original; 223).

There are certainly plenty of instances in the rehearsal notes when Stanislavsky unravelled the subtext behind the Given Circumstances of the play. These explanations were never indulgent affairs, because they were directly linked to what the actors were presenting, to their draft material which Stanislavsky would then deepen and clarify. During a rehearsal dated

23 January 1933, Tarasova expressed confusion about the scene where Negina reads Meluzov's and Velikatov's letters. Stanislavsky here proceeded to explain the nuanced love which Negina feels towards the former: she is rejecting her own happiness with him for the benefit of her acting career. He developed this reading in great detail, over two pages of notes in fact (224–6). Across these pages, but also during other rehearsal moments, Stanislavsky comes across as being very rational in his approach to directing, carefully explaining Ostrovsky's use of pauses for instance or how contemporary audiences would react to Negina living unwed with a man. Another rehearsal approach involved asking questions to the actors. Instead of transmitting his knowledge of the play, Stanislavsky used questions to elicit from the actors a deeper understanding of the Given Circumstances.[19] One such rehearsal took place on 16 January 1933, when Stanislavsky probed the actress Zueva about the importance of a character's entrance (220–1). The use of images and metaphors from everyday life to immediately connect with the actors also emerges as a further rehearsal approach. During these instances, Stanislavsky spoke about acting through the images of diving into a pool, opening doors, ripping off necklaces, playing chess, riding horses, painting a wall, a swan unravelling its neck and so on, some forty such metaphors in the space of twenty pages in fact.[20]

Throughout the notes, however, it is Stanislavsky's oscillation between specific moments of rehearsal and over-arching acting techniques that strikes me as the most consistent approach. Following his heart attack in 1928, Stanislavsky understood that he was working on borrowed time. Using rehearsal also as a space for the transmission of acting technique underlines his wish to maximize the time he had with the actors. As in the example given above, the transmittable acting techniques extrapolated from the rehearsal situations are italicized in order to give them more emphasis. Eighteen such examples of italicized techniques are evident, with the following being just a few examples:

> *Always, forever, start from yourself,* in all the characters you are performing. *It is me,* acting in those given circumstances that the author gives (214).[21]
> *Involve the partner into your images; force her to see everything with your eyes* (223). *An actor who tries to feel or stage a character is not a good actor. An actor who begins with the 'what if' will find the right path to the role* (228). *A role cannot be left in a fragmented state. A multitude of small actions and tasks have to be absorbed by bigger tasks and, finally, the bigger tasks will, in turn, be consumed by one unifying main task.* [...] *Spontaneity and improvisation on the stage are what best of all refreshes the role and breathes new life into it.* (242)

Ultimately, Stanislavsky distilled the essence of convincing acting in three succinct points, namely (i) knowledge of the logical through-line of action (ii) the ability to enter into the role in a fresh manner that is reflective of the 'here, today, and now', and (iii) playing for the partner (231).

The rehearsal notes of *Artists and Admirers* are also important because they provide evidence of how Stanislavsky negotiated the shift from the small rehearsal space to the big stage. This is another instance of transmission, negotiated not between different people, but as a movement of practice from one workspace to another. The adaptation and processing synonymous with transmission are also invoked. 'A terribly dangerous moment' is how Stanislavsky was quoted to have described this period of work on a play (reproduced by B. V. Zon in Vinogradskaia 2000: 244), which could lead either to the play's successful realization on the big stage or to the whole process hitting a brick wall. The production of *A Month in the Country* (1909) was a case in point. Benedetti described the move to the big stage as catastrophic, further quoting a letter of Stanislavsky in which he griped that the exercises in attention and communication, which had shown promise in rehearsal, simply disappeared on the big stage, and 'what had seemed fine at the table, emerged as weak. All the actors spoke quietly, could not expand their voices' (Stanislavsky quoted in Benedetti 1999: 192). Earlier on, when working on *Othello* (1896), he had marvelled how a senior actor like Tommaso Salvini could play in the huge Bolshoi Theatre while he could barely finish a rehearsal in a small room (Stanislavski 2008a: 148).

The shift from the small rehearsal room to the big stage was worked on during the dress rehearsals of 14 and 16 May 1933. Zon attended both rehearsals, which he described as an important learning opportunity to which even seasoned actors like Ivan Moskvin and Leonid Leonidov attended. During these rehearsals Stanislavsky gave substantial importance to the outer dimension of the performance. The scenery, props and costumes had been prepared beforehand of course, but it was at this moment that they were confirmed or tested out in practice: 'The actors enter the stage one by one. The meticulous study of the costumes and make-up begins here' (246). Consequently, V. A. Verbitsky's physical characterization of Prince Delubov was changed slightly, with folds of fat removed from the back of his head and the waist reduced in size. In this way, the 'somewhat elaborate form was simplified' (246) because, Stanislavsky explained, the inner design that Verbitsky constructed did not require it.[22] Zon remarked that this was the first time that every detail was seen in relation to the totality of the production.

Following this work, Stanislavsky moved to create mises-en-scène with the actors. These had to be found anew because of the major shift in the workspace. An entry dated 16 January 1933 gives us an indication of the work environment at Stanislavsky's apartment:

> V.A. Verbitsky, playing Dulebov, appeared from behind the bookcase, which in Stanislavsky's office served as the side-scene for all the rehearsals. He gave Domna Panteleyevna (who was being rehearsed by N.A. Sokolovskaya) his hat and walking stick. After talking to her, he sat down next to the table where Stanislavsky was also sitting. A.K. Tarasova (playing Negina) sits down as well, next to that table, and they start communicating between themselves in a low tone. (216)

The restricted rehearsal space emerges clearly in this quotation, and it still exists for anyone to get a feel of when visiting Stanislavsky's apartment, now his museum. Faced with the size of the MAT stage, the actors were tasked with finding a new physical expression to their behaviour. This behaviour had not only to function on the bigger space but also to remain faithful to the inner logical lines of the actors' actions. The flip side was that by keeping to their inner lines, the actors were making the shift from the small rehearsal space to the big stage.[23]

In concrete terms, the shift from the rehearsal room to the stage took place as follows. Stanislavsky asked the actors to take the stage, which was set up as Negina's apartment, and to get familiar with the space by entering it, walk around, sit down, touch things, lean against the furniture, etc. This work was carried out individually. In this manner, 'everything, or at least most of the things, were being recognized by the actors for the very first time' (247). The participants were thus asked to connect with the space first and to remain sensitive to what the new surroundings were suggesting: 'As they move for the first time from the rehearsal room to the stage, the actors occasionally find unexpected tools for the solutions of the set tasks' (249). It is this element of the unexpected that Stanislavsky particularly valued in these moments, in line with his broader technique of encouraging the actor to check himself against the 'here, today, and now' moment of a specific performance or rehearsal situation.

After getting a sense of the space, the actors were asked to start connecting with one another. They did this by acting according to the inner designs of their roles: 'They meet and talk quietly. They interact with the objects. In other words, they *live*' (emphasis in the original; 247). Through these interactions, groupings on the stage start emerging, which Stanislavsky asked the actors to remember. These groupings were also noted down: 'Notice – he tells his assistants – this arrangement. It is a group. There's warmness in it' (247). Finally, he checked the new arrangements to make sure that they fit within the technical requirements of the stage. In this particular case, he walked around the auditorium to confirm that a particular grouping looked good from different angles. The process was repeated for Act 2, which was set as the backstage of a provincial theatre. In the rehearsal, the MAT actors, playing the roles of provincial actors in the play, entered the scene, and Stanislavsky reacted by casually expressing his thoughts on the scene. The actors reacted to his instructions but seemingly gave attention only to the stage and without looking at Stanislavsky himself. They shuffled around, sat down wherever they wanted and interacted with one another. However, 'from this "wherever they wanted", and through gradual corrections, they once again delivered "from within", a live (not photographic) group' (249).

The international dimension of the Stanislavsky acting tradition

The well-known Moscow Art Theatre's foreign tours were only one example of Stanislavsky's casting his net outside of Russia. In looking internationally, Stanislavsky was being markedly modern in his approach to theatre making. He was certainly not alone in this. The amount of correspondence and sharing of ideas between Moscow, Paris, Berlin, Prague, London and New York shows that the modernists envisaged themselves within an international tapestry: 'modernism has for many embodied a kind of internationalism fundamentally at odds with the parochial, regional, and monolingual. [...] Pervasive border crossings – geopolitical, psychological, spiritual, sexual, moral, and aesthetic – underline the cultural imagery of modernism' (Stanford Friedman in Eysteinsson and Liska 2007: 35). Theatre makers like Jacques Copeau, Edward Gordon Craig, Erwin Piscator and others were clearly driven by their desire to renew their 'home' theatre culture, but their localized projects rippled outwards and stimulated a broader and more international project of theatre renewal. Turn-of-the-twentieth-century globalization also played a significant role in the internalization of theatre, especially with the significant improvement in transportation which eased the movement of people and of whole touring companies. Alison Hodge says that the 'cross fertilisation of ideas and practices between [...] practitioners is complex' (Hodge 2010: xxiii), meaning it can take multifarious forms and generate different kinds of impact. Examples of such cross fertilization in modernism abound. These include Copeau's interest in Emile Jacques-Dalcroze's eurhythmics and Adolphe Appia's scenic work, Stanislavsky's study of Isadora Duncan's work, and the assimilation, if not without criticism, of acting and staging techniques from Oriental theatre, including Bertolt Brecht's adoption of Mei Lan-Fang as an example of epic acting.

Stanislavsky's (and the MAT's) international character is evidenced in the words of non-Russian practitioners. It says a lot about the Soviet politicization of Stanislavsky that whereas in Russia his persona was used to define and represent a particular theatre culture, that of socialist realism, practitioners outside Russia treated him as a common ground for the bringing together of international theatre practice. Contrast, for example, the very national tone encapsulated in the various reverential accolades given to Stanislavsky by Soviet authorities from the 1930s onwards (e.g. 'Our Pride', in Carnicke 1993: 22), with Stanislavsky's role in cross-border activity as articulated by Eduardo de Filippo, where the Russian director is eulogized as 'a basis on which all the theatres of the world aspiring to real art could unite' (in Stanislavski 1963: 211). John Gielgud makes a similar statement when he described 'Stanislavsky's now famous book [as] a contribution to the theatre and its students all over the world' (in Stanislavski 1963: 220).

These foreign practitioners encountered Stanislavsky's ideas from what Ian Maxwell referred to, in relation to Stanislavsky's impact on actor training in far-away Australia, as the 'tyranny of' or 'effect at a' distance. This is the very real distance that stops people from making direct contact with one another and which consequently hinders transmission processes (Maxwell in Pitches and Aquilina 2017: 325–30; see also Pitches in Pitches and Aquilina 2017: 319–20). Such a distance, which Copeau described as one 'that seemed out of reach' (in Stanislavski 1963: 170), is, for example, how the French director described the indirect transmission routes through which he came to know of Stanislavsky's work. These included a number of Craig's writings and the stories recounted by travellers coming back from Moscow. Misinterpretations are often a corollary of this distance, with sources being either missing or extremely partial. Indicative of this misinterpretation is, for example, Copeau's inflated assertion that Stanislavsky's 'theatre could, thanks to immense material support, indulge securely in research' (in Stanislavski 1963: 170). While distance can make transmission channels both limited and limiting, it can also help fuel a more critical disposition towards a source technique. In Russia Stanislavsky was idealized as a national hero who was beyond criticism. Foreign practitioners, on the other hand, still idealized him – and the correspondences and addresses of Copeau, Antoine and Jean Vilar are peppered with such eulogies[24] – but their geographical detachment allowed them a point of view and a predisposition to read Stanislavsky through the prism of their own theatre culture.

The 'critical disposition at a distance' permitted practitioners to be highly selective in the techniques or practices they appropriated from Stanislavsky.

This was evident from Jaroslav Kvapil's interpretation of Stanislavsky. A Czech poet, playwright and librettist, Kvapil was appointed in 1900 as a director and dramaturg of the National Theatre in Prague. In this position he coordinated the composition of the Manifesto for Czech writers, which delineated the role that the literary sphere had to play in the drive for Czech self-government (Burian 2000: 24). His background, therefore, was in formal theatre institutions of a national composition, and it comes as no surprise to note that even though Stanislavsky did send him stage material like sets and costume sketches to use in his productions (another instance of Scenic Transmission), what struck a chord from the MAT tour of 1906 were the supposed national tendencies emanating from *Tsar Fiodor*, *Uncle Vania*, *Three Sisters* and *The Lower Depths*.[25] Kvapil describes these as 'excellent national traditions', with the elements of directing, acting and production being 'deeply rooted in their national soil [and] based on wonderful theatrical traditions' (in Stanislavski 1963: 162).[26]

Michael Redgrave's reading of Stanislavsky similarly highlights how cultural transmission allows practitioners to choose and select from a range of ideas and practices. Distance makes a source technique hazy to its receivers, allowing them to 'fill the blanks' and make choices that reflect not only the receiver's most immediate needs but also the cultural leanings within which they operate. Redgrave encountered Stanislavsky's work through two transmission channels, namely the 'glimpse' offered by Russian actors acting in Hollywood movies and the documentary evidence offered by books such as *An Actor Prepares*. Technical lessons Redgrave appropriated from *An Actor Prepares* included the acting tenet of organic development, where a role is given the time necessary to develop without rushing any of its developmental stages. A second technical lesson was the importance of a solid imaginative foundation when building a character (Stanislavski 1963: 215). More than technical, however, Redgrave indicated that Stanislavsky's impact on his theatre practice, as situated within British theatre of the early years after the Second World War, was ethical in nature. He argued that running throughout *An Actor Prepares* is a 'degree of serious respect for craft [...] [emphasizing that an actor's] work can at its best be creative and achieve not merely *réclame*, but dignity' (in Stanislavski 1963: 218). Redgrave believed that such an ethical disposition, encapsulated in Stanislavsky's maxim 'love art in yourself and not yourself in art', was missing in British theatre. This is, of course, another very general and contentious statement, but Stanislavsky's ethical zealotry, at least as expressed in *An Actor Prepares*, pushed Redgrave to say that the book 'will probably make him [the actor or actress] profoundly dissatisfied with the conditions of work prevailing in Britain' (Stanislavski 1963: 218). It is a dissatisfaction that serves as a first stepping stone for the renewal of that particular theatre tradition.

Similar to Kvapil half a century before, Redgrave's appropriation of Stanislavsky was therefore partial and preferential and, in underscoring the ethical dimension, revealing of the potential which context has to underscore certain transmission choices over others. Purists might argue that such a partial and preferential appropriation of ideas would not have met Stanislavsky's approval, especially when one considers the seriousness with which he stressed the organicity of the System. A recurrent concern for Stanislavsky was to find a way of articulating the relationship between the System as a whole and its constituent parts (imagination, concentration, magic 'if', tempo-rhythm, relaxation of muscles, etc.). Most famously he represented this relationship through a drawing, reproduced in Sharon Marie Carnicke's *Stanislavsky in Focus* (2009: 123) and in Rose Whyman's *The Stanislavsky System of Acting* (2008: 40–1). Patrick C. Carriere also reproduced in translation Stanislavsky's notes accompanying the drawing, to argue that '[t]his graphic depiction of the System provides a concise summary of Stanislavski's thoughts on how the different elements within the System functioned together' (Carriere 2010: 154). Stanislavsky's favoured approach to reach the System in its totality seems to suggest psychophysical unity via the System's constituent parts, of using fragmentation to reach the whole: 'The "system" has to be studied in its separate parts and then grasped as a whole, so as to understand its overall structure and fundamentals' (Stanislavski 2008b: 612).

Practical examples of Stanislavskian transmission, however, seem to suggest otherwise. Indeed, he himself evidenced a selective approach when interacting with other cross-border theatre realities. Mei Lan-Fang understood this characteristic in Stanislavsky: 'He [Stanislavsky] took the fine national legacy close to heart and selected the best from the art of other peoples very skilfully' (Stanislavski 1963: 189). Therefore, in cross-border interaction Stanislavsky was himself selective, partial and preferential in what he appropriated. Stanislavsky's most famous case of cross-cultural appropriation is perhaps evidenced in his experiments with the Indian techniques of Yoga and Prana. An important component of the research at the First Studio, these techniques were adopted to relax the muscles from unnecessary tensions and to stimulate silent communication between the actors (Gordon 1988: 69–70). Yoga was also posed as a model to advance Stanislavsky's research in body-mind synergies, unsuccessfully as it turned out (Kapsali 2013: 157–8). Another example of a selective approach is evident in Stanislavsky's appraisal of Ernst Possard (1841–1921), a German tragic actor who played frequently in Russia. Stanislavsky described Possard as 'an actor in the best and worst sense of the word' (Stanislavskii 1954: 420). While valuing Possard's comic characterizations, seeing them as models of simplicity and subtlety, Stanislavsky distanced himself from the German actor's tragic roles, which in comparison he considered bombastic and declaimed using 'the methods of the false German declamation' (Stanislavskii 1954: 420). Stanislavsky's application of the French acting tradition as a training ground was equally selective: he valued the skill in gestural composition of French actors while being critical of their predilection to represent rather than experience emotional states (Autant-Mathieu in Pitches and Aquilina 2017: 68–71).

In all these cases, Stanislavsky's critical disposition is to be noted, a critical disposition which he elevated as a working method when interacting with other theatre traditions, locally but also cross-culturally: 'Even in the old theatre, there were elements of high and beautiful art that we are looking for now. We should carefully, and with a lot of attention, analyse (study) the old, in order to learn better the new tasks' (Stanislavskii 1958: 466). Careful study implies a proactive disposition rather than a blind or wholly acceptance of a source technique: selectivity is one form which this critical disposition takes. It encourages receivers to create their own links between disparate theatre cultures to, as Stanislavsky himself would recommend, not depend slavishly on a source technique, but to develop a practice that answers the technical needs and contexts of work of a receiver.

Stanislavsky's international disposition came particularly to the fore when he addressed non-Russian audiences. In one such address during the American tour, he thanked American support which had alleviated the technical problems of the MAT (a lack of canvas, paints, bulbs, fabric, etc.). He also took the opportunity to suggest a reciprocal exchange where Russian institutions would provide cultural rather than material products. This will be done 'in the name of general human culture' (Senelick 2014: 398). With an international audience, Stanislavsky's attention therefore shifted to cross-border synergy. Another case in point is the following address to the Jewish actors of the Habima: 'In art, there are no differences, of rank, religion, nationality. Art is the realm in which brotherhood of people might exist' (Senelick 2014: 469).

The desire to unite theatre across borders was a micro-expression of the macro drive for international unification between countries. This is a recurring motif in Stanislavsky's letters to foreign colleagues. In this regard his was not a lone voice as Stanislavsky's internationalism was a reflection of the times. The warring times bequeathed by the modern world set in motion various efforts to prevent a repetition of the First World War. The strongest among these was the formation of the League of Nations in January 1920, whose principal objective was to promote world peace and international cooperation. The concept of internationalism was at the time already a fluid one. It was not imprisoned in binary articulations. Peace, for example, was seen possible through the combination of larger-scale efforts by the governments with the smaller independent cells operating at the local levels. Furthermore, post–First World War internationalism contained the 'paradoxical mix' of 'one world', i.e. the awareness that some concerns and qualities are shared, and the idea of 'multiple nations', with their unique cultural inflections and problems (Cuddy-Keane et al. 2014: 131). In this reading cultural uniqueness was not seen as an impediment to cooperation because nations had enough recurrences on which to construct international bonds. Stanislavsky supported the latter understanding. In his Appeal to the Union of Moscow Actors, he laid down his programme for a First studio that was to provide space for the convergence of the various artistic schools that were evident at the time. These included realism, stylization, impressionism, futurism and others. Beyond issues related to the theatre forms spearheaded by the revolution, however, Stanislavsky saw this First studio as a space for international cooperation between theatre workers. This was possible by understanding what practitioners shared, their points of contact so to speak, but placed in a positive tension with the qualities that rendered them unique. Stanislavsky thus spoke of recurrence and difference:[27]

> We judge someone's artistic principles on gossip, hearsay, according to the lectures of scientists and theorists who do not understand our art, and only know how to speak beautifully about it. [...] Confusion creates strife where people could understand each other.
>
> The Actors' Union must create its own studio, which could unite people from all directions for closer practical examination of all sides and depths of our art. [...] The main task of this studio is not to convince people of another direction or to pull them to their party. No. It would be a great mistake to encroach on artistic freedom and individuality. [...] In the Studio's practical experiments *there will be the promotion of separate directions but also the ground for convergence when that is possible* [...].
>
> [...] Who knows, perhaps, of the many small and autonomous regions there will rise a huge federal artistic republic which will spread not only in Moscow but throughout all Russia. And perhaps amongst these studios there will be Russian branches and actors from institutions of other countries.
>
> After all, before the war, there was a discussion about such an international studio. It will help to create if not to a rapprochement then at least a mutual spiritual understanding of people, through their

literature and art. I believe that this important mission of rapprochement and understanding has been assigned to us.

Art, as the most sensitive of feelers, probes and opens the specific characteristics of individuals and of whole nations. It is our duty to work in this direction. (Stanislavskii 1959: 29–31; emphasis added)

Stanislavsky's international outlook was enhanced further by the very international repertoire he worked on. This was most clear at the First Studio. The Second Studio produced many Russian texts and adaptations,[28] while the more tendentious nature of productions like *Days of the Turbins* and *Armoured Train 14–69* led to the abortion of a possible American tour in the late 1920s (Senelick 2014: 497–8). The First Studio, on the other hand, exhibited a very international repertoire. It staged works written by Herman Heijermans (a German), Charles Dickens (an English), Henning Berger and August Strindberg (both Swedish), and Henrik Ibsen (Norwegian). Its internationalism might have been fuelled directly by Sulerzhitsky himself, whose wandering adventures had taken him all around the world.

The international dimension of the Art Theatre itself came to the fore when it opened its doors to visitors from abroad. The most famous example is perhaps that of Craig and his co-production with Stanislavsky of *Hamlet* (1911), but other theatre makers visited the Theatre on the pretext of watching performances, but in reality to study its methods. A case in point is that of the English theatre maker Harley Granville Barker, who was in Moscow in February 1914 'to learn the art of the Moscow Art Theatre' (Vinogradskaia Vol. 2 2003: 423). He watched *The Cherry Orchard*, *The Three Sisters*, Maeterlinck's *The Blue Bird* and productions of Goldoni, Molière and Knut Hamsun (Purdom 1955: 153). His analysis of the MAT was again channelled through the prism of distance, this time generated by time. Granville Barker published two newspaper articles on this visit, both in 1917. Like Copeau, he inflated the MAT achievements, describing both productions of Chekhov's plays as 'perfection of achievement in the theatre' (*The Guardian*, 7 July 1917).[29] He was also under the impression that MAT productions opened only when they were considered ready and never 'aborted' prematurely to fit a schedule. He even downplayed the financial and profit-making considerations that underline an institution as big as the Moscow Art Theatre.

The 'lessons' which Barker derived from this visit to Moscow were both technical and ethical in nature. Technically, he was particularly taken by the musical dimension of *Three Sisters* – the knitted scheme of Act 1, the entrances and exits of the actresses, the busy dinner table, the hushed talk on the balcony – and the way that it gave unity to the performance. As a result, he was unable to discern the specific contributions made by the cast, the director or the playwright (*The Guardian*, 7 July 1917). He was also very impressed by Olga Knipper, particularly her use of stillness to convey meaning (Mazer 2013: 80). These instances might have compelled Granville Barker to assert that at the MAT 'character counts for more than theme' (*The Guardian*, 7 July 1917). On the ethical plane, it was Stanislavsky's understanding that theatre practice impacts the actors' everyday life that seems to have made an effect. Elsewhere, I argue that Stanislavsky saw the ethical behaviour underlining actor training – discipline, group work, diligence, commitment – as spilling out of the studio to impact on the students' everyday life (Aquilina 2012c). This understanding is reflected in Granville Barker's analysis of Stanislavsky's work:

> Stanislavsky was telling me [...] that what he always needed was a company of good citizens. 'Acting is not acrobatics, but the expression of life; and of life at its normal not less than at its moments of crisis.' [...] [Y]ou must think of art in terms not of profit or success but of life, and of normal life. And that life interpreted through art has double power. And that the theatre served aright, keenly, sweetly, merrily, with passion and thought, is not the least life-giving of the arts by which we both live and know we are alive. (*The Guardian*, 7 July 1917)

Consequently, an agreement seems to have been made with Stanislavsky so that two of Granville Barker's students could receive training at the First Studio (Vinogradskaia Vol. 2 2003: 423).

Granville Barker's case is a curious one. His artistic trajectory before this 1914 visit ran along similar lines to Stanislavsky's, a fact which several biographies on the Englishman readily acknowledge. Eric Salmon, for example, argues that Granville Barker's approach to theatre – especially in his emphasis on the inner unravelling of the dramatic world and of its various characters – chimed with what Stanislavsky was doing in Moscow.[30] Salmon goes on to argue that such unintended parallelisms are not unheard of in both theatre and science, when two 'explorers in the same field, responding to the form and pressure of the time, make the same series of discoveries simultaneously, co-incidently, without reference to or knowledge of each other's work' (Salmon 1983: 109–10). It is a parallelism that features in modernism broadly construed, not least in Peter Brook's coming to know about both Jerzy Grotowski and Antonin Artaud. Brook's encounter with their work and theories came in the 1960s, after his ideas were already substantially formed. He described this encounter as an exciting moment, when he realized that the more research-oriented approach to theatre production that he was developing at LAMDA had contemporary as well as antecedent reference points. On Grotowski, Brook remarked that the knowledge that someone else 'at the other end of the earth [...] is trying to do the same experiment makes us want to know the results'; on Artuad he wrote that '[w]ithout realizing it, for years the ground had been being prepared and so I was ready to be deeply impressed' (Brook 1988: 40 and 41). Similarly, Granville Barker's pursue of detailed rehearsal work was corroborated by his Moscow trip, offering it a parallel reference point and measuring yardstick. Modernism revelled in such international parallelism.

Conclusion

It is remarkable that lacunae and gaps remain even in our knowledge of Stanislavsky, whose name has generated a vast number of secondary sources. This is perhaps inevitable, not only because of the range of work that he attempted throughout a half-a-century career, but also because with the application of critical theory in the study of theatre and performance our interpretative strategies are also bound to expand. This chapter has hopefully shed light on a few such gaps, by using transmission as a focus to read Stanislavsky's relationship with Ludwig Barnay for instance or his rehearsal work going into the production of *Artists and Admirers*. In his commitment to transmission processes, at the First Studio, in rehearsal, but also in his more informal encounters with colleagues, such as over correspondence, Stanislavsky contributed to the renewal of the Russian theatre tradition. In the nineteenth century, this tradition was strongly defined by its writers like Gogol and Ostrovsky, while Shchepkin provided a crucial acting reference point. Developing into the twentieth century, a strong pedagogical current was infused into this tradition, bequeathing a studio culture which practitioners from all over the world sought to study, if at times, not uncritically.

Suggestions for practice

The Gorky Method

Attempt the Gorky Method of creating a play through the improvisations of the actors. Assign the role of director-facilitator from within the group to help keep the improvisation within the set scenario. Improvisations can often become indulgent affairs, with actors developing their lines and characters with little concern to the whole. As a director-facilitator you need to be alert to this. You might also wish to assign the role of the playwright, who can be tasked with providing the opening scenario. Depending on how far you wish to take the exercise, the playwright might also record the improvisations and develop these into more formal dramatic pieces. The following scenarios are the ones which Gorky himself had suggested to Stanislavsky (Gorkii 1955: 263–4).

Scenario 1

Some people, sitting in a room during a winter evening, are waiting for a man. He is a father or a relative who has been tried in the district court. The man is responsible for the livelihood of the family. They justify his crime, even though they all know he has done it. The dialogue can be very interesting, where the people try to convince themselves of something which they do not believe in. They can also sincerely consider that the convicted man is innocent: this, of course, is another interpretation. In this case, the people will frighten each other with the possibility of accusation. You can show different degrees of anticipation and impatience. The man is freed. He is cheerful, drunk. He may also not be a criminal but a rich relative who brings gifts and favours. He, however, shows up and behaves very differently. Disappointment ensues. The people are upset.

Scenario 2

Show people waiting in a room before they take the exams to enter the Art Theatre school. This can produce both dramatic and comic moments. People are sitting, talking, trying to hide their excitement; some are funny, arrogant – they are talentless of course – while for others the exams are a matter of life. They enter the examination room and come out. Gloating, sympathy, envy – all feelings can be shown in this short scene.

Your own scenarios can also be suggested. Experiment with different scenario lengths: a one-liner, a paragraph, an extended piece of writing, a more developed piece like a short story. How does the length of the scenario impact on the improvisation? Does a short/long piece facilitate the improvisation? Does it hinder it? Analyse your work processes throughout. The following questions are there to help you: which scenarios were the most conducive to improvisation? Why? Can you identify any 'plot-driven' improvisations? Were others more 'character-driven'? How do these two approaches differ? What are the salient qualities of each?

3

Misinterpretation of theatre practice: Stanislavsky-Smyshlaev

Why cultural transmission?

In Chapter 1 I provided a first definition of what cultural transmission is, with particular emphasis on its dual process-product nature. I also discussed actor training as a case of cultural transmission. However, while it is all well and good to identify actor training as such, I would like to investigate further in the hope of identifying unique perspectives on Russian modernism which are made possible by the application of these theories. In this chapter, I will develop further this idea, by focusing on the following question: in what ways does an application of cultural transmission theories broaden our understanding of theatre and performance in general and of Russian modernism in particular? In other words, how does the application of cultural transmission theories serve the study of theatre and performance without it becoming an end in itself?

The application of cultural transmission to theatre is worth developing when it serves as a critical tool to unpick a particular performance phenomenon. Such theoretical framing is only one example of a much broader debate about contemporary theatre historiography and the role which critical theory plays in the conceptualization of our methods to reconstruct the past. The debate has ranged from a certain wariness with respect to the use of theory in historical study, because of the danger of turning theatre events into 'formulaic illustrations of a system or theory' (Postlewait 2009: 10), to a more open attitude based on the understanding that it is '[f]ar better to acknowledge the ideas that are influencing one's own opinions rather than to assume naively that one is untouched by theoretical positions' (Davis 2011: 92). The general trust of this debate seems to point to an acceptance (and use) of what Jackie Bratton refers to as 'theorised theatre history' (Bratton 2003: 4) or a balance between rigorous archival research and personal imaginative interpretation, the latter framed around concrete theoretical models. These models typically include gender, materialist and psychoanalytic frames. The discipline of history itself has contributed at least one example of such theoretical framing around cultural transmission, namely Anthony Grafton and Ann Blair's edited volume *The Transmission of Culture in Early Modem Europe* (1990). In this study, cultural transmission is used as a means to uncover material which has previously tended to remain in the background, in other words by shifting our focus from the study of conventional and well-trodden historical canons to lesser-known, marginal and minor exponents of a particular historical milieu:

> In the realm of intellectual history, for example, the study of transmission has led us to see that the canon of texts now considered central to the intellectual history of the West does not include some of the most original and influential texts ever written. Works of fundamental originality and impact have been defined as peripheral by critics and historians [...]. They [the essays in the volume revolving on cultural transmission] force us to contemplate texts and artefacts less appealing than the canonical ones of the older cultural history. They divert our attention from familiar and evidently rewarding enterprises [...] to less familiar and evidently difficult ones. (Grafton in Grafton and Blair 1990: 4–6)

Cultural transmission therefore shifts our focus to lesser-known works by broadening a context beyond the established few names that define a tradition. The figure of Valentin Smyshlaev, on which this chapter is based, is one such example of a lesser-known theatre practitioner. At best, he appears only as a footnote in the grandeur project of Russian modern theatre, and often only in relation to canonical contexts, namely as a student of Stanislavsky, member of the Moscow Art Theatre and the First Studio, and as a director at the Moscow Proletkult theatre. What had particularly weighed Smyshlaev down were the accusations which Stanislavsky had made against him, of plagiarism, and of simplifying and even misinterpreting key acting ideas which he had been developing in the privacy of the studio or rehearsal room but which Smyshlaev had gone public with by writing a book titled *The Technique to Process Stage Performance* (*ТЕХНИКА ОБРАБОТКИ СЦЕНИЧЕСКОГО ЗРЕЛИЩА*; 1922, 2nd edition). As a result, he is rarely given much scholarly attention, and I have to still read the first study in English that tackles his work in detail.[1]

Relegating Smyshlaev to a footnote in Russian modernism is one example of what Douglas Mao and Rebecca L. Walkowitz have labelled 'bad modernism'. This is an effort synonymous with the classification of cultural products depending on their supposed artistic value and the consequent creation of hierarchies based on received notions of 'high-low' (in Wallace 2011: 7).

Figure 5 Valentin Smyshlaev. © The Museum of the Moscow Art Theatre.

Jeff Wallace underlines further this effort to create hierarchies, arguing that 'new modernist studies' have been preoccupied with 'unsettling the notion [...] of modernism as distantly superior to the burgeoning of early twentieth-century mass society and popular cultural forms' (Wallace 2011: 6). The creation of hierarchies between artistic products has certainly seeped into our understanding of modern theatre, and while it has given primary importance to names like Stanislavsky, Copeau, Craig, Brook and Grotowski, it has also slowed down the 'rediscovery' of realities like melodrama, clowning, street theatre and nineteenth-century forms of musical theatre (Bratton 2003: 9–10). Smyshlaev's work has similarly suffered from such marginalization. In this chapter I will seek to reposition him as an important figure in Russian modern theatre. The notion that cultural transmission develops, where receivers of cultures are treated as active and not passive agents in the transmission process, who 'collaborate' with the transmitter of the practice to shape the process of transmission, will be the key theoretical tool in this repositioning. Similarly to the way that archival researchers are today not treated as neutral beings but as interpreters of archival material who have their own ideological viewpoints, receivers in contexts of embodied transmission process knowledge through a complex matrix that is made of such dynamics like will, skill, preparation, previous knowledge and purpose, but also receptivity and openness to other ideas. In Smyshlaev's case the latter was particularly relevant, and I will argue that more than a misinterpretation of Stanislavsky's ideas, his acting theories were a product of a disposition towards hybridity which allowed a number of his mentor's techniques to be reconfigured within a context that made collective work its artistic and political driving force. In other words, and as I will argue, it is the link with the political and cultural discourses of the time which made Smyshlaev's theories less a misinterpretation of Stanislavsky's ideas and more of a hybrid development, one that married production processes to political relevance. Key documents in this study are Stanislavsky's letter denouncing his pupil, the aforementioned book *The Technique to Process Stage Performance*, and Smyshlaev's own diary entries of 1917. The latter two sources in particular have, to my knowledge, never been tackled in contemporary studies about Russian modernism.

Smyshlaev's diary: January–December 1917

Smyshlaev's diary shows a person responding to the surrounding environment as it was changing around him. In its pages Smyshlaev considered not only what was happening in the world of the theatre, of the Moscow Art Theatre and the First Studio, but also the broader political arena during those faithful months in 1917. Crucially, he drew connections between the two, in a manner that recalls Meyerhold rather than Stanislavsky or a group of theorists who at the time were looking at defining proletarian culture, like Alexander Bogdanov, Valerian Pletnev and, particularly, Platon Kerzhentsev. In his diary, which is reproduced in the collection *The Moscow Art Theatre in Diaries and Notes* (Anrusenko

2004), Smyshlaev adopts a political frame to articulate the role (i.e. the moral function) of theatre. This he did not by advocating the staging of propaganda or ideological statements, but by foregrounding the then fashionable 'collective practice', or 'collectivism', as a viable way of producing theatre. The diary chimes with Jochen Hellbeck's sociological study of how and why diaries were used in early Soviet Russia, as 'chronicles [to] map an existential terrain marked by self-reflection and struggle' (2006: 4). In this sense diaries are not an assorted compilation of recollections, but a locus for self-evaluation, criticism and ultimately transformation. Smyshlaev's diary is similarly reflective and transformative and can be divided into the following three parts:

- the romantic parts;
- the political dimension;
- the theatrical matters.

These sections emerge as separate and distinct from one another with some difficulty, considering the more intertwining mode of writing that Smyshlaev adopts throughout. What I refer to as the romantic parts exemplify this.[2] In these sections Smyshlaev depicts himself as a sensitive and introspective person, in possession of 'a soul full of inexpressible feelings' (75). This impacted not only his relations with fellow artists but also the way he experienced everyday realities.[3] Everyday occurrences, such as a group of workers going through their daily business, are draped in a language which critical theorist of everyday life Henri Lefebvre would negatively refer to as 'mystical' or 'the mystic metaphor'. This mysticism implies a disposition to curtail the potential of everyday life as a locus to engage with purposeful behaviour and creative human relationships (Lefebvre 2008a: 124–5). For Smyshlaev, the sounds of the workers repairing the rails coalesced with the silence of the night and his own 'bright plans and dreams, […] [taking him] far, far away' (49). Theatre work is similarly articulated in a romantic and idealistic fashion. The word 'suffering' is often invoked, with the following being a typical passage:

> The wish [to create art] is so strong that my soul suffers, till it eases in a process of creation, the supreme act of satisfaction. I want to satisfy it, and I am suffering because I cannot do it quickly enough. I am suffering, and the stronger the will, i.e. love, passion, is, the more painful is my suffering. Suffering makes me want to satisfy the will, i.e. the reason of the suffering. And in this hunt there is the essence of creation.[4] (52)

Smyshlaev uses this tone even when speaking about other performers. For instance, instead of analysing the technicalities behind Feodor Chaliapin's skill, he described the singer as 'a great priest of real Art [from whom he has] [...] received communion by the edge of my soul' (44). Smyshlaev did create a problem for himself when discussing theatre and acting principles and laws, a topic of great importance in the Stanislavsky acting tradition, past and present, where these principles are elaborated into the laws of organic and creative nature (Stanislavski 2008b: 21; see also my discussion about *Artists and Admirers* in Chapter 1).[5] I, say, created a problem because whereas for Stanislavsky these laws were technical considerations, to be methodically explored in the studio or recreated on the stage, for Smyshlaev they became tinged with his romanticism: 'In the mobilization of the spirit, a man draws out a grain of the Eternal. [...] The Eternal is a law, not a fact. A fact is a passing moment. To seek for the Eternal means to seek for the Truth' (54). In these entries, therefore, Smyshlaev obfuscates rather than explores the organic laws of creativity and, consequently, acting processes.

His romantic tone is obliterated as the 1917 events unfolded. When writing during Russia's final catastrophic months of participation in the First World War, his sensitivity was transformed. He himself treated it as a reflection of a bygone era and what he referred to as the 'old, nasty, capitalist law' and world view (62). His sympathy, particularly as his narrative develops, was unequivocally for the Bolsheviks, even exclaiming 'I am a Bolshevik' (62).[6] His allegiance to the Bolsheviks was also fuelled by their promise to end Russia's involvement in the war. Like many artists and members of the intelligentsia, he considered the war a futile and barbaric crime which only served to advance the imperialistic machine and unleash man's basest instincts (62–3). Smyshlaev considered the February Revolution and its aftermath as 'the most miraculous phenomenon in History' (53), but in the summer months he was already hoping for the advent of another revolution, a proletarian revolution (67). As a result, he was suspicious of the Provisional Government and wondered if it was about to 'sell' Russia to Germany in the wake of the latter's advance on Petrograd. Ultimately, it was the Bolsheviks' promise to empower the proletarian that won him over:

> I would tell them [my colleagues] that unity is the best way – that is the tactic of the Bolsheviks. The essence is simple: do not agree with the bourgeoisie. Be the Proletarian party, organize the working classes, the classes that make all the material value, because in the end the Proletarian class will win, and the sooner it happens the better, the less blood will be spilt, the closer true freedom will be, true fellowship, true equality. Unity

is the strength of the Proletariat, but not unity between the Proletariat and the Capitalists. (67)

The diary also sheds light on the theatre which he wanted to see after the revolution. This is a theme he would appraise in several post-revolutionary articles, published in proletarian newspapers like *Gorn* (see Chapter 4). As the revolution drew nearer, however, he had already hinted at a two-pronged theatre regeneration. Central to his thought was the understanding that the proletariat are creators, 'who created everything in the world' (70). Consequently, while lauding the efforts of those who wanted to bring the classics to the workers, Smyshlaev supported the potential of the masses to take theatre and art in new and uncharted directions, creating forms that were undreamed of (99).

In essence, his writings became more political as the revolution drew closer, reaching a culmination in the narration of those latter October days of the Moscow uprising (100–5). He described the state of war that engulfed Moscow, how the city became a war zone. He also recorded his colleagues' reactions to the revolution and was critical of their apolitical character, of 'the blindness of my comrades [at the First Studio]' (70). He felt the pulse of the time, when 'a storm is raging', while his colleagues, because of their bourgeois soul, 'curse the Revolution that brings the Freedom they talk about so inspiringly in their Art; they blame the emancipated people for "laxity", the very folk they describe so well in their Art' (70).[7] A blind sensitivity to artistic matters became not a mark of an elevated spirit, but escapism from the realities outside. Holed in the studio, with fighting in the streets, First Studio members were 'sad and dream[ed] about Art. They [were] confused and dispirited' (104). This was a time when Smyshlaev felt detached from the First Studio, fearing that his role would become that of an ordinary bureaucrat with only the salary to keep him there (71). His tone in the latter writings therefore adjusted to the times, and his romantic tone gave way to political fervour. This is clear in a September 1917 entry, where, while talking about the 'bottomless' sky, and 'the sparkles of moonlight coming into his soul', he asserted: 'What an abyss of beauty and strength in the Proletarian, what a thirst for life are in the eyes of those who are enthusiastic about the Revolution!' (75). Later diary entries, therefore, expose an urge to write himself into the developing sociopolitical order of the time. It comes as no surprise, therefore, to note his involvement in post-revolutionary theatre, as a writer of articles in proletarian newspapers, an acting teacher with an emphasis on working with young workers and a theatre director with the Proletkult, while still keeping his connection with the Moscow Art Theatre and the First Studio and, eventually, the Second Moscow Art Theatre. His contexts of work, therefore, were themselves multiple and heterogeneous.

Theatre references in Smyshlaev's diary

Smyshlaev's account of the tour undertaken to the front by a group of actors from the Moscow Art Theatre during the summer of 1917 offers a first-hand narrative of the difficult touring conditions experienced. He wrote of overcrowded theatres, impossible acoustics (in Kharkov for example), poor stage facilities (in Ekaterinoslav), and uncomfortable transportation and dressing rooms. In Ardasa the company performed on a makeshift stage, on a platform surrounded on three sides by camps, and with the adjacent roofs full of soldiers (64–8). The quality of the performances suffered, with Smyshlaev noting the coarse overacting used to at least carry one's voice and gestures across the performance space. These conditions, however, took second place because 'a few merry moments [were brought] to those miserable people thrown in that dirty dead hall by the hand of the imperialists' (66). Everywhere they performed, the soldiers were delighted with their performances. Performances were also used to provide the soldiers with the news of the day. Smyshlaev did not really approve of this and argued that the political speeches were actually hindering the performances:

> In the evening the garrison of Khamsiny will watch our play. Again Syren will talk with a half-cadet, half-socialistic, language about the brave demonstration of the Bolsheviks, again Boleslavsky will give the speech that he has learnt by heart. And it is what we call bringing the 'live word' to the front. It is ugly, gentlemen. (63)

Other references in the diary shed light on the operations of the MAT and its satellite studios. It is unsurprising that Smyshlaev made reference to the 'Stepanchikovo debacle' that was engulfing the MAT on the eve of the October Revolution. This was the production that widened the already considerable rift between Stanislavsky and the Moscow Art Theatre, when, close to opening night, he was removed from performing in Fyodor Dostoevsky's *The Village of Stepanchikovo*, a production which he was also directing. The reasons for this centred on his inability to bring the role of Rostanev to life. Smyshlaev described the Moscow Art Theatre's disarray with the following words:

> Yesterday there was a dress rehearsal of *The Village of Stepanchikovo*. The play is not a military one, and it does not live up to its expectations. And the expectations are great. The Art Theatre has not staged any new performances for two years now, giving excuses like work or war or

something else ... The real excuse is that it is able to hold on by the old repertoire, not spending money on new performances. Indeed, during these two years the Art Theatre received a great amount of money. And now, after two years the Theatre has to produce a new play and there it is, *The Village of Stepanchikovo*. In front of the audience watching [at a dress rehearsal] there was a break, some misunderstanding with Konst[antin] Sergeevich. In fact, they took the role of the uncle and gave it to Massalitinov, who had to act with little practice. And what is remarkable is that K[onstantin] Sergeevich was not present for the last rehearsals of this year. The old man is hurt with something. Something happened between him and the Theatre. And tomorrow is the general (the last paid) rehearsal of *The Village of Stepanchikovo*, and K[onstantin] S[ergeevich] scheduled a lecture at two o'clock. What is it – a demonstration? It's curious. Yes, it is a pity, but the Theatre has reached the final line, the Theatre is in a deadlock, the Theatre is dying, and maybe only our young Studio can save it, but only if K[onstantin] S[ergeevich] becomes its head. (77)

The failure in the role of Rostanev particularly pained Stanislavsky. He had already played the role as an amateur actor in 1893, and even twenty-five years later he still considered it to be one of his best roles ever (Stanislavski 2008a: 120–2). During the lecture he delivered on 24 September 1917 he spoke about the difficulty of giving birth to a role and about the *Stepanchikovo* failure in particular (78–9). The audience was comprised of gymnasia students and young actors, all of them in their late teens, highlighting his popularity with the young.

Affairs at the First Studio were hardly better, and it was still reeling from Sulerzhitsky's death in December 1916. A lot of work was taking place at the First Studio, and Smyshlaev makes reference to the rehearsals of *Twelfth Night* and the performances of *Wreck of the Ship 'Hope'*. Rehearsals for *Twelfth Night* were not progressing well, with Smyshlaev remarking that on occasion they were a waste of time and that the idleness that had engulfed the Art Theatre was spilling into the First Studio (78). This was particularly unfortunate because the First Studio needed a success out of *Twelfth Night*, considering that its repertoire was full of old productions.[8] There was also some internal bickering on the casting of the play (86). While this might appear as a superficial detail and hardly deserving attention, Smyshlaev deemed casting difficulties important enough to discuss them in a chapter of his book ('Division of the roles', Smyshlaev 1922: 13–14; see below). The actors' behaviour was also discussed at a council meeting, as certain actors were simply not turning up for the performances. This state of affairs might

Figure 6 I. V. Lazarev in the role of Boss, in the First Studio production of *The Wreck of the Ship 'Hope'*, 1913. In a 1920 letter to the Narkompros (Aquilina 2012a: 83), Stanislavsky mentioned that Lazarev was organizing, like Smyshlaev, a studio for workers, thus opening a wholly new transmission context. Courtesy Laurence Senelick Collection.

explain the Second Studio's reluctance to merge with the First Studio.[9] In reaction to this artistic stagnation, the running of the First Studio was reorganized in late September: Smyshlaev remarked that the general spirit was that artistic standards of the First Studio were to be improved (81). The reorganization of the First Studio was suggested by Vakhtangov, and it entailed the setting up of an accountable central committee made of the old council and newer elected members. Smyshlaev was not elected on this committee (82).

While the Moscow Art Theatre and the First Studio were proving unsatisfactory, gratification came from a new project with which Smyshlaev would be soon associated. In early September 1917 plans were set in motion by the Union of the Youth of the Third International to open a drama school to 'help the comrades interested in Dramatic Art' (73). This school was to provide free lessons in acting and related subjects, like make-up, the construction of scenery, the history of folk theatre and the theory of music. Smyshlaev took several acting classes, rather nervously at first (75–6). The school strongly echoed his own political beliefs. In fact, it wanted to transmit acting techniques while also forming students politically. The two aims were intertwined: 'Comrades who wish to study every kind of art, you are welcome in this school, and let it become a promise of the new, bright, and joyful future in the building of the new life' (73). The lessons were based on aspects of Stanislavsky's System. One lesson tackled public solitude for example, with a final improvisation allowing a practical insight in the practice. Smyshlaev was excited by this work, finding it both 'wonderful and simple' (94). He also noted that Stanislavsky's System and dramatics were popular among the masses (94). By the first week of October the number of participants attending the lessons had increased considerably.

In transmitting elements of Stanislavsky's System to these youngsters, one can say that Smyshlaev was locating himself into an untapped niche in the market. Similar to the way that Richard Boleslavsky would place himself as a spokesperson of the System in American through his master-student association with Stanislavsky, Smyshlaev also situated himself within the early efforts of transmitting acting techniques to a new and vast audience coming from the working classes. By associating himself with the school of the Third International, Smyshlaev facilitated his integration into the new cultural and political milieu, constructing his place in the future world through the transmission of technique. He will bring this construction to maturation by being closely associated with the Proletkult, as I will discuss in the next section. The rift with Stanislavsky, however, loomed large above the work that he was doing in the early 1920s.

The Stanislavsky-Smyshlaev rift: Collective creation

One concern of cultural transmission is the extent to which transmission processes change a source practice. Historically, the discipline of cultural transmission rests on this very concern. The first wave of transmission scholarship can be traced back to the founding and early phase of work of the Warburg Institute (1900–21). This institute suggested that transmission is a one-directional process where 'the original message was assumed to be pure and perfect' (Grafton in Grafton and Blair 1990: 2). Changes and alternations to a source were treated as necessary but undesirable, occurrences therefore that cannot be done away with, but which were still 'a corruption, not an enhancement, of the original' (2). The institute propagated the idea that misrepresentations of a source are something to keep an eye on, because 'only a set of adaptations of inherent forms and ideas seemed to be organic expressions of genuine thoughts and feelings; others were dismissed, for no evident reason, as banal and sterile' (2). A substantial portion of contemporary Stanislavsky studies manifests the Warburg Institute's turn-of-the-twentieth-century preoccupation with the misinterpretation of a source object. In reality, there were several instances of supposed misinterpretations of Stanislavsky's ideas, roughly concurrent with the institute's early work. Smyshlaev was certainly not the only case in point here. Other examples included Stanislavsky's thinly veiled criticism to Olga Knipper when she left in tears a rehearsal of *A Month in Country* (Benedetti 1991: 276–8) and the often-referred tug of war between Stella Adler and Lee Strasberg on whether Stanislavsky's acting approach was at its core physical or emotional. Perhaps inevitably, more recent literature has also directed us to instances of '[g]etting Stanislavsky wrong' (Marowitz 2014) and to '[r]ecurring misconceptions in Stanislavski's translations' (Martins 2017).

The tug of war between what constitutes a processing of a source technique as opposed to its misinterpretation is evident in the rift that developed between Stanislavsky and Smyshlaev. The rift between the two was rooted in the book *The Technique to Process Stage Performance*, which Smyshlaev published in 1921, with a second edition appearing a year later. Stanislavsky's draft remarks about this book have survived and are reproduced in Volume 6 of his *Collected Works* (Stanislavskii 1959). Possibly, these were the basis for an unpublished article or letter. In this text Stanislavsky voiced his displeasure with Smyshlaev's book. First, he accused Smyshlaev of plagiarism and of lifting his ideas. Laurence Senelick already drew attention to this when translating sections from Stanislavsky's letter (Senelick 2014: 393–4). The following complements Senelick's selection:

You can requisition a person's house, his apartment or real estate, and take diamonds from the person, but you cannot requisition his soul with impunity, his dream, his life's purpose. You cannot appropriately own it, you cannot pass someone else's idea for your own and graciously share it with others as if it was your own property, without even asking for permission.

But V. S. Smyshlaev has a different opinion.

My former pupil Smyshlaev published a book titled *The Technique to Process Stage Performance*. In this book I did not find any new thought, not a single practical advice that belonged to its author and which deserved the publication in a new book. To my surprise, it is full from beginning to end with my thoughts, my practical advice, and theoretical positions. Even my expressions and my terminology are preserved. Reading the book, I recall the rehearsals during which I spoke about those ideas, and I recall the bent figure of Smyshlaev, constantly writing down my notes. (Stanislavskii 1959: paras. 1–3)

The second criticism was more technical in nature. Writing in 1921, Stanislavsky appears aware of the disparate elements which make the actor's creative process but less secure in his knowledge of how these connect together, their order so to speak and logic:

My cupboard bursts with notes and material, manuscripts for a future book which I could have printed fifteen years ago. But there are reasons which do not allow me to do so. The issue of utmost importance is the sequence and gradual development of the creative process to create a role. And until the practice teaches me and indicates me such an order, a gradualness to the main line of artistic work, I do not dare publish any books. Everything else, that is, all the composite and separate creative processes, have been studied by me, tested, and accepted by theatres, artists, and students who follow my instructions. (Stanislavskii 1959: paras. 6–7)

In publishing his book, Smyshlaev can therefore be seen to have gone against Stanislavsky's wish.[10] Whole sections of the book are easily linked back to Stanislavsky. These include chapters on dividing an act into bits and the identification of corresponding tasks (Smyshlaev 1922: 16–23), the logic of the actions (46–51), rhythm and tempo (175–85), and attention (69–72). Stanislavsky, however, severely admonished Smyshlaev for oversimplifying and therefore misinterpreting his techniques:

In his book Smyshlaev has muddled and misinterpreted my so-called system, even preserving my experiences and unfortunate terminology, which I am trying to gradually correct. [...] He was a bad and retarded student. He writes about tasks and writes incorrectly. He distorted my thoughts. [...] What he writes is wrong. (Stanislavskii 1959: 269)

The crux of the matter was collective creativity, which Stanislavsky believed Smyshlaev was trumpeting by pushing mass scenes on the stage and the collective work going into the creation of new plays. The latter is the same collective work which I discussed in Chapter 2, carried out, Stanislavsky here confirms, by Gorky, A. Tolstoi and Sulerzhitsky within the remit of the First Studio. In an earlier version of this text Stanislavsky pointed out that Smyshlaev had indeed participated in these experiments, albeit as a student and not as an instigator of the practice (Stanislavskii 1959: para. 9). Again, he accused Smyshlaev of taking the practice and passing it as his own, without giving credit where credit was due. To somehow rectify his position Smyshlaev did write in the foreword of the second edition that Stanislavsky was indeed the first to systematize the work of the actor and that the System made further development of acting and theatre techniques possible (Smyshlaev 1922: 1).

However, placing Smyshlaev's book in his context shows that Stanislavsky's understanding of the book and its theories might actually be missing some of the finer points.[11] In other words, in equating collective creativity to mass scenes and the collective writing of a play Stanislavsky limits the reach of Smyshlaev's ideas. This is partly fuelled by a lack of contention with the fact that the sociopolitical context had changed markedly between 1912 and 1917. In other words, whereas working collectively in 1912 to create a play can 'only' be seen as a theatrical development, in 1921, i.e. within a context that was actively using collective work to rebuild itself, the same work became a theatre practice tinged with political weight. Collective creativity in Smyshlaev's vision, therefore, cuts deeper than Stanislavsky allowed, because it was informed by the then contemporary theories on collective theatre, especially those developed by cultural theorist Platon Kerzhentsev (1881–1940).

Kerzhentsev is often remembered as a catalyst to the repressive environment of the 1930s. It was he, after all, who precipitated the closure of Meyerhold's theatre in 1938 (Braun 1998: 288–9). However, his theories about collective creation, written in the years immediately following the revolution, are much more positive because they made a strong case for the creative potential of the masses. Instead of a theatre *for* the masses, where performances are made accessible to the workers, Kerzhentsev proposed a theatre *of* the masses, i.e. one which was built on the creativity of the workers. Kerzhentsev's theatre vision was as open and inclusive as it could be. Productions were to be produced by a community, be it a factory, neighbourhood or district, with all members pitching in the acting, direction, writing of the musical scores, construction of the scenery, sowing of the costumes and so on. Future spectators were also encouraged to attend rehearsals and offer their preliminary advice and feedback. Eschewing professionalism and specialization, Kerzhentsev's early theories argued that collective work is possible only in amateur contexts where there is equality between the members of a group. In the same way that notions of a 'privileged class' were supposedly dismantled in an environment that was vigorously being defined along socialist lines, Kerzhentsev reproved the professional theatre's resolve to foreground the hierarchical and authoritarian figure of the director. Equality in a theatre collective was possible because participants involve themselves in all areas of theatre production and not only those that were strictly their main area of specialization:

> [T]his system of [collective] work will be fruitful only on the condition that each member is, if possible, a universal worker, and that he not only understands clearly the general conditions of the theatre but is also familiar with all its details. To achieve that we shall let all the participants carry out, at least partly, the work of the author, stage director, decorator, and actor. Everyone shall create his own plan to direct the play, give the play his interpretation, work on the play's text (in literary terms), go over some roles (like an actor), think of the decorations and maybe sketch them, take care of the musical side of a play, and so on.
>   It definitely does not mean that all this complicated work will fall in full on the shoulders of every participant. Surely a stage director or a person drawn to that work will pay more attention to the staging, while a writer or lover of literature will work mainly on the play itself and so on. But it is important for each person to acquire different skills, so that no one is confined to his profession but has done the work of others.
> (Kerzhentsev 1919b: 39)

Kerzhentsev saw the Proletkult, an independent organization that tasked itself with the creation of a proletarian culture, as a possible practical outlet for his theories. Consequently, he supported this organization, often positively and publically invoking its attributes, while also presiding on several of its boards (Aquilina 2014: 29). Smyshlaev's own work at the Proletkult – he directed, for example, the Moscow Proletkult's opening performance, a dramatization of Émile Verhaeren's poem *Insurrection* (Chapter 4) – would necessarily have drawn him very close to Kerzhentsev's circles and made him aware of the latter's theories on collective creation.

In rooting his practice in Stanislavsky's System, but framing it around (Kerzhentsev's theories of) collective creation, Smyshlaev created a hybrid practice which merged acting considerations with contemporary political relevance. Stanislavsky framed theatre practice around an investigation and on-stage recreation of the organic laws of creative nature; Smyshlaev shifts this onus to collective work and makes that the defining theatre principle. This is evident from the opening sections of his book:

> The stage-director should clearly understand that the essence of creative work in the theatre is not in despotic methods, where pawn actors are placed on the stage as he likes, where they are made to speak in different voices for reasons which he prefers – no, the stage-director should make it clear that the form of art we call theatre can withstand art criticism only on condition that the creative work is strongly based on collectivism (коллективизм).
>
> The essence and secret of theatre art is in this collectivism, in the 'community' of action, in the friendly comradely solidarity of all the individuals working in the collective. (Smyshlaev 1922: 11)

In framing his book on collective creation, Smyshlaev therefore takes a different and unique turn, away from a deep and solitary engagement with Stanislavsky and more towards a combination of his teacher's creative process (then relying on an analytic understanding of the role and dissection of the play) with the discourses on collectivism developed at the time. The latter, fuelled by his support of the proletarian, and exposure to the working classes, was, in the terms developed by cultural transmission, his 'bias of learners' (Smith et al. 2008: 3471).

Smyshlaev directed collective work towards multiple objectives. It is not a condition to be taken for granted, but one which the leader of an ensemble must be careful to nourish right from the start of the work. This will create the appropriate collegial atmosphere. Work to create the collective precedes the actual rehearsals. It is not a waste of time because it moulds the group into a tightly knit unit and readies it for creative work (Smyshlaev 1922: 11–12). On a superficial level, Smyshlaev's collectivism might not appear as anything deeper than the basic behaviour (politeness, respect and so on) that makes the day-to-day running of a theatre group possible. However, for Smyshlaev, collective work was a modus operandi to produce theatre. It is first evident when the group is choosing the play, an important moment that sparks the creative work. The group, Smyshlaev suggested, should choose a play which the majority of the participants want to produce. Once the choice is made, an initial discussion on the piece is made involving 'not only the director but necessarily all the members of the creative team' (Smyshlaev 1922: 12). In reality, while titling this chapter in his book 'Choosing the Play', Smyshlaev opted to develop a rationale for the use of improvisation to create and devise stage performances. He identifies a tripartite relationship between the group as a collective, improvisation and the creation of stage material:

> You do not need to look for finished plays, but at least for material for staging, themes for improvisation. [...] It should not be understood that everyone must necessarily write a play. No, in such cases stage material, a play, is born here in the collective, created by a series of open improvisations in which participants exchange words, repeat those they like most, and then select their favourite. And only then, when it is sufficiently identified, is the piece recorded. (Smyshlaev 1922: 12)

The trigger starting the process of improvisation could be anything – an image, song or poem – partaking in Christopher Balme's contemporary concept of a theatrical text, i.e. 'any kind of textual blueprint that is intended for or attains performance' (Balme 2008: 125).

Irrespective of whether a play text is devised or not, the group is to transform the casting of the play into a collective exercise. In this case, the director allows the actors to improvise on a number of sketches based on the tasks and facts of the play. Any actors who want to play a particular role would participate in these improvisations, and 'when the competition is finished the team determines who will play which role' (Smyshlaev 1922: 24). The whole group is encouraged to attend all the rehearsals, 'because every person in a collective is a very valuable collaborator and necessary for the success of the enterprise' (Smyshlaev 1922: 15). Collective work also facilitates the psychological analysis of a role. Peer feedback, Smyshlaev says, can be more vivid and more 'valuable than a dissertation or a scientific study of a character' (Smyshlaev 1922: 25). Working collectively also helps a director to find new interpretations to a play he or she previously staged. It unpicks 'something new in the play, new possibilities, new interpretations of the scenes and characters' (Smyshlaev 1922: 15). Consequently, there are no definite bits – as defined by Stanislavsky – to a play, as their articulation depends on the particular collective involved in the work.

In Smyshlaev's vision, therefore, what we might refer colloquially as group work can be seen to cut across the whole process of stage production. A final form of collective creation involves the contribution to theatre production of the other arts, like music, painting and dance. Along the lines advocated by, among others, Kerzhentsev (1919a), Smyshlaev also argued for the need of the arts to come together within the theatre medium. The staging of *Insurrection* benefitted from such an integration with the other arts. The contributions of the painters and the musicians were not ancillary, but supportive of the creative process, taking it in unplanned territories: '[In *Insurrection*] they brought us their own thoughts and feelings, new to us, and we absorbed them. They merged their creativity with our own' (Smyshlaev 1919: 90).

The use of improvisation

Many of Smyshlaev acting principles revolve around the use of improvisation. For him, improvisation is a multi-layered technique. It is a tool to devise and create performances, as I have discussed above. Improvisation is also a key way to distribute roles, because it makes evident the external and internal potential of an actor wanting to play a role (Smyshlaev 1922: 14). Improvisation features throughout the whole production and rehearsal process, during which it further moulds the group into a collective. It also features strongly in the post-mortem phase, within a practice which Smyshlaev labelled 'second day performance'. Second day performances were special evenings of constructive criticism, during which former spectators were meant to improvise in front of the cast their views on the production. Smyshlaev saw second day performances as a valuable acting and training exercise, not only for the spectators, but also for the original performers, who were thus able to spot any shortcomings in their interpretation. To these technical considerations Smyshlaev also added a political dimension to improvisation work. Technically, improvisation improves the actor's skill in imagination, initiative and taste (Smyshlaev 1918: 54). It also develops what Stanislavsky called communion on stage, i.e. the ability to respond and be open to what the stage-partner is doing. In a context which was seeking to rebuild itself through 'collective and public' means (Kiaer and Naiman 2006: 1), however, improvisation also gained political significance by giving its practitioners a direct experience and understanding of 'the principle of collective work which [during the improvisation] is carried out in full' (Smyshlaev 1918: 54).

It is through an emphasis on improvisation that Smyshlaev's ideas gain in significance, especially when juxtaposed with Stanislavsky's own final experiments, within the practice that later became known as Active Analysis. As mentioned in Chapter 2, improvisation is a key feature of Active Analysis. In reaction to the more rational and cerebral approaches of Stanislavsky's Round-the-Table work, Active Analysis places the actors in an embodied rehearsal environment where they are 'no longer sitting at the table [...]. They now did their research *on the stage*, looking into their own human lives for whatever information they needed to achieve their characters' "tasks"' (Merlin 2003: 30; original emphasis). The following key points define the use of improvisation within Active Analysis:

- an initial freedom in relation to the words of the play, where the actors do need not to stick to what the author wrote but can rather improvise on the basic skeleton of the Given Circumstances. This is done in the knowledge that subsequent improvisations will eventually lead back to the playwright's text;
- the use of improvisations to ground the actor in the behaviour with which he is most familiar, i.e. his own everyday life and actions.

These two aspects appear in Smyshlaev's use of improvisation, at least in its theoretical formulation. For example, he treated bits as 'milestones for improvisations' (Smyshlaev 1922: 16), which the actors work on by improvising dialogues and moments that do not appear in the text. The director's role, then, is very much that of a 'helmsman' (Knebel in Thomas 2016: 90) who, in collaboration with the collective, moves these improvisations closer to the text:

> The director gives a theme to the cast, who play an étude using not only their own words but also adding new acting which the author did not give, adding to the action new episodes prompted by their imagination. The étude can also be repeated several times; meanwhile the director, together with the participants of this improvisation, gradually narrows the action, bringing it close to the scene in the play. The second bit and the ones that follow are worked out in the same way. (Smyshlaev 1922: 20-1)

What results is a process which, though open and flexible, already contains an impulse towards structuring by steadily moving towards the stability of a text. It is a process made possible because of the collaborative environment that has been created, one that calls upon the inputs of the actors, directors and, even if not physically present in the room, the playwright. Smyshlaev's improvisations, therefore, are a step towards the democratic levelling which Stanislavsky had himself attempted at the First Studio (see Chapter 2).

Along similar lines which Stanislavsky would propose in the 1930s, the first improvisations in Smyshlaev's vision 'have to be as near as possible to the everyday life of the actors, while the theme is kept the same [as in the text]' (Smyshlaev 1922: 21).[12] For example, an improvisation on a bit titled 'A Meeting with Friends' implies the use of the physical behaviour (the greeting, eye contact, body language, etc.) which the actor himself performs in his own everyday life when meeting friends (Smyshlaev 1922: 21). The more studios approach of Round-the-Table Analysis is not forgotten, but its primary and initial position is taken over by the actors' improvisations. It will appear at a later stage in the rehearsal process, when the improvisations become more complex and when the actors gradually add new circumstances arising from the detailed evaluation of the Given Circumstances (Smyshlaev 1922: 21). The more rational (Smyshlaev called it 'mechanical') analysis, therefore, is not dry or over-calculated but coloured by the experiential involvement of the actors' improvisations.

For Smyshlaev everyday life also served as a space for rehearsal. Rehearsing in everyday life involves the actor donning the character in his daily encounters and seeing how people react. This was a practice Stanislavsky adopted when he staged *A Practical Man* at the Alekseev Circle (1883). In this play Stanislavsky played the part of a poor ugly student who was in love with a rich girl. The cast prepared for the performance very seriously. They trained, rehearsed and studied, and as Stanislavsky wrote, '[I]t was in the school of life that we learnt' (Stanislavski 2008a: 40). Regular improvisations were performed as follows:

> [I]n order to approach a part better and get into its skin, we needed to get used to it, do regular exercises. Here is what they were. For the whole of one day we had to live not as ourselves but as our character within the circumstances of the play and whatever happened in the real life around us, whether we were walking, gathering mushrooms, boating on the lake, we should be guided by the circumstances described in the play, using the inner nature of each of the characters. We had as it were to transpose real life and adapt it to our roles. (Stanislavski 2008a: 43–4)

Stanislavsky called this approach of rehearsing in everyday life 'a new working method' aimed at gaining a better understanding of the role. It made the actors aware of the 'soul's cast' that constitutes the essence of the characters (in Vinogradskaia Vol. 1 2003: 60). While Stanislavsky would eventually downplay this rehearsal approach, the use of everyday life as a rehearsal space remained an integral part of Smyshlaev's approach to creating a character:

> Having defined the task, an actor strengthens it through a number of études, which he performs not only in rehearsal, where he is an object

of his peers' criticism, but also at home, in the street, while riding a carriage, and in any spare moment of his everyday life. [...] I know the desire of the first task; now, anywhere possible I perform études, which my creative fantasy grounds in all circumstances of my everyday life. [...] An actor performing the études will snatch the opportunity and perform his task in a way that no one around him realizes he is playing an *assigned improvisation*. (Smyshlaev 1922: 23; emphasis in the original)

It is worth highlighting that when using everyday life as a rehearsal space, Stanislavsky was still an amateur actor making his first tentative experiments in understanding how to construct a role. This amateur context was at one point also shared by Smyshlaev, when he delivered the classes to the young workers for instance, who presumably would have lacked acting nuance. He described these lessons, it has to be remembered, as 'wonderful' but 'simple'. Working with amateur actors always entails a struggle for time, with rehearsals taking place late in the evenings after long hours at work. Using everyday life as a space for rehearsals thus becomes a way for practitioners like Smyshlaev working in amateur contexts to extend rehearsal time.

Work processes in *The Technique to Process Stage Performance*

I will now move to conclude this chapter by expounding further on Smyshlaev's book *The Technique to Process Stage Performance*. My discussion will be restricted to the first chapters (Smyshlaev 1922: 5–30). I will do so not only for reasons of space, but also because in those pages Smyshlaev gave primary importance to working on Act 1 of a play which I find both unique and peculiar:

> Act 1 is always the most difficult for the director to work on: not only because the foundations of the images and characters are laid here, but also because it is where the direction of the whole work is determined. (Smyshlaev 1922: 15)

While there is nothing new in treating Act 1 as the initiator of the dramatic curve, Smyshlaev goes a step further by identifying the work on Act 1 as being para-dramatic, i.e. as also serving as a space to nourish the group's collective ethic. This accentuates further Smyshlaev's over-arching framing of theatre practice around collective work. The two (i.e. working on Act 1 and developing the collective ethic) support each other congenially: 'The first task in working on Act 1 is to find the general colour of the collective, depending on its individuals; this is possible exclusively through improvisation' (Smyshlaev 1922: 15). Collective work and improvisation again appear as through-lines that go through these chapters, creating a sense of flow between choosing a play; the first impressions which it generates; the division of the roles between the members of the cast; and the identification of bits, tasks and psychological analysis of the scenes.

The following are the chapter titles of Smyshlaev's book:

Foreword
1. Choice of Play
2. First Impression
3. Division of the roles
4. Work on the first act of the play. Improvisation – études
5. Division of the first act in bits and identification of the tasks
6. Psychological analysis of the role
7. Feelings of a memory
8. Dreaming
9. The method to perceive surrounding circumstances
10. The method of today
11. Improvisation outside an act
12. Researching an era and the facts of a play
13. Logic of the action
14. Connection between the actors acting on the stage
15. Colours
16. Characteristics
17. Attention
18. Dynamism
19. Use of circumstances appearing on the stage
20. The method to memorize the words
21. The method to get rid of memorized intonations
22. The Method of the main thought
23. Preparation to enter the stage
24. Building up the act
25. Main scenes
26. Mass scenes
27. The change of the scenes in the act, intervals, additions
28. Mises-en-scène
29. The appearance of the stage and the actor

30. Meter, rhythm and tempo
31. The period of the last rehearsals
32. Performance and the art of the spectator
33. Conclusion

The work on a production starts by noting the first impressions which a text or, if the work is more devised, an idea or theme makes on the collective. Smyshlaev likens these reactions to reading a new book. The same applies to theatre. The initial fascination which actors have with the production material is a point which Stanislavsky did not fail to recognize, one, which fast forward a century, Bella Merlin would make a key component of her own Stanislavsky-informed methodology (Merlin 2003: 130). In underlining the first impressions generated from a play, Smyshlaev is therefore not only in line with Stanislavsky's own practices but also reflects more contemporary readings of the Stanislavskian source. Somewhat surprising, seeing his emphasis on collective work, is Smyshlaev's suggestion to have one reader produce the first reading of the text. This was a common occurrence at the time but one which today does not hold much credit:

> [The importance of the first impressions] is why it is very important that the play is read to the audience by a good reader, who is able to both identify strong points but also obscure its disadvantages. After all, this reading or, rather, the enthusiasm aroused in the actors, serves as the initial material, which is quite real and tangible, with which the actor will initially work. (Smyshlaev 1922: 13)

What follows next is typical of Smyshlaev's writing style in this book, where clear parts rich in practical details combine with visionary sections that read more like a manifesto. Consequently, he asserts that a series of exercises is necessary for the actor to rediscover that initial fascination, without however expounding any further on the nature of these exercises.

Much more detailed is the chapter dealing with the division of Act 1 into bits and the identification of corresponding tasks (Smyshlaev 1922: 16–24). This chapter reads strongly like a guidebook or manual. The 'whole play, and Act 1 in particular, is a whole structure consisting of a number of connecting elements' (Smyshlaev 1922: 16), these elements being the bits. The division into bits is essential because neither an act nor a play can possibly be grasped intuitively as a whole. The identification of these bits creates 'a score […] of the role and the play which an actor would use to act on the stage' (Smyshlaev 1922: 16). Anticipating discourses that would become central to acting processes in the second half of the twentieth century, Smyshlaev argued that through the score the actors are not left wandering the stage 'empty-handed' but are rather given secure grounds on which they can build more creative moments. The score is made of a series of tasks that bring the bit to fulfilment. The following example from *Boris Godunov* illustrates Smyshlaev's thinking:

Bit 1: 'New guests in the tavern'	TAVERN ON THE LITHUANIAN FRONTIER
Acting tasks:	
Hostess: I want to give my guests a warm welcome.	MISSAIL and VARLAAM, wandering friars;
Varlaam: I want to rest and enjoy my time in the tavern.	GREGORY in secular attire; HOSTESS
	HOSTESS. With what shall I regale you, my reverend honored guests?
	VARLAAM. With what God sends, little hostess. Have you any wine?
	HOSTESS. As if I had not, my fathers! I will bring it at once. (*Exit.*)

Bit 2: 'Missail and Varlaam are interested in Gregory' – 'A stranger in the company'	
Acting tasks:	
Missail: I want to find out who is this man that joined us on the road.	MISSAIL. Why so glum, comrade? Here is that very Lithuanian frontier which you so wished to reach.
Gregory: I want to get out of the conversations in order to stay incognito.	GREGORY. Until I shall be in Lithuania, till then I shall not be content.
Varlaam: I want to discourage the lad.	VARLAAM. What is it that makes you so fond of Lithuania!

While bits are self-sufficient entities, because they have a clear beginning, middle and end, moving from one to the other allows the actor to rediscover the organicity of an act. This is possible when small bits are placed together to form bigger ones (Smyshlaev 1922: 20). Again, Smyshlaev can be seen to have anticipated more recent developments in acting theory, namely those which do not see a dualism between fragmentation and organicity in the actor's work.

In suggesting a work process based on bits and tasks, Smyshlaev threads very strongly into the Stanislavsky acting tradition. What seems unique to him is the emphasis he placed on moods (*настроений*). Smyshlaev reworks bits to have them define and encapsulate specific moods. This emerges in at least two occasions. For example, naming a bit 'New guests in the tavern' immediately

> underlines that the action is taking place in the tavern; that various visitors often drop by; that the hostess is happy to see the visitors. The word 'guests' creates the impression of fatigued wanderers who come to the cosy room where they can get warm, satisfy their hunger, drink a reasonably good wine, and feel welcomed. This definition emerged as a result of talks with the given collective, and it immediately brings all the actors playing this scene into a particular circle of circumstances and moods. Everyone understands the result that the audience has to perceive in the given moment of the play, in this bit on the stage. (Smyshlaev 1922: 18)

Similarly, the articulation of a bit as an instance where tired travellers are happily settling in the warm room waiting for dinner and wine to be served defines 'the mood of all the characters: everyone prepares for rest and pleasure, which redoubles as the Hostess comes in with the wine' (Smyshlaev 1922: 19). The mood in this case is seen in the creation of a very visual understanding of the scene, of a moving image which encapsulates its general feeling, and which informs the levels of energies (e.g. settling in the warm room) that are needed.

Following the identification of bits and tasks, Smyshlaev shifts his attention to what he called 'feelings of memories' (*Чувства воспоминания*), a clear adaptation of Stanislavsky's own technique of Affective Memory.[13] Smyshlaev speaks about memories, distant and forgotten memories which can be brought back to the surface when stimulated by external details like lines, colours or sounds. The example Smyshlaev gives is that of a woman who burst into tears while looking at the mirror because the dress she was wearing on that day reminded her of a funeral. The dress brought back the memory and its corresponding emotion, showing that while emotions are fleeting and elusive, their connections with external details are strong and accessible. The creation of these connections is a characteristic of the human brain: everyone experiences this process of memory and emotional recall, but it is part of the actor's technical skill to know how to stimulate them at will. This involves the relocation of emotion from everyday life to 'similar and comparable but not identical [scenarios] in the play' (Smyshlaev 1922: 31).

Feelings of memories are complex because they connect the actor to his past (as in the example of the crying woman), while also having the potential to project forwards towards an imaginary future.[14] For instance, while walking down a street, the melody played on a mandolin and guitar transports a person to Italy, 'and the [actual streets], the patches of sunlight, the faces of men and women coming towards you are immediately transformed' (Smyshlaev 1922: 28). Smyshlaev argued that human beings are constantly perceptive. They also record the details that they take in, with the actor's technique again involving the knowledge of how to bring back these recordings and use them as and when needed. This know-how includes what Smyshlaev referred to as 'anchoring' (30–1). The actor starts by identifying tasks to perform on stage, which he colours by invoking parallel feelings from his personal life. Both the task and the corresponding material are worked upon via improvisation, where they are thought over with as many details as possible. Smyshlaev suggested that this work is eventually put aside for a few days to 'wait until the task reappears in your soul' (Smyshlaev 1922: 30). The actor is still proactive during this period of wait, closely observing life around him, 'looking and listening carefully because some external trigger [...] will suddenly, like a lightning bolt, illuminate the emotion he is looking for. [...] In such case to wait means to observe oneself and the life around you' (Smyshlaev 1922: 30). The actor then has to anchor this fleeting emotion in an element of work that is more technical and tangible, such as a word, phrase or action. It is a necessary phase of work which allows the actor to provoke the appropriate emotion at the right moment.

Conclusion

In her study of Vyacheslav Ivanov's interpretation of Dante, Pamela Davidson argues for the necessity of using an interpretative lens when studying cultural realities. A possible methodology that she suggests is that of studying and interpreting one reality through another:

> Generally speaking, the study of refraction of one culture through another, or of one's writer's works through those of another, can afford

many insights into the psychology of the receiver of the influence. A writer's interpretation of another author's works often highlights the features which are most characteristic of that writer's spiritual outlook and creative process. (Benjamin 1989: 10)

Smyshlaev's openness to the cultural scenarios that were developing after the revolution served as one such interpretative lens through which he read and processed Stanislavsky's work. His teacher's accusations of plagiarism and misinterpretation have weighed Smyshlaev down, turning him into a 'less appealing' figure, similar to how the emphasis on Kerzhentsev's censoring role in the 1930s obfuscated his not insubstantial contributions to post-revolutionary theatre. The discipline of cultural transmission restores such marginal works by identifying as a further area of study not the salient characteristics of either Stanislavsky or Smyshlaev, but by focusing on the mechanisms operating between the two. Foregrounding Smyshlaev's own background and character as a receiver of practice, reactive as it was to other forces apart from Stanislavsky, helps to requalify his reading of the System as less of a misinterpretation and more of a separate entity that had collective creation at its core.

Suggestions for practice

From individual to group work

The situation which Smyshlaev returned to so often in his book, that of the need to mould a group of participants into a collective, is certainly something which many of us encounter in our work with actors or students. The moment when a group of people comes together for the first time in a rehearsal room or studio reminds of two people meeting each other for the first time: an initial contact is made, first impressions are generated and the seeds of a possible encounter planted. Alison Oddey describes the need to work on this moment and not leave it, so to speak, to its own devices:

> Group practical work and 'getting to know each other' exercises are vital to [theatre] exploration. Exercises in communication, concentration, trust, sensitivity, movement, voice and improvisation are all required for group development. In my experience, this preliminary but necessary work can be applied to all new groups coming together at any level, be they professional, amateur, young people, drama teachers in training or undergraduate students of theatre. (Oddey 1994: 25)

Personally, my own work in higher education places me face to face with new cohorts of students on a yearly basis. They always come from very different backgrounds, with equally different levels of skill. The class is also often enriched by visiting/exchange students from abroad, mature students, as well as the occasional participant from other faculties taking the class as an optional credit. In view of these disparate backgrounds, the first few sessions necessarily have to carry an underlining group-building objective, along the lines and preoccupations expressed by Smyshlaev. The exercises suggested below help participants to feel comfortable working together, while developing an environment of trust and openness. In simple words, they are team-building exercises.

The suggestions for practice below are structured on three sessions. Session 1 has students working together in the same room, but individually. This individual work serves as a basis for Session 2, where partner work is introduced. Work in larger groups, as large as the whole class, is then attempted in Session 3. In this way, a sense of progression is generated, where a collective atmosphere is developed organically from individual work to small groups and finally large collectives. It is hoped that in these three sessions participants receive an embodied understanding of Smyshlaev's concern for 'the creation of the atmosphere of mutual trust and comradeship between the members' (1922: 11).

The exercises can easily be carried out with a class of about twenty students, but this is by no means a requirement. Several of the exercises will also be familiar to readers. Many of us, for instance, have certainly started sessions using variations on the basic 'walk and fill up the space' exercise. This and other exercises have seen a substantial amount of adaptation and development from my end, and the reader is certainly free to do so himself. Having said that, I will on occasion give proper accreditation when a particular instance of practice has a clear link with a source, practitioner or context. Any omissions in this regard are regretted.

Atmospheric music can also be used with many of these exercises. In this case, the leader should be aware that music can both help and hinder the process, and particular attention is to be given to choosing pieces of music which stimulate rather than control the work. As we all know from our practice, music impacts on the mood and atmosphere of a session. Pieces of music which I have used in the past include Maurice Ravel's *Boléro*, Pink Floyd's *Shine on You Crazy Diamond* and Jon Lord's *Concerto for Group and Orchestra* (Movement 3). The leader should also pause regularly to ask for and give feedback on the exercises being carried out.

Session 1: Individual work

Icebreaker

Before entering the studio, collect the group in a line outside the studio. Ask them to close their eyes and to picture themselves performing an action, movement or gesture which signifies that they are detaching themselves from their everyday life. They are, so to speak, to suspend temporarily their everyday concerns. Give about twenty seconds for the students to mentally picture this activity. The action chosen can be realistic, abstract or a combination of both. Possible suggestions include 'removing' daily worries as if one is removing a shirt and throwing it or folding it away, burying an imaginary box, etc. Students are instructed to enter the room silently and perform the action as a loop or sequence.[15]

Exercise 1: Walking exercise

- Walk around the room, taking in its details. Instruct the students to fill up all the space.
- To introduce urgency and focus, walk in straight lines and diagonals or introduce a walking grid.
- Change the focus of the eyes, and follow with the walk.
- Stop the group and check the balance of the space.
- Place a number of chairs in the room, randomly, about one-third of the number of participants. Either (i) stop at a chair and improvise with it by getting familiar with its weight, texture, colour, form, through different ways of handling it, etc., or (ii) sit down briefly on a chair and observe. What did you observe? What are the other participants doing? Are there any recurrent patterns emerging?
- Even sitting down, you are still in the studio and open to the gaze and attention of the others. Do not switch off. How can you make your 'sitting down' more engaging?

Exercise 2: Physical tuning

- Find a space, and make sure you can see the session leader.
- Adopt a relax stance, and look straight ahead.
- Shake your wrists, starting by locating the action to the wrist but then extending this to the whole body.
- Stretch arms up, and let them fall. Sigh out while doing so.
- Draw circles with your hands and arms, starting from small circles, but then extending these to the whole body.

- The bodies of the participants are covered in dust. Remove the dust, slowly at first, but then more energetically. Use your whole body. A variation of this is to work with the image of itchiness.

Exercise 3: Open/close body

- Go into a closed, ball position on the floor.
- Open yourself completely, expanding the reach of your body and position. Work on the image of becoming larger and larger.
- When you reach the largest point possible, keep that position briefly and then perform the opposite – move back to a closed position by imagining that you are getting smaller and smaller.
- Repeat the process, always looking at new ways of opening and closing the body.

Exercise 4: The plant exercise

- Take a similar position to the previous exercise, i.e. a small ball on the floor, this time imagining that you are a seed that grows and grows.
- Once the plant grows to its maximum potential, reverse the process and go back to the seed.
- Repeat, but use the elbow as the leading point in the growing of the plant. The elbow, in other words, leads the movement.
- Repeat with other body parts: the nose, the back of the spine, the shoulder, the other shoulder, the chest, the back of the head, the wrist, etc.

Exercise 5: Movements of different sizes

- Make a series of large, broad movements. Make use of the whole body.
- Some suggestions include: saw a large log, dig a hole in the ground, beat a hammer on an anvil, drag a large box on the floor, kick a ball, paint a large wall. In all cases, it is important that the actions are not localized to a specific body part (e.g. the wrist and hand if you are painting), but work on and with the whole body.
- Reduce the action in size by 50 per cent. Repeat reduction.

Note: You may wish to split the participants in two groups for exercises 1–5. This will allow the participants to observe each other. Also consider ways of joining the exercises together or even encouraging students to create a montage from the emerging material. Are there any movement patterns that emerge repeatedly? How can these be structured in a routine? How can the routine be kept fresh and alive?

Session 2: Pair work

Icebreaker

Divide class in pairs. Both participants sit down on chairs, facing each other. Participant A starts an action, which could be realistic, abstract or a combination of the two. Give attention to make the action as clear as possible. Examples could be playing a violin, putting on make-up, stirring tea (the teacup could be huge), etc. Participant B signals 'stop' and reproduces the position suggested by participant A. He starts another action, taking the action somewhere else. Repeat.

Exercise 1: Walk in the space

- Repeat elements from the walking exercise of Session 1. Add the following layers.
- Walk around the space, and nod or smile when you make eye contact with another participant.
- Shake hands with a person whom you make eye contact with. Introduce yourself, by giving your name. Do not rush, but let this brief encounter take its natural course. Listen to your partner. Consider instructing the participants to use an invented name.
- While walking lightly touch a person on a shoulder, and gently push him to the floor. Do not rush, and establish the contact first.
- If touched, find a composed way of falling to the floor. Try not to use your hands. Lie down on the floor.
- Help those lying on the floor back to a standing position by pushing them gently from behind their back.
- Experiment with a composed way of standing up. Try not to use your hands.
- Walk, and change the direction of another participant by pushing him/her slightly on the shoulder.
- Walk, put both hands on someone's shoulders and jump.16
- Clap, 'meet' someone else and describe to them your day so far. You can invent.
- Follow another person without making it obvious who that person is.

Touch can certainly be a sensitive issue for many participants, even when practised lightly as suggested here. In undertaking similar touch exercises with students of the Department of Theatre Studies of the School of Performing Arts (University of Malta), Jakub Korčák, of the Academy of Performing Arts (DAMU), Prague, suggested that the exercises should be carried out 'carefully, gently, and with empathy' (in Aquilina 2019: 17). This is certainly how students should approach touch work. Exposing students to emphatic touch is, however, an important contributor to the creation of any collective.

Exercise 2: Imaginary ball exercise

- In pairs, the students throw an imaginary ball, roughly the size of a football, to one another.
- Get a sense of this throw-catch-throw sequence. React to the throw and the catch. In other words, do not isolate the action to a particular part of the body, in this case the hands, but react accordingly.
- On catching the ball change its size. It can become very large or small like a marble, and anything in between. Throw the new ball. The receiver must make sure to catch the ball in the size that it was thrown. Once the ball is caught, its size changes again.
- Throw and catch the ball using different parts of the body, like the head, elbow, pelvis, shoulders, chest, back, feet, etc. Internalize the imaginary ball so that you can, for example, catch it with a shoulder but throw it with a knee.

Exercise 3: Statues in two

- Students are again divided in pairs. One takes a physical position, typically with some space in it (e.g. a star position). The position can be realistic or abstract.
- The other student comes in and fills the space. In other words, continue the image in a way that is logical, i.e. in a way that makes sense to the participant.
- The first student leaves the position, and continues the image created by his partner. Repeat.
- Give attention to the transitions. How am I moving from one position to the other? In a flowing way? In a disconnected manner? Quickly? Slowly? With one part of the body leading? In the latter case, material arising from the exercise of the seed (Session 1) can be recalled.
- Variation: include higher status and lower status.

Exercise 4: Wrist work

- Two students connect together by touching their wrists.
- The wrists are circled but their contact is kept. Expand the contact and the circling by having the latter inform the whole body of the participant. In other words, transfer the impulse from the wrists into the whole body.[17]

Improvise on exercises 2–4. Give attention to the transitions from one exercise to the other. What prompts these transitions? Is there a leader in the pair?

Exercise 5: Situation

Define a situation with two people involved. Give attention to details such as the following:

- Who are the two people?
- Where are they?
- How does the piece begin?
- What happens?
- How is the scene resolved? How does it end?

Briefly rehearse and present the scene.

Session 3: Larger groups and ensemble work

Icebreaker: Shoe sizes

Form a circle around the room, without talking. Participants find their place in the circle according to their shoe size, from the smallest to the largest. Repeat until a correct progression of the shoe sizes is achieved.

Exercise 1: Walking

To start with, go through the various levels of the walking exercise, as attempted in the previous sessions. Consider adding other levels.

Exercise 2: Rhythm in a box

- Form three groups of nine participants each. Place the participants in a 3 x 3 box.
- Each group takes a corner in the studio.
- The outside person in the front row is the leader, who starts a rhythm which is then reproduced by the rest of the box. Initially at least make the rhythm a simple one, like step-step-clap.
- The whole box moves forwards with the designated rhythm and stops once the wall in front is reached.
- Once the box stops, turn 90° clockwise. In this way there is a new person in the outside position of the front row, who becomes the new leader. He starts a new rhythm, which the others follow while again moving forward.
- Repeat.

This exercise always takes a bit to get going, but students are significantly engaged once they get the hang of it. Encourage them to keep the size and shape of the box and to walk in unison.

Exercise 3: Create a shape and move

- In pairs, and as quickly, quietly and efficiently as possible, physically create a dragon. Repeat the exercise in group of three, four, five, six, seven and so on and as appropriate to the size of the group. Repeat until the whole group is engaged in creating one dragon.
- Does the dragon have symmetry? Is the tail too long/short? Is it a logical design?
- Ask the various groups to 'fly' the dragon. How difficult is this? Keep the shape and size of the dragon.
- Repeat using other images that allow movement: a car, airplane, train, boat, etc.

Exercise 4: Scenario

- Divide the class in three groups of about seven participants each or as necessary.
- A scenario is given. It is a street in a suburban town, with large houses and beautiful lawns. The houses have a fence separating the lawn from the pavement and the street.
- One student goes out with an imaginary can of paint in hand and starts painting the fence.
- One by one, all students go out and contribute to the scenario. Some might read a newspaper, cook a barbeque, sunbathe, play with a ball, etc.
- Interaction is added gradually. What happens if a ball falls on the barbeque? If someone plays loud music?
- Bring the scene to a logical conclusion.
- Experiment with realism but also with stylization (i.e. perform one action repeatedly, like a machine).
- Repeat the exercise using different scenarios and different group sizes. Ideally, the exercise should finish with the group contributing as a whole. Another popular scenario is actors backstage preparing for a performance. What do they do? How does their behaviour change one hour before the performance? Half an hour? Fifteen minutes?

4

Amateur and proletarian theatre in post-revolutionary Russia

Aesthetics and theatricality on the amateur stage

The theatre inroads that the workers had made by 1922 are proudly and positively trumpeted in 'The results of the new theatre', a central chapter of Platon Kerzhentsev's book *Tvorchesky Teatr* (*The Creative Theatre*). A crucial supporter of amateur creation and key figure in this chapter, Kerzhentsev's review is coloured by a clear and biased identification with what the workers were doing, a bias that could only emerge from one of the most ardent supporters of amateur theatre. For example, at one point Kerzhentsev says: 'The experience derived from the past two years [1918–20] has taught us that the revolutionary creativity of the popular masses in the fields of the arts is capable of achieving major victories' (Keržencev 1979: 97).[1] However, underneath this championing, one can find a number of examples that shed light on the practices adopted by the workers when creating their theatre pieces. One such description of an amateur production runs as follows:

> A dramatic text that treated the theme of the revolution was collectively created by the workers, the majority of whom had never set foot in a theatre before. One particular scene depicted the workers bringing down a wall that represented the old times. As the actors onstage shouted and hurled themselves against the wall, the spectators instinctively stood up as one from their seats to help the actors in their struggle. The victorious notes of the Internationale were played when the wall was destroyed, to which the whole hall participated. (Keržencev 1979: 97)

Many of the qualities of post-revolutionary amateur and proletarian theatre – collective creativity, use of improvisation to produce material, aesthetic crudeness, dramaturgical simplicity and audience participation – are clear in this anecdote. They will recur throughout this chapter, which tackles the transmission processes evident in the theatrical underbelly spawned by the revolution, namely the amateur theatre organized by and for the workers.

This chapter is divided in three parts. In the first section I will give a brief overview of the scene, in this way expounding on what I feel are the salient features of post-revolutionary amateur theatre in Russia. More than giving a full description – the vastness of the scene cannot possibly be reproduced within the restrictions of a book chapter – I plan to discuss first how a study of amateur theatre raises several historiographical questions which any historian must contend with when attempting the reconstruction of past theatre events or realities.[2] Among the historiographical difficulties raised by amateur performance are (i) the issue of naming, (ii) the reliability of sources and (iii) periodization. In the second part of the chapter I will tackle some transmission issues emerging from the scene. How does a study of amateur theatre help our understanding of transmission processes? A key form of transmission in proletarian theatre will be located to contexts where professional directors and instructors were roped in to raise the standards of amateur work. Such instances of amateur-professional hybridity suggest that transmission processes are effective when performance realities allow for the fragmentation and eventual reconfiguration of their constituent elements, either with each other or with other elements brought in from outside. I will conclude the chapter with an exposition of two short case studies. Each will foreground a different aspect of transmission. These case studies are (i) Valentin Smyshlaev's production of Émile Verhaeren's poem *Insurrection* at the Moscow Proletkult (1918) and (ii) the 1924 essay 'Unified Studio of the Arts', sourced from the Proletkult publication *Art at the Workers' Clubs*.

The meteoric increase in amateur theatre produced by the workers was a consequence of the emancipating momentum generated by the revolution. A thin amateur scene did exist before the revolution, of workers coming together to produce theatre, but this paled in comparison to the numbers witnessed after the revolution.[3] Chroniclers of the time are joined by more recent sources in explicating the vastness of the scene. Kerzhentsev, for instance, wrote that 'proletarian drama clubs […] sprung out like mushrooms after rain' (Kerzhentsev 1918b: 5). More recently, Konstantin Rudnitsky wrote that 'there was no club or factory without a theatre' (Rudnitsky 1988: 45). Reasons for such an explosion vary.[4] These could be as mundane as the workers relishing the prospect of staying indoors in a heated environment and gaining access to the club's buffet. Other reasons were more political. In a context which saw a marked increase in public meetings and tumultuous political debates in the newspapers, amateur theatre became a vehicle for the workers to express their personal and collective concerns on matters they deemed important. It also satisfied man's natural instinct to share in the company of others, in coming together and engage in common tasks. Theatre also offered a respite from the repetition and bleakness of everyday life, where even the most basic necessities like food, water and coal were in short supply. Nikolai Lvov, another strong supporter of amateur theatre, described the rush of ordinary people to produce theatre in terms that are directly resonant with the moral dimension of the Russian theatre tradition. In fact, he argued:

> The desire to experience the new, and to feel previously unexplored feelings, is very natural – to transfer into someone else's image, to live someone else's life, in another world, which you have created during the stage transformation and among electrical lamps. Such is the strong pull which keeps a person in the theatre.
>
> And now, when new ideas have been thrown among the broad masses of the people, when new opportunities for life have opened for them, an unrestrained rush to the stage immediately inflamed these classes: here they find an outlet for their aspirations, for a different and brighter life. They have the opportunity to broaden their spiritual world with new and unexplored experiences. (Lvov 1919: 8)

Pavel Markov, on his part, referred to the upsurge in amateur theatre rather negatively, as a theatre epidemic or fever in fact (1934: 137).[5] It would quickly produce an ambivalent position in Soviet debates on culture. While the efforts of the workers to choose edifying activities such as theatre were to be lauded, preoccupation was raised on a number of levels, including matters of control and direction, contents of the repertoire, and production standards. In other words, amateur theatre work provoked both apprehension and pride. Most of the groups turned out to be ephemeral and transient affairs. Memberships were in constant fluctuation as workers were often enlisted in the Red Army to fight in the Civil War. As Lynn Mally writes, '[i]t was on shifting ground – with limited resources, physical impediments, and unreliable memberships – that the first Soviet amateur theatres took shape' (Mally 2000: 29).

The picture that emerges from eyewitness accounts is one of rough-and-ready performances, with a crude theatricality that was however countered by the workers' inventiveness in maximizing the sparse resources available. Typically performed without scenery, make-up or costumes beyond what the actors were immediately wearing, amateur theatre needed little more than a floor, the will of the actors to perform, and the imagination and participation of the audience. An example given by Huntly Carter, for instance, evidences the existence of a basic and simple post-revolutionary amateur style. He spoke of an unnamed production as 'an improvised and co-operative performance' performed on a rudimentary stage erected at one end of a stuffy and small room. No footlights were available. A section of the auditorium was 'divided off by a grey-curtain, and the gangway on either side is hung with a grey curtain. Directly in front of the audience is a grey screen representing a wall. This is the stage, auditorium, and scene' (Carter 1925: 98). Such anecdotes confirm the voice of one contemporary writer who underlined that amateur practitioners 'did not have a tenth of the resources of the high theatrical culture, of [its] technique, craftsmanship or finance' (in Rudnitsky 1988: 46).[6] Evaluations of theatrical and aesthetical standards, however, can only be relative, because they are made against context-based and therefore shifting parameters. Surely, the simplicity of the workers' productions gains in relief if a comparison is made between, say, Nina Gourfinkel's description of a Blue Blouse production called *Stenka Razin* and Stanislavsky's 1896 production of *Othello*. In the former, actors simply sat down on the floor and hinted at the presence of a boat through the movement of their hands, while Stanislavsky created the whole locale in minute detail, including a gondola floating and rocking on the water.[7] No such striking scenography could be envisaged by the amateur actors that took the stage after the October Revolution, but then realistic authenticity is a mark of developed theatricality only in performances that attempt the reproduction of life. A striking aesthetics in amateur theatre was offset by the form's communal potential to bring worker-actors together. A lot of theatre was being staged during and after the revolutionary era, even though theoreticians felt distressed because a post-revolutionary repertoire had failed to appear. It was as if the revolution had not touched the theatre (Mally 2000: 37). The revolution however did impact on the theatre. It opened the doors not only to a new audience, but also to a new class of amateur actors and theatre makers. Recent scholarship underlines the communal potential of amateur theatre. Even on the smaller pre-revolutionary scene, Swift writes that 'it was not the skill displayed in the performances but the fact that they were created by and for workers that seems to have mattered most' (Swift 2002: 198). Mally agrees: 'The quality of performances was usually indifferent [...]. But a polished presentation was not essential for audience or actors – the important thing was that the performance was taking place at all' (Mally 2000: 11).

The rough-and-ready nature of amateur theatre was reflected in the spaces used. With access to conventional theatre buildings difficult, amateur theatre was produced in communal and shared spaces like factories, streets, public spaces and cafeterias. For instance, Leach gives the following example of a performance titled *Labour*. It was staged in 1920 by the Moscow Proletkult, 'from the backs of lorries and on mobile stages in the city squares and at workers' clubs' (Leach 1994: 70). However, this lack of a proper space worked in the groups' favour in that they played on a newfound responsibility of

Figure 7 A poster of the Blue Blouse. © A. A. Bakhrushin State Central Theatre Museum, Moscow. Like the Proletkult, the Blue Blouse formed a bracket within the larger amateur-theatre context. The first Blue Blouse was formed in 1923 under the auspices of the Moscow Institute of Journalism. By 1927, it had transformed into a movement of thousands of Blue Blouse groups, out of which four or five were professionals. The Blue Blouse particularly incarnated the simple and direct aesthetics of amateur work. Their manifesto read as follows: 'We are against bright beauty and realistic sets and decoration (no little birch trees and rivers), no clumsy props and set' (in Stourac and McCreery 1986: 30).

bringing the theatre to the people, often performing on the same level of the spectators and choosing material which both actors and spectators shared. On paper this must have created quite a strong bond between the two, although actual practice would always show the actors' difficulty in controlling and focusing the audience's attention, a characteristic of open-air performances. Another example of this street theatre proceeded as follows:

> For the 1 May 1919 festivities, Leningrad was literally covered by four mobile theatre companies. One of these companies staged a Petrushka, the text of which was written by Lunacharsky. A year later an original experiment was attempted. In that year, the power station worked with great difficulty. Power cuts were so common that each manifestation of energy was met by a general outburst of joy and cheering. Twelve trams travelled across the city through half devastated streets. They were equipped with open air platforms, and decorated in drapes and with painted canvas. They were transformed into mobile theatres. During the frequent power cuts, the actors, who had changed in the tram, took to the stages and gave short presentations of ten to fifteen minutes.
>
> In the next years, these experiments were developed further; in Leningrad alone, one could count three hundred mobile companies. A part of these companies travelled the city and mingled with the crowds. They either used platforms which had been prepared beforehand or acted at the same level of the street or pavements, circled by the spectators. Another group of these companies occupied the platforms more permanently. Trucks were used. (Gourfinkel 1979: 125–6)

Workers' clubs proved a particularly fertile ground for amateur theatrics, throughout the 1920s and after (Mally 2000: 24). Any space where a group of workers congregated to partake in theatrical activity was thus transformed into a theatre space, on lines that link with recent theories about performance space being construed not through the delineation of a formal and tangible theatre building but through the active agency of those who inhabit it.[8] In Kerzhentsev's understanding space is not necessarily a given space, an *a priori*, but one that is generated through the process of performance and the work of the actors in close contact with their audiences:

> The inert and traditional theatre space must necessarily be left behind. [...] The neighbourhood theatre will not need to close itself behind the four walls of the theatre building. It will take its work outside in the streets and squares. It will form small groups of three or five actors who on feast days or in the evenings will go round the city and stage

semi-improvised performances in the parks or the streets' corners. They will perform as readers or gather around them groups of people who, under a tree or somewhere similar, will hear them read poetry and prose. (Keržencev 1979: 62–3)

Neighbourhoods were considered a strong source for amateur theatrics because they were underscored by bonds, or 'familial ties', that were alien to bourgeois circles. Kerzhentsev attributed 'a very particular importance to the territorial proximity among those who organise a neighbourhood theatre, because only this condition allows for an active and extensive participation in the theatre' (Keržencev 1979: 56). With these words he reflects an understanding, typical of its time but today seen as narrow, where communities are solely defined by close spatial proximity, understood as 'a static, utopian ideal of neighbourliness and locality' (Heddon and Milling 2006: 142). Staging amateur theatre, for example, was a means for the neighbourhood to celebrate itself.

One prominent reality in the context of early post-revolutionary amateur theatre was the aforementioned Proletkult, a non-governmental institution formed on the eve of the October Revolution which tasked itself with the creation of a proletarian culture.[9] Proletarian culture was in itself a highly contentious and divisive term, with many voices offering conflicting definitions (Biggart 1987). It variously meant the integration of past traditions to the contemporary socialist age (as opposed to other clusters, like the Left Front of the Arts (LEF), who would have happily consigned these traditions to the pre-revolutionary bin), the identification and propagation of appropriate revolutionary themes (such as the relationship between the individual hero and the mass), or even a shift away from artistic production to the overarching organization of everyday life. The latter effort sought to define a kind of proletarian moral ethics with indications about which books to read, how to dress, raise children, talk in public, and so on (Mally 1990: xx). Theatre came to play a prominent role within these debates about proletarian culture, as a vehicle that could both create and transmit the culture of the working class. To the Proletkult proletarian culture first of all meant a process leading to the empowerment of the proletariat – another highly contentious term – in order to transform them into cultural producers. The organization offered the hopeful believe that even those who were once considered as the most insignificant members of society could contribute to the construction of a new world. A key Proletkult characteristic was that its leaders fashioned it as an autonomous entity, independent even of the party and the government. These were statements which from late 1920 would put the Proletkult in very dangerous political waters, with Lenin himself involved in a very open and public attack on it. During the years of the theatre epidemic, however, the Proletkult 'was able to gain a national following and [became] a major voice in cultural debates' (Mally 1990: xxvii).

The early Proletkult was closely linked with the theatre epidemic. Central studios were opened in Moscow and Petrograd, but the institution created a veritable, if chaotic, and equally epidemic movement throughout the country. By 1920 some 400,000 members could be counted within Proletkult ranks (Mele 1990: 10). A theatre division was typically at the core of the activities of every cell. Such divisions were sometimes led by a professional director or instructor. It is important to underline that the Proletkult was only one part or section of the post-revolutionary amateur theatre. It did not define the context, which was much broader and heterogeneous. The Proletkult was, however, a very visible entity. It was housed in an imposing villa formerly owned by the millionaire Savva Morozov (Bergan 1999: 69). Its publications commanded a substantial readership. Such a strong visibility made it quite at odds with the more rough-and-ready amateur examples described above. My subsequent writing in this chapter will take in consideration the incongruity between the Proletkult and the larger movement of amateur theatre. It will treat the Proletkult and its exponents as one example of post-revolutionary amateur theatre, a bracket within a much larger movement.[10]

Apart from the studios in Moscow and Petrograd,[11] which had better resources and could count on the direct participation and supervision of professional directors, a lot of Proletkult theatre was similarly characterized by the crude theatricality synonymous with amateur theatre (Mally 1990: 152–3).[12] Standards remained a concern for the advocates of amateur theatre well into the 1920s. It made amateur theatre an easy target of criticism, especially by government organs who found its diffusion hard to keep tabs on. To improve their standards amateur practitioners were eventually asked to take their models from the professional world (Mally 1993: especially 203 and 211). In fact, the relationship between the amateur and professional scene can be treated as the defining debate surrounding the role and reach of amateur theatre. Are the best amateur actors to leave their day jobs and turn professional? Should amateur theatre remain wholly amateur, or should its doors be opened to professional directors and instructors? If professional instructors, who had developed their skills in pre-revolutionary theatres, were to be welcomed in, how were their counter-revolutionary and 'bourgeois' tendencies to be kept in check? What was to be taken from these professional models, and what needed to be discarded? Can one today speak, therefore, of an amateur-professional hybrid? These questions will be at the core of the discussion that I will develop below on the transmission issues arising from the study of amateur theatre, but before going into that discussion I will raise some historiographical questions associated with the scene.

Historiographical difficulties

One of the difficulties raised by the study of post-revolutionary theatre is that of naming (Mally 2000: 20–4). Naming phenomenon is not an inconsequential affair, as choices made impinge on the identity which an object wants to transmit to its audience – a basic marketing concept (Doyle 2011). Several variations were tried out, each foregrounding a different facet of amateur work. For instance, in his use of 'neighbourhood theatre', Kerzhentsev chose to underline the community-based element of amateur work. Carter's use of 'club and factory theatres', on the other hand, emphasizes the locus that housed and nourished amateur productions (Carter 1925: 94). In another instance, he used the appellation 'cellar and club' performances to underline not only the locus of performance but also the crude theatricality of the pieces (1925: 97). The word 'cellar', in fact, implies small, dark, stuffy and underground rooms, far removed from traditional theatre centres. Other options which Kerzhentsev toyed with stressed the openness of the movement to the largest possible number of cultural players ('mass theatre', 1918a: 63), in contrast to other instances when he opted for a more class-sensitive appellation ('socialist theatre', 1918b: 6). A short-lived term was that of 'worker-peasant theatre', which ran over strong criticism due to its artificial amalgamation of two social classes which had little in common with one another (Keržencev 1979: 103–4).

The encompassing name which Mally uses is that of amateur theatre, but only after explaining that amateur theatre implies a do-it-yourself attitude that relies heavily on independent initiative (Mally 2000: 20–4; see also Swift 2002: 204). 'Do-it-yourself' is a rather cumbersome translation of *samodeiatel'nost'*, literally 'autonomous action' or 'self-activated' (Mally 2000: 15 and 23), which is why she uses the simpler English wording of 'amateur theatre'.[13] Notions of 'amateur footballer', 'amateur photographer' or 'amateur painter' are easy to grasp, as are the implications that amateurism calls for less skill from its participants. There is also no expectation of making a living out of the practice. Advantages of the *samodeiatel'nost'* appellation include its elimination of class connotations, removal of any links with popular traditions (often treated as too humble or vulgar for edifying tasks) and, most importantly, the outright eschewing of dilettantism, what Valerian Pletnev described as 'shallowly skimming the pinnacle of art without delving deeper' (1919: 32).[14]

Until now I have developed my argumentation around the use of the term 'amateur theatre', but in the knowledge that in the context of post-revolutionary Russia 'amateur theatre' also meant 'proletarian theatre'. To me 'a proletarian theatre that was also a form of amateur practice' is the most logical way to describe a theatre that was organized by and for workers. Proletarian theatre implies a theatre that has the proletariat as its producers and consumers, staging material that is of relevance to the workers. It also implies the use of proletarian organization and proletarian production methods. The term is strongly rooted in Kerzhentsev's juxtaposition between a theatre *for* the workers, one made by professional actors performing for the workers, and a theatre *of* the workers:

> The transformation of the central theatre in a theatre with a fixed group of professional actors, even if these are coming from a work environment, contradicts, in my opinion, the essential principle of proletarian theatre – its tight link with the masses. I am convinced that a theatre organised along those lines would inevitably lose the link with the masses. It would become a normal and old-fashioned theatre. Only the repertoire would differentiate it from the rest, and not its basic principles. Such a theatre might stage good socialist dramas, but it will not become *the creative proletarian theatre*. (Keržencev 1979: 66; emphasis added)

The Proletkult was a strong supporter of the effort to create a proletarian theatre. It brought it in conflict with the so-called Left artists and the avant-garde, who 'represented theatre made for the proletarians' (Allen 2013: 131). Using literature as an example, Kerzhentsev underlined that the Proletkult should not be content with bringing the best literature from the past to the workers. The organization also needed 'to discover and unite those writers, mainly from proletarian circles, who themselves create elegant literature in the spirit of a new socialist culture' (Kerzhentsev 1918c: 8).[15]

A second historiographical difficulty raised in the study of proletarian theatre is that of the completeness and therefore reliability of the sources. Thomas Postlewait argues that solid historical research is built on the six historiographical questions of 'who', 'what', 'where', 'when', 'how' and 'why'. He adds that while historians can be relatively secure when answering the first four questions, the 'how' and 'why' often remain open to interpretation (Postlewait 2009: 1). The scale of the proletarian theatre epidemic, compounded with the dubious scholarly methods used by the movement's first chroniclers (Senelick 2000: 49), however, means that even the first four questions often remain unanswered. The examples cited above from

Kerzhentsev and Carter were typically incomplete. To the opening example quoted in this chapter, Kerzhentsev offered very little concrete details about the context of the production beyond the fact that the performance was staged in Starogorkinsk (under the Moscow governorship). Of course, he had no obligation to follow scholarly rigour in recounting the scene, as his work was at the root visionary and theoretical rather than documentary. He skived certain details, however, which would be at the core of any contemporary reconstruction of the event. Who are the actors performing the piece? What are their backgrounds? How experienced were they? What is the title of the piece? How was it received beyond its immediate spectators? What was the exact date of performance? Why was it staged? Certainly, with so many details missing, studying post-revolutionary amateur theatre can become a historiographical nightmare.[16] Similar shortcomings in depicting a fuller picture are present in Carter's account. He spoke of the staging and the plot without divulging on the date, place or producing context.

The difficulty in assessing the reliability of sources is compounded by the biased views that were often voiced. Critics and supporters of proletarian theatre rarely attempted a reconciliation.[17] The eclecticism of the movement meant that many people were proposing contrasting ideas – a characteristic of the 1920s rather than the 1930s – and forming in turn what in transmission theory is known as 'transmission clusters' or 'transmission groups'. These clusters are formed when people come together because their reactions to a particular phenomenon are in some way relatable (Aquilina 2019). In Russian modernism, clustering was evident around the various competing art movements that developed, each with a separate credo and literary café (Bergan 1999: 66). Groupings were already evident at the second conference of the Moscow Proletkult, where some delegates favoured a turn towards professionalism while others openly denounced it (Pletnev 1919: 31). Any statements made on proletarian theatre have therefore to be traced backwards and unpicked against such contrasting clusters.

Archival work is of course necessary in our attempt to reconstruct any past theatre event, including proletarian theatre. Several scholars today underline the plethora of material and new insights on Russian modernism unearthed with the relative opening of the Russian archives (e.g. Senelick 2000: 48; White 2014: 4). Naturally, even archival work needs to be problematized, and the idea that archives are repository of historical truths resisted. Maggie Gale and Ann Featherstone, for example, have spoken about 'the *creative* archival process' (in Kershaw and Nicholson 2011: 37; emphasis in original), which they locate in the encounter between the material and the researcher. The latter is never a neutral being but one who is informed by personal agendas, skill and specific research aims. The (partial) opening of Russian archives has allowed the discovery of whole new figures whose names were cancelled from the annals of Russian theatre history or sidelined because they were seen as marginal.[18] (Andrei Malaev-Babel's recent work on Stanislavsky's student Nikolai Demidov is one prominent example.) Previously unavailable sources also question some of the most conventional and readily accepted ideas about the scene. For example, it is often said that the government wanted to preserve the old theatres, seeing them as the best custodians of Russian traditions. Kerzhentsev expressed these voices in the following way:

> In an effort to save from destruction the best examples of bourgeois theatre, the government even went, in my opinion, a little too far. As if wishing to parry the accusation of 'Bolshevik barbarism' and their hate of culture, Soviet theatre workers often showed a completely unnecessary piety to, for instance, the former imperial theatres. (Kerzhentsev 1918a: 9)

This protective attitude entered into the lore of post-revolutionary theatre. Further research does not negate this interpretation but problematizes it. More varied views among Bolshevik leaders on the bastions of pre-revolutionary art emerge in a January 1922 memo which Lenin sent to Vyacheslav Molotov. The memo shows Lenin's indignation towards 'Lunacharsky's utterly indecent proposal to preserve the Bolshoi Opera and Ballet' (in Clark and Dobrenko 2007: 24). He suggested a massive reduction in the company's personnel and the redirection of the funds towards fighting illiteracy and the opening of reading rooms. Past and present scholarship create a picture that the government wanted to safeguard the old theatres, and while there is plenty of evidence that shows the government giving special privileges to the Academic Theatres, there is also the evidence of a more disparaging attitude. Our reading of the scene is thus problematized, highlighting the liminality rather than organic nature of the first post-revolutionary years.

In the case of proletarian theatre, archival research questions the romantic image of the sacrificing worker in constant search of self-improvement. Swift paints an vivid picture of this idealized worker, one who developed an interest in the arts, dressed neatly, spoke appropriately, and ultimately 'tried to raise the consciousness of his less "advanced" fellow workers' (Swift 2002: 183). Lunacharsky himself used rhetorical devices to paint a glorious image of the proletariat: 'The great proletarian class will in time upgrade culture from top to bottom. It will establish its majestic style, which will be reflected in all areas of art. It will insert its own soul into it. The proletariat will change the very structure of science' (Lunacharsky 1919: 3). Archival research, especially when carried out by other disciplines and brought in by theatre studies as a multidisciplinary tool, paints a very different picture. For example, it is hard to imagine how Lunacharsky's vision could be accomplished through the worker-type found within the Komsomol (a political youth organization in Soviet Russia) and as described by Vladimir Brovkin in his sociological study of early-Soviet culture:

> As in the countryside, most Komsomol cells in workers' neighborhoods and townships were least of all concerned with grand political issues of the day. [...] When Komsomol membership did not interfere with young people's other activities and aspirations, they willingly joined. When, however, they felt that there was nothing particularly interesting to be gained from that membership, they quit without hesitation. (Brovkin 1998: 112)

The difficulty in assessing the reliability of sources is compounded by the divide between official and theoretical pronouncements and their practical implementation. This divide informs proletarian theatre. The movement had in Alexander Bogdanov one of its main theoretical articulators. At one point Lenin's direct competitor to the leadership of the party, Bogdanov's ideas carried substantial weight. His faith in the creative energies of the proletariat was unwavering:

> To win over nature, humanity has to organise itself in one powerful army. This was being formed throughout centuries, forming workers' collectives, from small family gatherings of the distant past to the modern coming together of a hundred million people. The latter might not know it yet, but it is fully possible. (Bogdanov 1919: 8–9)

While the party had been the architect of a political revolution, it was the task of such proletarian agencies like the Proletkult to create a cultural revolution, a revolution that was to touch the people intimately and transform their everyday life. Collective creation, or the workers coming together within a comradely environment to solve common tasks and gain collective authorship of the resultant products, was a key aspect of proletarian culture as theorized upon by Bogdanov and translated to theatre by Kerzhentsev (Leach 1994: 22–5). However, even Kerzhentsev's supposedly practical methods were difficult to implement. His appeal for the end of specialization in order to nourish the multi-skilled performer, who in a production process could take part in all aspects of work, be they acting, directing, writing, music composition, costume and scenery preparation (see Chapter 3), was impossible to create considering that theatre revels in specialized activity. In fact, Kerzhentsev's most realizable ideas were those that became mainstays of modernism, such as the bringing down of the barrier between the actor and the spectator and the use of unconventional theatre spaces.

The Proletkult suffered markedly from the theory-practice divide. Looking at the writings of the Proletkult leaders and supporters – which read as short and contentious pieces and therefore as typical manifestos of modernism – exposes the theoretical side of the Proletkult. These are the writings of Bogdanov, Kerzhentsev, Pletnev, Pavel Lebedev-Poliansky, Fedor Kalinin and others. The practical implementation of their theories in the provinces, away from the centres of Moscow and Petrograd, was however often left to its own devices. A key example related to the membership: while the centre argued that Proletkult members should be sourced from the proletarian vanguard, i.e. the industrial workers, group composition in the local districts was much more varied – skilled, non-skilled, factory and office employees, and even peasants (Mally 1990: 61–2). In fact, while central Proletkult committees sought to control the movement as it was developing, overwhelming demands for assistance from local cells meant that separate interpretations of the Proletkult's theories were common. The use of the pre-revolutionary intelligentsia is another example of the divide between theory/practice and centre/fringe. Mally argues that the centre's denouncement of pre-revolutionary intelligentsia 'mainly [served as] a rhetorical function [...] [because] lower class participants welcomed intellectuals' aid without any ambivalence at all' (Mally 1990: 96). Ultimately, the majority of the Proletkult's actual cultural products never amounted to much when compared to the leaders' pretentious and loud theoretical statements. The practical accomplishments were much humbler.

The third historiographical difficulty when tackling amateur theatre is that even in the short time span of the first decade or so of Soviet rule, amateur practices were shifting and changing at a very quick pace. Amateur theatre in 1918 was very different from that of 1929 or even 1925. All-encompassing statements on the scene are, therefore, to be made with great caution, if at all, because they rarely hold for the whole decade. An ever-changing practice gives rise to the problem of periodization. Periodization involves the creation of the frames and models that theatre historians use to organize and categorize past theatrical realities. Historian William Green describes it as the 'organizing principles upon which we write history, the priorities we assign to various aspects of human endeavour, the theories of change we adopt to explain the historical process' (quoted in Tillis 2007: 11–12). There is substantial discussion surrounding periodization in theatre and performance. Christopher Balme (2008: 106–11) underlines several milestones of this debate: the problem in using models derived from parallel disciplines like literary and art history, the predominance in historical studies to juxtapose large-scale historical periods (Ancient Greece, Ancient Rome, Middle Ages, Renaissance) with more national inflexions (Italy, France, Germany, Spain, etc.) and the typical separation between Western and Oriental forms. These categorizations might as well be inevitable, but the student of history does well to approach them 'with a sharpened awareness of their constructedness' (Balme 2008: 111).

Several models of periodization and therefore of the organization of amateur theatre can be found in relevant literature. Carter's exposition of the first years of the Proletkult is structured on strict artistic criteria, i.e. what the workers were producing, with the 'Period of Revolution' followed by the 'Period of Transition'. Five categories were evident to Carter: Preparation, Military and Revolutionary plays, Semi-Relief, Full Relief, and Construction. He is very clear-cut in his periodization, reducing the chaotic work of the time to a linearity which both the Proletkult and proletarian theatre did not possess. The categories are, in fact, described as 'definite stages of development' (Carter 1925: 87). Gorchakov's periodization is defined around a major historical milestone, that of the Civil War. He created a binary between 'Civil War' and 'post-Civil War' amateur theatre. This binary served Gorchakov well. It allowed him to delineate a clear difference between the more spontaneous forms evident during the Civil War years and the latter developments centred on theatre as a form of governmental propaganda. Periodization is always reflective of the author's agenda and objectives, and in Gorchakov's case it supports his overarching criticism of the party's involvement in the arts. In the case of amateur theatre, what was once 'a pleasure, under the Communist regime became "social work". [...] [M]ost of the amateurs lost interest in their dramatic circles immediately and began to leave en masse' (Gorchakov 1957: 152). Leach's periodization also supports the specific narrative that he wanted to construct. He identified a clear theatrical milestone – Eisenstein's joining the Proletkult and consequent collaboration with Sergei Tretyakov – to suggest that what he called 'revolutionary theatre' reached its apex with their work. When the paths of the two separated, 'the revolutionary theatre began to fade [...], but it did not simply disappear' (Leach 1994: 162).

Mally's periodization is possibly the best among these sources. It suggests shifts in the broader political arena as a model for the organization of amateur work. This is a helpful method, not only because amateur theatre was intrinsically linked with political developments, but also because changes in the political status quo were always clearly articulated and thus relatively easy to delineate. Surely, this does not mean that Civil War culture, for example, immediately made way once Lenin proclaimed the advent of the New Economic Policy (Brovkin 1998: 42–4).[19] Still, both modern and current scholarship mark the Civil War years, New Economic Policy, rise of Stalin, the First Five Year Plan and the Great Terror as particularly well defined pockets in Russian history. In Mally's periodization, each period is presented as having given rise to a respective form of amateur practice (e.g. the epidemic years coincided with the Civil War, the rise of the small forms with the New Economic Policy, agitprop brigades with the First Five Year Plan). Consequently, the aims of amateur theatre changed to reflect the shifting political environments, and as a result 'the meaning of amateurism changed from the 1920s to the 1930s' (Mally 2000: 214). As in the broader cultural contexts, specific amateur practices did not die overnight to be substituted by others, but Mally's organization works well because it allows her to discuss amateur theatre as a tension between recurrent principles (role of the professionals, production spaces, issues of control and organization, etc.) and more specific developments.

My decision (see below) to emphasize collective creativity and autonomous action practically dictated the period of amateur theatre that I will focus on. My choices in this chapter are book-ended by the October Revolution and the start of the Civil War on one side and the issuing in 1924 of a book titled *Iskusstvo V Rabochem Klube* (*Art at the Workers' Clubs*; Pletnev 1924) on the other. The publication of this book was overseen by the Moscow Proletkult. The amateur theatre spearheaded by the revolution and the Civil War is on the other hand perhaps best encapsulated in Platon Kerzhentsev's book titled *Revoliutsiia i teatr* (*Revolution and Theatre*; 1918a). James von Geldern describes this book as a 'practical program' (1993: 228), but this is a very relative assertion and practical only in relation to the longer and more 'theoretical' *The Creative Theatre. Revolution and Theatre* in fact still appears as a visionary work that offers action plans only in the broadest sense of the word. See, for example, how the nationalization of the professional theatre, a complex and protracted task, is described by Kerzhentsev in a rather simple three-point programme and formulated over the length of two pages (1918a: 16–17).[20] In contrast, the *Art at the Workers' Clubs* volume offers concrete guidelines about the disciplines that need to be studied at a workers' studio, the length of the sessions, a bibliographical index for instructors and so on. Concrete texts for Living Newspapers and Agit-Trials are also produced. The trajectory from *Revolution and Theatre* to *Art at the Workers' Clubs* is representative of a broader development from spontaneous and independent forms of amateur practice to more directed and controlled efforts. It is this trajectory that underlines my use here of the 1918–24 periodization.

Transmission point 1: Critical processing

Part and parcel of academia is the notion of critiquing. This is done to facilitate the development of knowledge, especially in its need to be constantly reactive to the ever-pressing changes of the contemporary world. Critiquing is not strictly synonymous with criticism. The latter signifies, at least in lay terms, one's expression of discontentment and recognition of the negative features or faults of an idea, theory or practice. Critiquing, on the other hand, implies a careful delineation between elements that are either positive (and, therefore, usable) or negative (needing 'improvement' or removal). Raymond Williams, for example, defines Marx's 'critique of materialism [...] [as one that] accepted the physical explanations of the origin of nature and of life but rejected the derived forms of social and moral argument' (Williams 1983: 200). The examples of proletarian theatre that I will discuss below share in this understanding of critiquing. I will refer to 'critical processing', a process which implies operating on a phenomenon to affect its transformation and, consequently, adaptation and preservation – in post-revolutionary amateur theatre, this critical processing or critiquing was construed in decidedly collective terms. The examples that I will refer to are two essays by Pletnev and Kerzhentsev, which both articulate the need to critique pre-revolutionary elements so that they find a place in the post-revolutionary world. The transmission of pre-revolutionary theatrical ideas and practices therefore will be tackled as needing critical processing if they were to be integrated in the new cultural climate.

Valerian Pletnev (1886–1942) represented that group of proletarian leaders with roots in the working class (he was a joiner by trade) and who took leading roles within the Proletkult by working their way upwards into the national organization. In fact, Pletnev was elected in 1920 as the national president of the Proletkult, a position he kept till the organization's demise in 1932. He turned out to be a rather less explosive figure than Lebedev-Poliansky, his predecessor, and worked hard to ride the waves of criticism which engulfed the Proletkult. Pletnev was an avid writer, whose many theoretical essays about the workers' creativity were supported by his numerous and popular plays (Mally 1990: 102–3). The essay that I refer to here is titled 'On Professionalism' (1919). In this essay, Pletnev made a strong case for the importance of training the workers to become the next generation of skilled cultural producers. He noted the voices of those students whose participation in theatre was cut short by the weariness of a day's hard work. A lack of time meant that 'the work of these students can only be random, incomplete, and amateurish' (Pletnev 1919: 31). In view of this, a faction within the Proletkult suggested that the most talented students should be released from their factory jobs, given a stipend, and thus turn professional.[21] Pletnev fully understood the importance of professionalism. It was necessary to create proletarian experts who were skilled in theatrical techniques.[22] In describing the process leading towards the formation of proletarian experts he disclosed his complex thinking about organic development. In line with Stanislavsky's own thinking that artistic processes – be they a character, a theatre institution or a tradition – need their own time to germinate naturally and independently of outside pressures, Pletnev argued that proletarian experts cannot be created on order. The first creative sprouts nourished by the revolution were to be given time to come to their natural maturity. He also argued that the formation of proletarian experts should be a restricted rather than widespread activity.

The shortage of proletarian experts was being felt when Pletnev wrote this essay. As a solution, he suggested using bourgeois experts trained in pre-revolutionary theatre. These experts needed to be carefully integrated in the new world. Their technical expertise was valued – Pletnev at one point referred to this technique as a 'skill in the forms [of art]' (34) – but their bourgeois ideologies (e.g. social hierarchies, predilection for individualism and the creation of art as a profit-making endeavour) were to be dropped. This separation between technical skill and ideology is one example of critical processing: one aspect of a practice was valued while another deemed damaging to the receiving context was dropped. It appears in Pletnev's essay under the guise of 'class struggle':

> It is necessary for the proletariat to conquer bourgeois art and culture, especially its extraordinary technique. […] [On the other hand], [t]he creation of proletarian culture is a process of struggle with the remnants of bourgeois culture, a struggle where the psychologically harmful influence of the declining bourgeois art on the proletarian masses is defeated.[23] (31–3)

The ideological content of proletarian theatre was to be derived from the workers and their close contact with collective-based work environments. Places like the factory or the club teach the worker that his creative potential does not lie in his individualism but in a tight cooperation with his co-workers. Together the workers create a 'unity of action, a collective creation in which one link follows the next'. With his choice of wording, Pletnev seems to have been critical of Ford's production line. He spoke of 'depersonalisation, the derivation of work from the automatic repetition of a single operation [which] […] turns a proletarian into a small screw in a giant machine'. Collective creation, on the hand, transforms 'a proletarian collective' into a creative body 'which takes the soul of a proletarian to the most sacred depths' (35).

It is through the transmission of bourgeois technical skill amalgamated with proletarian class-consciousness that a proletarian theatre hybrid was to be created. Such a hybridity defined Pletnev's understanding of professionalism. He was critical of that 'professionalism which is deeply convinced that it can create artists who are brilliant in their technique but shallow in their class content' (36). As already hinted in the opening of this chapter, there is plenty of evidence of proletarian theatre being construed as a cultural hybrid between amateur and professional players. Leach, for example, writes that in the Proletkult and outside it, '[t]he usual pattern for theatre work [...] consisted of a teacher leading about fifty participants, in classes broadly based on his professional experience' (Leach 1994: 69; see also 143). These teachers were allowed freedom in devising their programmes, which meant that teaching within Proletkult cells could vary widely, depending on the character and background of the teacher and on his own understanding of proletarian culture (Mally 1990: 13). The Tonal-Plastic Department was similarly made of workers wanting to produce theatre in their free time but led 'by professional leaders [who] provided a comprehensive curriculum' (Leach 1994: 70). It opened within the Moscow Proletkult in September 1920 in order to experiment with physical and collective acting techniques as an alternative to Stanislavsky's System. Chroniclers of the time also underline this coming together of amateur and professional practitioners. Kerzhentsev ultimately conceded that it was hard to put his theories into practice, and he gave several examples of performances staged between young professional actors and amateur worker-actors (Keržencev 1979: 99–101). Carter, on the other hand, discussed the worker-based membership of the Proletkult but added that the movement then had Lunacharsky, Kerzhentsev and Smyshlaev as its main theoretical interlocutors. They variously contributed ideas about the self-expression of the workers, the value of mass plays and suggestions about actor training (Carter 1925: 83).

Other examples of amateur-professional hybridity raise the point of compositional processes and skill. For example, the staging of *The Overthrow of the Autocracy* (1919) at the Theatrical-Dramaturgical Studio of the Red Army revolved around the soldiers bringing in the revolutionary ideas, themes and content (many of the performers had themselves participated in the actual February Revolution), which the professional director Nikolai Vinogradov then brought together through his skill in composition. In other words, he exhibited the knowledge of how to string disparate theatrical elements together to form a whole (von Geldern 1993: 126). The dichotomy between a content brought in by the amateurs and the skill in composition provided by the professional directors is evident in several other texts. It emerges in Kerzhentsev's discussion about professionalism, which is as complex as Pletnev's. Kerzhentsev similarly argued that professional instructors were to be welcomed only when they could prove their detachment from bourgeois ideology. This detachment was a prerequisite for the contribution they could give to proletarian theatre, in terms of their 'technical preparation of the performances, the artistic direction, and in the gestation of all other areas in which their experience and understanding is helpful' (Keržencev 1979: 61). Composition was one such technical skill which the workers lacked, as opposed to the 'revolutionary temperament' which Kerzhentsev believed they had in abundance. In another essay titled 'After the Holiday' (1918d), Kerzhentsev criticized the outdoor decorations used to celebrate the first anniversary of the revolution. He argued that they lacked a sense of organic composition. The decorations included banners, posters, paintings and the like. While applauding the energies of the artists, and some of the most tasteful and uplifting examples, Kerzhentsev remarked that a general feeling of disappointment crept in because many decorations did not match each other. The controlling hand of a skilled director was necessary if an overall unity was to be created: 'In organising future festivals, we will need to pay special attention so that this disharmony is not repeated. For this purpose, the decoration of each square should be given to one artist of a co-ordinated team' (Kerzhentsev 1918d: 3).

A further example of critical processing is found in another essay by Kerzhentsev, titled 'Adapt the Plays!' (1919c). In this essay, Kerzhentsev lamented the fact that a proletarian repertoire was still to be created, a common preoccupation after the revolution that was regularly associated with both the professional and amateur scenes.[24] In this essay Kerzhentsev spoke about the transmission of old scripts into the new cultural context. This transmission entailed the transformation of the plays or critical processing to render them relevant to the post-revolutionary era. This redoing or processing could be carried out in several ways. It might involve the addition of new materials and texts, or the alteration of the play's tempo or style. In effect, plays could be adapted by treating the text not as a durable whole but as a construct whose constituent parts can be untangled and reconfigured anew. Both Eugenio Barba (in Barba and Savarese 2006: 66) and Richard Schechner (2002: 227) agree that the etymological meaning of the term 'text' implies the action and know-how of weaving together different elements to make single and constructed artefacts. Critical processing as seen by Kerzhentsev seems to imply that the process of weaving different elements together to create single entities can actually be reversed. If an artefact is woven together from disparate elements, then it can also be untangled for its constituent elements to be reconfigured anew in different ways or even attached to outside elements brought in to hybridize the original artefact. The adaptation of a play text is one such example of critical processing that allows form to be separated from content or, as we have seen with Pletnev's example of professionalism, technical skill from ideology.[25]

The example Kerzhentsev uses to illustrate his theories about critically processing a text is that of *The Dawn* (1919c: 6). Written by the Belgian poet Émile Verhaeren, *The Dawn* became an enduring presence in post-revolutionary repertoires. Kerzhentsev often referred to it as an appropriate text (1918a: 31, 34; 1918b: 6). Meyerhold famously staged a version of the play in 1920, which Kerzhentsev duly criticized for emphasizing technical effects over revolutionary content (Braun 1969: 170). In fact, critically processing *The Dawn* meant underlining its political content first. Kerzhentsev was overall supportive of the play's political message. He felt that the text had the right amount of pathos, and the author exhibited great skill in elevating specific events into historical generalizations. These elements were to be maintained, and a production of the play was to foreground such themes because they contributed to make *The Dawn* a 'modern and sagacious play' (Kerzhentsev 1919c: 6). Other themes, like the passivity and even stupidity of the crowd, or the insecurity of Erenian, the main hero, were to be corrected because 'how can the play be successful if the proletariat is shown in an image which is not typical of our days?' The first level of critical processing therefore related to the updating of the play's content, namely the promotion of the crowd and giving Erenian a different character.

The second level of critical processing related to the play's technical form. Kerzhentsev felt the piece was overlong. It was more appropriate as a piece of literature. Critically processing the play's form entailed the shortening or removal of the long monologues and the elevation of stage action instead of the word. A third level of critical processing involved adding newly composed scenes in order to sharpen 'the psychology of the participants in the struggle' (Kerzhentsev 1919c: 7). These scenes were not to be composed by a playwright but by the collective of actors producing the piece. Kerzhentsev argued that the resultant piece would still be *The Dawn*, but it was a version of *The Dawn* with a form and content that had been critiqued and updated for contemporary times. Its main political theme – the transformation from chaos to synthesis, from destruction to creativity, and from war to revolution and peace – had to be 'kept safe', but the play was to become more 'articulate, dynamic, and economical' (6). In line with Kerzhentsev's theories on collective creation as the basis of proletarian creativity, the critical processing of a text was to be carried out by the particular collective at work, during collective meetings and while staging and rehearsing the piece. This collective work contrasts with the image of the bourgeois director holed alone in his ivory tower working on the mise-en-scène of a production.

Transmission point 2: Collective creation and independent action – from the studio to everyday life

In the previous sections I remarked how collective creation and independent action were key characteristics of proletarian culture. The two warrant closer inspection, seeing how collective work and the ethics of independent and autonomous action provided the foundation for much of the debate surrounding proletarian theatre. Collective creation is particularly foregrounded in Leach's exposition on proletarian theatre, via Bogdanov and Kerzhentsev (Leach 1994: 22–4). Mally, on the other hand, emphasizes independent action (1990: xxvi; 2000: 14–15), as does Swift (2002: 184 and 204). Collective creation and independent action, however, far from negate each other. They rather support each another in a congenial manner. Independent action comes as a result of collective creation. In a first instance, it directs production processes away from a reverential attitude towards the text as the be-all and end-all of theatre practice, what Kerzhentsev described as 'the cheap thrill given by the play text' (Kerzhentsev 1919b: 39). Second, independent action and collective creation also reduce the reliance on the director as the generating and organizational force of performance. In environments based on collective creation it is the group of practitioners which becomes responsible for a production, on lines not dissimilar to how contemporary devised processes give rise to notions of collective authorship (Oddey 1994: 56). The roles of the author and director are not removed in Kerzhentsev's vision of proletarian theatre, but their contributions are redefined and placed on an equal footing with the rest of the group. Kerzhentsev explains:

> Collective creation can work correctly and fruitfully only when there is a natural equality between its members and equal value is given to all theatre participants. The actor and stage director, prompter and stage worker, light-technician and artist, makeup man, and musician shall be considered as necessary creators of the scenic whole. [...] Bourgeois theatre only knew productions of the stage directors who, although conferring with experts, rested solely on their own vision and led all the work on a play. We have to break away from this tradition and form.
> (Kerzhentsev 1919b: 38–9)

Independent action is stimulated by what Kerzhentsev called dramatic laboratories. A distinction is made between dramatic circles and dramatic laboratories in a central part of *The Creative Theatre*. The former were the performance groups of the Civil War years which had quickly forged a connection with the Red Army. They were often led by some third-class professional actor and resulted in a lot of degenerative performances staged for the entertainment of the soldiers. Kerzhentsev linked the dramatic circles to the basest, most superficial and vulgar dramas of the bourgeois kind (Keržencev 1979: 68–70). Dramatic laboratories, on the other hand, were intended to penetrate these circles and reform them from within. The dramatic circles had to continue, but under the influence of the laboratories their work would become theatrically stronger and more serious. The laboratories would transmit a fully fledged theatrical education in technique, history and political implications of theatre work, while at the same time 'use all possible ways to stimulate the *initiative* and *autonomy* of the students' (1979: 71; emphasis added).[26] (Symptoms of such an extensive programme are certainly evident in the collection *Art at the Workers' Clubs* which I will discuss below.) Independent action, therefore, is attached to technical skill, and transmitting the latter allows the former to be nourished.

In environments based on collective creation, therefore, a big part of the initiative is given to each member of the group. The actors are the ones that start, focus and compose a performance piece. This is clearly evident in my discussion below of Smyshlaev's essay 'Experiment in Staging of Émile Verhaeren's Poem "Insurrection"', which documents his production of the poem for the Moscow Proletkult. Collective creation and personal initiative with independent action are also evident in the example which Carter gives of a play titled *Don't Go!* As always, we do not get much details about the context that produced the piece, because Carter is more interested in recounting how the work on this performance started from a picture, suggested by one of the members of the group, which was then 'collectively built up into a play, altering it here and there' (Carter 1925: 96). Improvisation played a key role in the compositional process. The examples which Kerzhentsev provided in his chapter 'Results of the New Theatre' also revolve around improvised and collective processes (1979: 97–102). He felt these examples vindicated his earlier statement, expressed in 1918, about the extensive use of improvisation and how it could contribute to the creation of a proletarian repertoire. The model which he suggested was that of *commedia dell'arte*, which 'has all the reasons to be reborn in Russia right now'. Improvisation was to be based on a few types or moments in the plot, while '[e]verything else – the dialogue, the plot development, and the culmination – will be improvised by the performers themselves' (Kerzhentsev 1918b: 7). The potential of improvisation within such devised contexts is easy to discern. It allows for variations to be tried out in practice. Improvisation also facilitates the pruning of the dramaturgical material into a discernible and organic whole. In suggesting a pre-revolutionary reality like *commedia dell'arte* as a paradigm for proletarian theatre Kerzhentsev was in actual fact also providing another example of critical processing. The improvisation techniques of *commedia dell'arte* were deemed valuable, but not its contents which needed to be reworked for post-revolutionary Russia. The idea of using types was retained, but these were to be sourced not from Renaissance realities but from Soviet life (e.g. the worker, the foreman, the peasant, the bureaucrat).[27]

Kerzhentsev's key text about collective work is an essay aptly titled 'Collective Creativity in Theatre' (1919b). It is important to expound on this essay because, typical of the context, collective creativity came to mean different things. For instance, in his work at the Petrograd Proletkult, Alexander Mgebrov linked it with choral declamation (Mally 1990: 148). Collective creation also meant production themes and stories depicting the collective, like scenarios in which individual protagonists choose to sacrifice their interests for the common good (see Gourfinkel 1979: 138–9). The relationship between an individual man and the revolution was envisaged too complex for the common man to understand. Indeed, the whole idea of the 'individual' was considered as counter-revolutionary. Conflicts of a social nature were much easier to grasp and more politically correct. Therefore, references to simple events were made, like an accident at the office between a worker and his foreman (Gourfinkel 1979: 138). Collective creation was also related to collective reactions from the audience, in the form of collective singing for example, evidenced during the mass spectacles staged in the period 1918–20.[28]

For Kerzhentsev and other people collaborating to post-revolutionary proletarian theatre, including, as we have seen, Smyshlaev, collective creation cut much deeper than all these practices, especially choral singing and mass participation which were deemed as 'a simplified [and mistaken] understanding of collective creation' (Kerzhentsev 1919b: 37–8). Kerzhentsev's theories treated the proletariat as creative beings who could come up with inventive solutions to their stage problems (e.g. the use of the wall mentioned in the opening quotation as a way of delineating a separation between the pre- and post-revolutionary epochs). Collective creation also included the future spectators, who could attend rehearsals to provide preliminary feedback. Criticism from every participant was particularly valued.[29] His understanding of collective creation also chimes with current twenty-first-century theories about embodiment. The work of Einar Schleef as expounded upon by Hans Lehmann helps to qualify this point. Schleef is particularly undeviating in his goal to make the spectators experience directly the physical presence of his performers. He is described as showing 'the possible future of a thoughtless and unscrupulous sportive, virile military body'. The performer's body is not a representation of this futuristic body. It is not depicted on stage through relevant futuristic scenarios for example. Through physical techniques, the performer's body is rather made to incarnate and embody (i.e. become) this vision of the future. The bodies 'in Schleef's theatre [do] [...] not "demonstrate", "show" or "communicate" the presence of a [different] body, but instead *manifest* [it]' (Lehmann in Murray and Keefe 2007: 26; emphasis in the original). Similarly, the version of collective creation expounded by Kerzhentsev did not rely on scenario work or representation. Like Schleef's physicality, it was to be embodied:

> Any participant in a collective shall consciously seek to embody the best interests of the whole and comprehensively identify the ideal of the proletariat: communism. Specific tasks should be made clear to everyone. Finally, creative organisation shall be based on the principles of partnership, while staying apart from any authoritarianism and allowing space for criticism. (Kerzhentsev 1919b: 38)

The question that can be posed here is one of reach: do collective and independent practices impact beyond the studio or rehearsal room, or is their reach restricted to these workspaces? The question is fundamentally a transmission concern, as it underscores the identification of transmission channels.

A 1924 essay titled 'A Unified Studio of the Arts' raises this very issue. The essay forms part of a broader collection titled *Art at the Workers' Clubs*. The volume is authored by several individuals, whose full names are however not disclosed.[30] The authorship of the specific essays thus remains somewhat unclear. We do know, however, that Pletnev served as the volume's editor (Pletnev 1924: 3).[31] The collection includes essays on theatre training (with entries on Biomechanics, acrobatics, voice training, application of different forms, stage exercises and so on), plans for literature and art sessions, relevant bibliographies, sample scripts, etc. It was, to all effects, a guidebook for developing the artistic work at the workers' clubs. The essay 'A Unified Studio of the Arts' is a central essay in the collection. It offers plans for a Unified Studio as 'the basis of the Art work in a club' (3). The essay also provides a template for the workers' holistic formation, one that drew from various disciplines like theatre, eurhythmics, physical education, literature, choral singing, fine arts and political theory. All the participants of the Unified Studio were meant to partake in this common curriculum.

The Unified Studio was not meant as a production house. Artistic production was of course an important aspect of club work. These artistic products included works in proletarian literature, dramatizations of current events, Living Newspapers, Agit-Trails, athletic parades, and propagandistic posters and banners. They were however to be created in specific and specialized theatre, music, literature and art studios. The Unified Studio, on the other, directed its operation towards the 'concept of art as life-building (the development of new modes of life)' (Pletnev 1924: 10). The authors clarify that a workers' club is not an institution that trains art specialists, but a studio which sets as its 'goal the harmonious and comprehensive development in its members of those conditions that are necessary for building a proletarian life' (10). The essay is valuable for its precision not only in identifying these conditions, but also in recognizing the everyday life of the workers as the locus where these 'new modes of life' will be implemented. In other words, training in the arts was to be redirected towards the workers' own everyday life. Everyday life was not treated as a mundane space, as the trivial and run-of-the-mill side of existence. Rather, it was seen as a space for transformation, with even Lenin asserting that '[w]e give little attention to that aspect of *everyday* life inside the factories, in the villages and in the regiments where, more than anywhere else, the new is being built' (Lenin 1974: 98; emphasis in the original). Soviet cultural theorists consistently treated everyday life as a space for transformation and the creation of the new Soviet Man or what Leon Trotsky called an 'improved edition of mankind' (in Hellbeck 2006: 5). The Unified Studio partook in this endeavour to transform everyday life, by using artistic practice to train the workers in 'socially productive and environmentally-oriented skills' (Pletnev 1924: 10):

> **A number of disciplines are obligatory** for the art work of a club. This follows from the fact that in studying these disciplines the attention is not on a purely aesthetic upbringing and education, and not on specialisation, but rather on their direct implementation in everyday life. Studying these obligatory disciplines becomes the foundation on which all further art work at the club is built. (10; bold emphasis in original)

Consequently, literature classes were not envisaged 'as a factory of poets and writers' (11), but as means of developing skill in verbal and written language which a worker could use to solve 'tasks arising from everyday life', while at the same time making everyday speech 'flexible, expressive, and straight to the point' (13); voice training aimed 'at the development of vocal qualities for their direct application and intonation in everyday life' (12); eurhythmics were meant to help 'develop psychomotor abilities' (12); physical education classes will not have the 'goal of preparing record-breaking specialists in some sports discipline' but 'to produce a normal, healthy, physically fit person' (12); physical education also had the more '"social" [goal] of developing effective orientation skills within an environment, in everyday life and in work' (12); choral singing was 'regarded in its constant application in everyday life' (13). It is worth noting that the conditions to be implemented in everyday life were seen as particularly physical in nature, in line with Toby Clark's exposition that while formulations on the 'new man' were 'generally conceived as an all-round development of mental and physical capacities, in the early Soviet period there was a particular preoccupation with the physical aspect, and the human body became a principal site for utopian speculations' (Clark 1993: 33).

At least two theoretical frameworks can be used to support the Unified Studio's provision that the transmission of artistic training can impact on and transform every day. The first is provided by educational theorist Robert M. Gagné (1916–2002), especially in his identification of 'attitudes' as one of the five varieties of what can be learned (the others being intellectual skills, cognitive strategies, verbal information and motor skills). Attitudes are character traits that inform a person's behaviour in life (Gagné 1977: 44–5). They advance a moderating influence that allows a person to manifest consistent reactions to contexts that are in some way comparable. For example, an individual who has embodied over time the attitude of precision can be expected to look at fine detail across various life scenarios. Other attitudes include competition, carefulness, rule abiding (or not) and, in the line with the discussion about proletarian theatre developed above, the inclination to participate in collective creation or to develop independent initiative. Gagné underlines that attitudes do not operate in isolation but are intrinsically linked to technical skill. Along the lines expressed in the Unified Studio essay, training skills like the use of gesture, vocal projection, pacing and timing, and eye contact allow the individual to speak with the attitude of confidence not only in formal settings but also in everyday scenarios.

The manifestation of skill and corresponding attitude across different contexts (like the studio, work and home) is possible when the skill is practised over a prolonged period of time. This allows an attitude to become an embodied attitude. A studio environment facilitates the embodiment of attitudes because contrary to a school or formal theatre, it provides the space and time necessary for such protracted work to take place. Modern practitioners and theorists underline the workshop potential of a studio, as a space where its participants can spend time together to collectively seek answers to common problems without the pressure of performance. This ethic is perhaps best encapsulated in Stanislavsky's original plans for the First Studio, especially when it was led by Sulerzhitsky (see Chapter 2), but theoreticians about proletarian theatre equally valued a studio's predilection for study, thinking and experimentation. This understanding of the studio emerged forcefully after the revolution. Mally, for example, argues that the Proletkult's self-definition as a laboratory to create proletarian culture (on terms of exclusivity and restriction) supported its early claims for autonomy (Mally 1990: 42–4). Kerzhentsev similarly underlined that a studio's 'tasks are not only to prepare and educate. The studios are laboratories for new discoveries. It's where the first experiments to create the proletarian theatre must take place' (Kerzhentsev 1918a: 52).

In simple terms, the essay 'A Unified Studio of the Art' identifies a channel or path linking artistic practice with everyday life. Across this channel, technical skills are transmitted and redirected away from specialization and towards the transformation of everyday life. The possibility for this channel is further supported by the theories of everyday life developed by Henri Lefebvre (1901–91). In his theories (2008a, 2008b), Lefebvre addressed the general association of everyday life with the most trivial and repetitive side of existence. He noted that the roots of these claims could be traced back to nineteenth-century literature's emphasis on the romantic and marvellous, which 'mounted a sustained attack on everyday life which has continued unabated' (Lefebvre 2008a: 105). Lefebvre's aim was not to describe or catalogue the practices of daily life, how a particular culture eats, drinks, dresses or builds houses. He wanted to critique the everyday in order to affect its transformation: 'There can be no knowledge of society (as a whole) without critical knowledge of everyday life [...]. Inseparable from practice or praxis, knowledge encompasses an agenda for transformation. To know the everyday is to want to transform it' (Lefebvre 2008b: 98). This sense of transformation also defined post-revolutionary understandings of everyday life. Daily existence was seen as that space where the major changes produced by the revolution on the level of official decrees (e.g. abolishment of Tsarist systems of ranks and private land ownership) could impact on the lives of ordinary people along the path that creates a new culture, mores and ways of life.[32] In their study of early Soviet culture, Christina Kiaer and Eric Naiman link this impact on everyday life directly with Lefebvre and argue that '[i]t is in the repeated, routine practices of everyday life rather than party edicts that the incomprehensible, world-shattering concept of revolution begins to take on meaning for subjects, begins to be lived by them, and begins to transform them' (Kiaer and Naiman 2006: 2).[33]

In Lefebvre's theories, one way of transforming everyday life beyond its superficial connotations is by evaluating different activities and realms not as separate realities but as each having the potential to 'cross-refer' one another. Everyday life is thus construed as a matrix of interlinked channels:

Take this tool-maker. He has a 'good trade' (relatively speaking). Up to a certain point he likes what he does. He 'earns a good living'. But this prompts the question: *what life does he earn with his work?* The life of a tool-maker. Yes and no. Looking carefully, we would observe that his work may leave an impression on him, so that traces of it can be seen in his life outside of the factory. [...]

[...] If we would watch him at work, we would doubtless perceive in his mannerisms and attitude (towards his superiors, his peers and his inferiors) and echo of what he 'is' when he is not at work – and vice versa. This is because in that 'substance' or 'matter' which is neither substance nor matter as the terms are usually understood, i.e. in the everyday, ever sector cross-refers to another. (Lefebvre 2008b: 51–2; emphasis in original)

For example, such cross-reference is absent in the life of a 'society woman' whose existence is compartmentalized in terms of the everyday against 'artificial means [like] society life, fashion shows, snobbery, aestheticism or the pursuit of "pure" pleasure' (Lefebvre 2008b: 51). These events exhibit a clear beginning and end, producing a high degree of independence and severance from one another. Lefebvre argues that such events only have a sparse effect on other spheres and as 'activities run the risk of disintegrating and disappearing' (Lefebvre 2008b: 53). In opposition to this separation and fragmentation, Lefebvre suggested an organic view of the human being, organic in the sense that binaries like 'work' and 'home' give way to a continuum where the same behavioural patterns emerge in multiple spaces, what the authors of the Unified Studio essay likened to a process of direct transmission and implementation of technical skills into everyday life.

Insurrection as an example of proletarian theatre

Smyshlaev's production of Émile Verhaeren's poem *Insurrection* offers concrete insights into the processes adopted to create a piece of proletarian theatre. I will use this example to conclude this chapter on amateur and proletarian theatre in early post-revolutionary Russia because the work going into the production, though perhaps idealized by Smyshlaev, ties up with many of the points raised here. These include the use of improvisation to create theatrical texts, acting processes, topical relevance, and a concern for both the form and the content of production. Underlining the work going into the production was a clear effort to use collective work and creativity, one that drew from the life experiences but also imaginative capabilities of the participants. This collectivism was, however, supported by Smyshlaev's significant professional expertise, accentuating the amateur-professional hybridity of proletarian theatre. The production of *Insurrection* was staged for the opening of the Moscow Proletkult on 6 November 1918.

What the collective could bring to the proceedings was valued right from the start of the work. Verhaeren's poem was in fact proposed by one of the participants rather than Smyshlaev or any other leader of the Proletkult. An inclusive environment was therefore set up right from the beginning. Smyshlaev expounded on the work processes adopted in an essay in the newspaper *Gorn*. He opened this essay on a theoretical slant, by saying that 'the most significant aspects of theatre are action and dialogue. [...] They are the two theatre essentials' (Smyshlaev 1919: 82). The criteria to choose a theatrical text as a blueprint for performance, in Balme's sense (see Chapter 3), were whether the poem offered potential to generate these two theatrical elements. Stage action and dialogue were to be laden with the correct political content, one that projected to the then contemporary and passionate view that the masses had been the main architects of the revolution. In the essay Smyshlaev spoke about the role of the masses as romantically as when Lunacharsky described the proletariat. In fact, he denoted 'the feelings of the masses, the feelings of the revolutionary crowd who is building a new joyful life through the destruction of slavery' (82).

The work on the production started in a very visual manner. The collective's first reading of the poem created a strong impression on all participants. The poem, Smyshlaev wrote, 'seized us and we wanted to perform it. [...] We began to immediately think how the poem could be produced when the impression from the reading was still so bright in our minds' (82). The noun 'chaos' was identified as the basis for the production. It was defined as the 'message' which the audience was to take from the performance. The choice of the noun 'chaos' as the trigger for performance is to be underlined. It contrasts with the use of a verb. Stanislavsky gave importance to constructing stage action around the use of verbs, which push the actors to stand up and start acting. Smyshlaev's initial work on the production took a different direction, becoming less technical but more imaginative:

> Together we drew a whole picture of the staging. The theatre is immersed in darkness; somewhere, formless, breaking sounds of music, appear, which gradually turn into an ecstatic hymn. The curtain opens slowly, but the viewer still cannot discern anything on the stage. Streams of golden sparks break the darkness, and merge with the stars. The roar of a formless, excited crowd, the trampling of running feet [is heard]. Little by little the red reflections of fire scatter in the darkness. The spectator starts

distinguishing some lines resembling corners of houses, window edges, doors. These are not definite lines, but trembling, broken, rebellious; the spectator sees a seething, excited crowd ... And over all this chaos, the words of Verhaeren's poem are heard ... The groups of people merge together and split ... human bodies fall down ... someone is above the crowd and gives a speech ... somewhere the enemies appear ... fight ... victory ... And everyone, through the burning buildings, is alarmed by the worrying call of the bells, and the enthusiastic and determined crowd is slowly coming towards the audience. [...] That is, in general, how we initially pictured the staging, how we thought it will be. (82)

Following the creation of this initial visual picture, the group turned its attention to the development of the text. Collective work was again at the centre of the process, with the group gathering together to read the poem and to pitch in material. In this process the script changed many times, and a lot of editing took place. A scenario was eventually worked out, which Smyshlaev reproduced in the main body of the essay.

The production process then developed as a combination of technical work, related to the composition of the piece, and personal recollections, proposed by the participants as the piece's content. It was this combination that made the process a micro example of the broader interaction between professionalism and amateur work. Smyshlaev, as the leader of the troupe, brought in his technical expertise, especially how this related to the use of improvisation and, as we will see, in crafting the performance's form. The participants, on the other hand, brought in the subject matter of the improvisations, 'elicited all the time from [their] live feelings' (85). This links with what Kerzhentsev referred to in *The Creative Theatre* as 'revolutionary temperament', which the workers cultivated from their own direct experiencing of the times. Many of the participants in the production had themselves witnessed the October Revolution, while some even remembered the 1905 uprising. Memories of these events were shared and used as themes for the improvisations. The critical processing which Smyshlaev provided with the group elevated these recollections from the plane of life to that of stage material, in turn distancing them from a direct and unembellished naturalism:

We built our dramatization on [the participants'] vivid feelings. And of course these sketches were not exact copies of the experience, they were not photographs of the reality – no! Warmed by the imagination of the creative artists, these memories turned into a reality very similar to the truth; from genuine truth they turned into a work of art. (85)

The next phase of work involved direct work with the actors on their parts. As mentioned above, the main role of the piece was given to the crowd, in line with Kerzhentsev's own recommendation to strengthen the crowd's position in, for example, *The Dawn* (see above). Smyshlaev's overt work on the crowd is what probably instigated Stanislavsky to be critical of Smyshlaev's approach to collective work, when collective work was equated by Stanislavsky to mass and crowd scenes on the stage (Chapter 3). The crowd in *The Insurrection* was made of different individuals, reflecting the infinite variety of human individuals one could observe in a crowd. The group's first task was to define the roles, and they identified post-revolutionary types like metalworkers, masons, tailors, soldiers, clerks, managers and the unskilled. They also included people who happen to be in the crowd by chance. The division of the roles therefore came quite late in the production process, allowing all the participants to get a sense of the play as a whole. Following the identification of the parts, the participants then worked to enliven their roles. To give, so to speak, life to the roles, Smyshlaev used an approach he called the 'method of today':

> Actors imagine a whole day of the persons they are playing. This method, in addition to developing the actor's imagination, is also remarkable as it affects the actors' souls. It brings the feelings necessary for the given case from 'rich' emotional impressions. (86)

The participants were also encouraged to record these 'dreams' or fantasies, which offered the opportunity for reflection and editing. One such dream narrated the story of a worker who, on hearing shooting in the streets, was compelled to leave the safety of his apartment to join the workers and soldiers in the uprising. Another fantasy narrated how a soldier deserted his squadron to join the workers in the fight. This method did not carry much of the technical complexity of Stanislavsky's System as it was applied in 1918 (concentration, detailed work at the table, identification of bits and objectives, etc.). In contrast to Stanislavsky's techniques, however, the value of 'the method of today' for amateur actors emerges as follows: instead of drawing from the participants' limited technical skill, the 'method of today' made the most of their imaginative capabilities as human beings, fuelled by their own recollections of the events. Smyshlaev concludes this part by saying:

> There is a lot of genuine, real truth, and the comrades who wrote these 'dreams' experienced once again what they had once experienced in reality. The significance of these fantasies for the staging is enormous: here is found the foundation of the role, where all further knowledge of the image is built. (86)

Ultimately, the work on 'the method of today' was used extensively, and about a hundred dreams were created.

The last part of the essay described Smyshlaev's work on the crowd. It should be noted that while the essay is about nine pages long, only about a third is devoted to the work on the crowd. Equal if not more importance was given to the work on the text and on the actors' use of the method of today. This reconfirms that while Stanislavsky was indeed correct to identify this aspect of work in Smyshlaev's practice, it also needs to be said that crowd work was only one facet of a larger collective performance process. The key point to create the mass scenes was 'that special feeling where each person in a crowd is linked to the whole group through some very special strings' (88). Improvisations were again used not only to find but also to consolidate this feeling. They allowed the participants to experience what it means to be in a crowd, even if the scenarios were not necessarily sourced from *The Insurrection* or worked out to form part of the final mise-en-scène. One such crowd scenario was titled 'Fire', where the participants improvised on a scenario where they were trapped in a burning building. Each individual could feel the connection with the crowd because the same objective was shared: to find a way out as quickly as possible. Smyshlaev referred to this as the basic desire.

The account of the crowd scenes in *The Insurrection*, where the feel of being in the crowd is worked on through a series of improvisations, is markedly different to the approach which Stanislavsky used at the Society of Arts and Literature and the early productions of the Moscow Art Theatre. In productions like *Urial Acosta* and *Tsar Fiodor*, Stanislavsky had made a name for himself as a very precise director who drilled the actors on stage to follow a clear production plan. This plan was made of clear actions, gestures, rhythms, voices, etc. Smyshlaev, on the other hand, turned his attention to the aspects relating to the form of staging a crowd only after the participants had gone through the group improvisations. These formal aspects involved the delivery of parts of the text by a section of the cast or even the whole collective. It also involved movement in unison. These aspects of the mise-en-scène were treated by Smyshlaev as 'external forms that express collective feelings, but first we tried to find these feelings, enormous, powerful feelings that are known only in a crowd' (89). It was in the creation of the production's form that Smyshlaev's skill was particularly necessary, to in turn concretize Pletnev's assertion that the professionals were valued specifically for their compositional knowledge. Smyshlaev identified the mass as an example of Stanislavsky's 'through action' around which the production was made to revolve. At the same time that Smyshlaev was producing this piece Kerzhentsev was speaking in the 'After the Holiday' essay about the importance of organic composition, where all parts of a performance fit together to create a whole. In his work on *Insurrection* Smyshlaev gave organic composition due attention, on the basis that 'every small, unfinished, and indefinite gesture or work of individual persons completely breaks the entire form' (90). He also gave attention to the articulation and composition of the actions so that they are all 'completely finished and defined, and also significant and magnificent […] so that everything could be in harmony with the rhythms of the new life that is coming' (90). The form was also supplemented by the contributions of other artists and musicians who helped the collective complete their dramatization.[34]

Conclusion

At a time when a new post-revolutionary life, inspired by notions of 'a universal brotherhood' (Gorky 1995: 8), was being built, questions related to the relative potential of amateur theatre, and its contribution to the creation of this new life, were raised. Whether a satellite of the Red Army, or adjacent to factories, neighbourhoods or clubs, amateur and proletarian theatre exhibited an attachment to the life of the workers, in terms of the stories that were brought over to the stage, the materials used and the spaces utilized. In my final analysis of proletarian and amateur theatre, I would like to make reference to the theories on the practice of everyday life developed by Michel de Certeau. De Certeau's studied how everyday practices like reading, walking and storytelling contain within them the seed of resistance against authoritarian drives. His study revolved around the singular. For instance, he spoke about the worker who writes a letter on company time and using company material. His case studies are therefore about the reader, the walker and the narrator, all in the singular. However, the repercussions of these actions, while individually authored, reverberate beyond the single person and impact the group as a whole:

> In the very place where the machine he [the worker] must serve reigns supreme, he cunningly takes pleasure in finding a way to create gratuitous products whose sole purpose is to signify his own capabilities through his *work* and to confirm his solidarity with other workers or his family through *spending* his time in this way. With the complicity of other workers (who thus defeat the competition the factory tries to instil among them), he succeeds in 'putting one over' on the established order on its home ground. (de Certeau 1988: 25–6; emphasis in original)

Figure 8 Cover image of the journal *Rabochii i teatr* (*Worker and Theatre*), which published material relevant not only to worker-spectators but also to worker-actors. From the author's private collection.

A number of links with amateur theatre emerge from this quotation. The impulse towards creative action and a non-profit-making ethic are two recurring qualities of any amateur work: apart from the desire to stage the best theatre which the scarce means make possible (and to become known for it), underlying any amateur work is a desire for some shared hours to counter the rigidity and stress of everyday life. The amateur actor values the encounter with his peers in a relatively tranquil environment, i.e. the communal aspects of the work, what de Certeau refers to as the 'solidarity with other workers'. As I have discussed through Kerzhentsev's theories, such a solidarity, evidenced in the collective work undertaken and the consequent shared ownership which such work engenders, was seen as the basis on which to build a new and politically relevant amateur theatre.

A lot of theatre was staged during and after the revolutionary era, even though several theoreticians felt distressed because a post-revolutionary repertoire of a certain consequence had failed to appear. It was as if the revolution had not touched the theatre (Mally 2000: 37). However, the revolution *did* touch the theatre. For a brief period of time, and before policies and strict guidelines overtook the predilection towards improvisation, proletarian theatre opened the doors not only to a new audience, but also to a new class of amateur actors and theatre makers. Some 'effect' on its amateur doers was possible by theatre, a transformation which de Certeau acknowledges in everyday practices in general, as his discussion about the narration of stories proves. For de Certeau, storytelling acquires value 'more by a way of *exercising itself* than by the thing it indicates. And one must grasp a sense other than what is said. It produces effects, not objects' (de Certeau 1988: 79; emphasis in original). The same can be said about amateur theatre and its creative potential which was often evident not in the final 'objects', i.e. the performances, but in the communal 'effects' created and transmitted by the collective processes adopted. These processes, one can say, were the foremost characteristic of amateur work and provided the practice with its inherent transformative value.

Suggestions for practice

Amateur aesthetics and collective practices

1. Much of amateur theatre work, especially during the years of the Civil War, revolved around a crude and simple aesthetics. With few theatrical materials (lights, costume, make-up, scenery, etc.) at their disposal,

workers tended to trust their imagination, adopt collective work and experiment with physicality to solve stage tasks.

In groups of different sizes, create physical images representing the following:

- house
- car
- dragon
- ship
- room
- countryside
- airport

For each image reproduced think of the constituting parts and how these fit together. Also give attention to movement if this is relevant to the image. In moving, does the shape remain whole and clear?

2. Develop the physical and static representations attempted above towards more political sloganeering. These slogans can be sourced either from the internet or by browsing current electoral campaigns. Some examples could be:

- We stand for the Proletariat!
- Workers of the World Unite!
- Eight hours for work, eight hours for sleep, eight hours for what we will!
- Your boss needs you. You do not need him!
- Together everything becomes possible!
- All the world is at our feet!

3. Choose one slogan to work on with the rest of the class. Divide the class in small groups. Each group works separately to create material based on the same slogan. This could be a set of poses, a short physical routine, a piece of text, a poem, a song, a painting or sketch, etc. Each group shares their creation with the rest of the class. A discussion ensues about how these various pieces can be brought together to form a short performance. The performance is briefly rehearsed and presented. In this exercise it is important that the leader (e.g. the teacher) only gives brief indications about how the piece could develop, so that the main decisions related to the choices, editing and composition of the piece are made by the collective. Participants should also make the most of their talents or skills, like singing, dancing, acrobatics and juggling. These can be used to enliven the piece.

Political scenarios and improvisation

In her book *Théâtre russe contemporain*, Nina Gourfinkel presented the following two examples as typical scenarios on which amateur actors improvised (Gourfinkel 1979: 138–9):

> A working-class family. A father and his son work at a factory, while the daughter is engaged to another worker. There is a strike which is followed by all members of the family. However, the daughter's fiancé chooses to distance himself from the strike and, consequently, the girl renounces the love of this class traitor.

> An old man has two sons. The elder has a college education. He is an intellectual, a sweet human being with strong ideals. The second son is a worker and Bolshevik. The two fall in love with the same girl. She prefers the older, who exhibits good manners but reacts to the events of the civil war in a cowardly and fearful way. On the other hand, the Bolshevik dies a hero. The girl collects the Red flag which has slipped from the hand of the young man and pushes the workers forward for another attack.

Attempt the creation of a short performance on the basis of these scenarios. The following methodology can be helpful, but feel free to explore other approaches. The ultimate aim is to produce the scenario and to highlight with clarity its political 'message'.

- Identify a number of pivotal moments in the scenario. In the first scenario, for example, these might include the moment when the workers decide to strike; in the second, when the girl expresses her initial love for the elder son.
- Improvise a scene on each important moment.
- Show the scenes to the class, who comment, especially on whether the choices of the actors were theatrically clear or not.
- In these improvisations the role of the director or instructor is more important. His or her task is to keep the improvisations on track, by ensuring that each fragment fits within the larger logic of the scenario and that the improvisations do not turn into indulgent and over-sentimental affairs.
- With the involvement of the actors, edit the improvisations down into a series of manageable components forming a whole.
- It might help the composition of the piece if the characters are treated as broad types each representing a clearly defined personality trait.
- Repeat using scenarios of your own composition. Again, these can be sourced from current newspapers and based on topical issues.

5

Meyerhold: Bias in transmission processes

Researching Meyerhold: From bias to myth-making

As already hinted in Chapter 3, one of analytical frames brought forwards by cultural transmission is that of 'transmission bias', or the background and baggage brought by participants into transmission activity. Colloquially, bias is used as a pejorative term to imply unfair and inconsiderate prejudice, an attitude or belief that precludes one from seeing bigger pictures. In cultural transmission, however, the presence of bias is taken as a necessary given to denote the active filtering which practices go through when transmitted from one individual or group to another. R. Boyd and P. J. Richerson have argued that transmission bias 'allows humans to effectively and efficiently acquire beliefs, ideas, and behaviours from the immense amount of confusing and contradictory information presented by the external world' (in Schönpflug 2009: 16–17). It is often linked with learners but also, and as I have argued elsewhere, with teachers and transmitters who put their own transmission biases in motion when they set out to prepare transmission material, workshops or situations (Aquilina 2019: 12). Transmission bias may include the learner's ideological background, previous experience of a particular technique or his intention to appropriate a practice as a means of validating his own work. It is also exemplified in the transmitter's desire to work with a particular group of people and the constraints of a specific set of operational conditions. In all of these cases, bias impacts on the transmission process.

Reading Meyerhold from the point of view of transmission bias allows us to draw through-lines cutting across a career that not only spanned four decades but also embraced (and discarded) many of the forms and genres that defined modernism, such as naturalism, symbolism, traditionalism, futurism and constructivism. In other words, the use of transmission bias offers a way of organizing Meyerhold's impressive range of theatrical experiments. In this chapter I will start by arguing that transmission bias distils recurrent elements in Meyerhold's work – in a first instance, the grotesque – without, however, obliterating the unique characteristics of his many work phases. The methodological 'how' that I suggest here, therefore, is one where recurrence, or the recurrent bias, is treated in tandem with difference, or shifting work conditions and aesthetic choices. I will also underline Meyerhold's efforts to establish a recurrence or continuation between past theatrical traditions and his own practice, especially as it was developing in the decade or so before the revolution. More than a simple expression of a passing trend, Meyerhold's study of the past will be seen chiming with our own contemporary understanding of Practice as Research (PaR). Seeing instances of Meyerhold's work as an early example of PaR in turn offers strong possibilities for the rediscovery of his practices today.

What are the difficulties posed by contemporary Meyerhold studies? The organization of historical material is something which every theatre historian has to contend with at some point in his or her work. For good reason, as the way in which the historical material is presented impinges directly on the way it is read and understood. A chronological organization of Meyerhold's (and Russian) theatre is predictably anchored by the October Revolution.[1] This choice is not without its problems as the relative usefulness of a particular organizational frame will always be a matter of debate. Daria Krizhanskaya, for instance, critiques the use of the revolution to delineate Meyerhold's career in two, seeing it as an over-simplification. She speaks, for example, of the 'myth of the Revolution [which has] enchanted Westerners', adding that 'the theory which divides Russian art into two disconnected pre-revolutionary and post-revolutionary epochs is lazy' (Krizhanskaya 2000: 160). Another bane in the study of Meyerhold (and the modernists in general) has been the transformation of events, situations and individuals into myths. A myth is a belief which has distanced itself from verifiable fact. This is the kind of myth, already critiqued in Chapter 1, that defines High Modernism as a blatant moment of rapture with its past, as manifested for example in the scandalized uproar that seemingly met the opening performance of Alfred Jarry's *Ubu Roi* (1896).[2] A sense of mystification is also evident when Mirella Schino refers to Meyerhold and his contemporaries (Artaud, Appia, Craig, Copeau and Stanislavsky – note how selective this list is) as 'great masters' (Schino 2018: 13–30).[3] Informed by this particular bias, Schino's reading of the turn of the twentieth century as a time of hope and desire, of the young dancing naked in nature, of the 'dream of a less unjust society' (Schino 2018: 14), contrasts with Jeff Wallace's more sombre account. Wallace's reading evidences a diametrically different bias, in his argument that the centuries-old process of modernity had promised peace and a better life but instead delivered the death and destruction of the First World War (Wallace 2011: 18 and 21).

In the case of Meyerhold, myths appear when extreme and unbalanced readings are developed of his work. For instance, two scholars like Robert

Leach and Edward Braun created a very conflicting image of Meyerhold's work at the Theatre Studio of 1905. Leach argues that the more dictatorial approach allegedly used by Meyerhold – fuelled undoubtedly by Stanislavsky's view that Meyerhold moulded his actors into shape as if they were putty (Stanislavski 2008a: 249) – conflicts seriously with another reading that foregrounds a more exploratory, collaborative and open-ended work the Russian director adopted with the actors (Leach 2003: 53). That Meyerhold was repressive of the actors working with him is a typical reading, with Leach adding that this understanding was developed in the 1930s to validate Meyerhold's own political repression in the Soviet Union. It was, however, strongly denied by many of his collaborators (Leach 1989: 46).[4] Another myth has been generated around his final public debate of December 1937. In this case the myth of Meyerhold as one who heroically took the offensive in his criticism of the stifling censorship and work conditions of the time was constructed as a fabled account by a certain Yury Elagin, an émigré musician whose bias was to discredit Stalinism in every possible way.[5] Laurence Senelick, who tasked himself with reconstructing the events surrounding Meyerhold's speech, argues that 'rumour and wishful thinking can falsify the historical record, often for the best of motives, and [...] politics alters the cultural memory to suit its own needs'. More specifically: 'Wishful thinking fills the gap left by documentation. If a heroic Meyerhold did not exist, he would have to be invented' (Senelick 2003: 158 and 167). Myths are, in other words, created.

Figure 9 Meyerhold with composer Sergey Prokofiev and painter and set designer Alexander Tyshler, during a rehearsal of Prokofiev's opera *Semyon Kotko*, 1939. Such encounters were not uncommon in the cross-boundary environment that was modernism. ITAR-TASS News Agency Alamy Stock Photo.

It is important to keep in mind the emergence of conflicting interpretations, not so much to find which is correct and which is erroneous, but to widen the gap between reconstruction and transmission processes. In reconstructing the opening night of *Ubu Roi*, Postlewait did well to discredit conventional wisdom that the performance was met with a riot, because rigorous historical research evidences otherwise. With transmission, on the hand, attention is given to the means through which a cultural memory is constructed, in many cases over a prolonged period of time. In other words, transmission speaks not only of the original environment which created the event in the first place, but also tackles the various moments that link a source to us, because 'changes in an original form, text, or idea were charged with meaning [...] – they normally represent conscious artistic and intellectual decisions rather than failures to reproduce a primal truth' (Grafton in Grafton and Blair 1990: 1). In this sense, the many myths surrounding Meyerhold offer ample possibilities for historians to unpick Meyerhold's work within his own cultural milieus (an example of reconstruction) in juxtaposition with his reception in other environments, including ours (i.e. transmission).

It is certainly important to keep uncovering new material about Meyerhold: as late as the year 2000 David Chambers and Nikolai Pesochinsky had argued that Meyerhold's 'tragically silenced voice [...] [needs] reawakening' (Chambers and Pesochinsky 2000: 24). Such efforts have been in evidence ever since Meyerhold's rehabilitation started in the 1960s.[6] It was fuelled further with the partial opening of the archives and, more recently, the availability online of many Russian sources.[7] Then again, the notion (myth) that an archive is a repository of historical truth is to be resisted.[8] Even the primary sources that I use here are often made of fragments, hurried notes jotted down by Meyerhold's students or those attending public debates. They rarely carry notes about the context of delivery for example. One personally nagging lacuna is an indication of whom Meyerhold was addressing during a specific lecture, whether these were, for example, students from his own workshops, seasoned actors, representatives of other theatres, workers and so on. It would also be interesting, for example, to research more about Mikhail Korenev, the student who Meyerhold entrusted to organize material for a publication about Biomechanics (Normington 2005: 118).

One way of questioning the archive is to keep in mind, and therefore to unpick, the fact that its organization is never haphazardly done. The organization of an archive predisposes its own, often concealed, set of biases, 'largely centred on questions of who creates the archive, for whom it was created and how it is used' (Gale and Featherstone 2011: 17). The bias of the researcher is another variable that needs unpicking. These biases often make the researcher skim over certain details, sources or whole events in his or her attempt to foreground a particular set of materials and their interpretation. In Chapter 4, I have argued that the researcher cannot be neutral in his interpretation of the material at hand because he is always informed by his theoretical choices, intentions or work context, in short by his biases. Before interpretation even begins, however, I will now add that the researcher's biases are there to impinge on his selection of the material. For instance, my own bias in this chapter on Meyerhold rests on my intention to use available sources but also to shed light on instances and corresponding texts and materials which we might have shunted to the side. It is because of this bias that I discuss Meyerhold's research in past theatre traditions as an instance of transmission, why I invoke contemporary debates about Practice as Research, and why I draw attention on his 1930 European tour and the entries about him in Western newspapers.

Recurrence and difference in Meyerhold's work

The contemporary challenge in Meyerhold studies is therefore three-pronged: excavating new instances of work and corresponding materials; contextualizing these within our common assumptions about the man and his work; and processing them with renewed analytical models. In relation to the latter, I would like to suggest the idea of 'recurrence and difference' as a possible analytical frame. Recurrence draws directly from bias. It extracts persisting and cross-cutting elements across disparate realities, contexts and work practices. Within the oeuvre of a particular practitioner, recurrence often takes the form of a deep-seated quality which recurs as a work staple. Difference, on the other hand, prevents recurrent practices from becoming myths, impeding a one-dimensionality to a practitioner's career which figures like Meyerhold did not have. Looking at theatre realities in terms of both recurrence and difference allows us to see a phenomenon in terms of

- progression between *different* phases, which, though critiqued by periodization on grounds of engendering a false linearity to theatre history (Balme 2008: 106–11), still provides an initial, if insufficient, way of organizing performance material by foregrounding key milestones;

- through-lines, or seeing phases not as self-contained and independent of one another, but as entities that connect through certain *recurrent* elements.[9]

Recurrence and difference are especially helpful to identify underlining work principles. In science, a principle is a general theorem or law which finds numerous applications across a wide field. Cars, for example, all operate on the same set of basic principles, as a wheeled motor vehicle used for transportation, even though of course there are endless models and variations on this basic idea. Storytelling functions in a similar manner. National stories are culturally specific: a child growing in England might be familiar with the stories of King Arthur, in Germany with those of Goetz von Berlichingen, in the United States with Tom Sawyer, and in Italy with those of Pantamerone. Underlining these contextual variations, however, is the suspension of time and space and transportation elsewhere of the listener. It is this principle which recurs as an organizational frame and on which storytelling rests and functions. In other words, while the contents of the stories celebrate difference, the principle evidences a recurrence that makes specific acts of story-telling not isolated phenomena but part of a bigger weave. The actual stories underline uniqueness, while the recurrent functional principles transcend borders to link together the acts of story-telling.

What are the recurrent principles in Meyerhold's work? One aspect – the grotesque – is easily discernible. Jonathan Pitches argues that Meyerhold's pre-revolutionary writings appear 'extended and lyrical', while those after 1917 read as 'polemic and politically strategic'. The grotesque, on the other hand, appears as a central leitmotif throughout (Pitches 2016: 10). Dassia Posner describes it as 'a defining characteristic of all Meyerhold's productions' (2015: 372). At its most fundamental level, the grotesque is a vision of theatre that embraces extremes and contrasts.[10] It confounds conventional notions of logical and cause-and-effect sequencing. Crucially, the grotesque uses contrasts as raw performance material in the composition of artistic wholes:

> The grotesque mixes opposites, consciously creating harsh incongruity and *relying solely on its own originality*. [...] The grotesque synthesis opposites, creates a picture of the incredible, and invites the spectator to solve the riddle of the inscrutable. (Braun 1969: 138; emphasis in original)

It was Meyerhold's practical means to turn the spectator into a creative performance partner. He despised spectators who took their complacency with them to the theatre. According to the actor Mikhail Sadovsky,

Meyerhold 'aimed at wrenching the spectator out of the familiarity of everyday existence, attempted to rip off his comfortable house slippers' (in Schmidt 1981: 47). Through the grotesque, Meyerhold articulated the role of the spectator as one who is constantly kept on his toes, expecting one thing but receiving another, in the same way that in life tragedy and comedy are often bedfellows.[11] He searched for this participatory spectator in his symbolist years, as Dr Dapertutto, when staging constructivism and in his post-revolutionary stagings of the classics and of new texts, even if what constituted 'a participatory spectator' tended to fluctuate depending on contextual, especially political, factors.

Examples of contrasting elements tucked together in performance abound in Meyerhold's work. The following are only some instances that show the recurrence of the grotesque as a performance practice. One form of the grotesque involved a juxtaposition between the fictive reality created on the stage and the tangible experience of being a spectator sitting in an auditorium watching a performance. The forestage in *Don Juan* (1910) played directly on this dynamic, serving 'not as a boundary but as a threshold between the fictional world and the world of the audience' (Posner 2015: 371). In *The Magnanimous Cuckold* (1922), a grotesque contrast was evidenced between the actor who could both play and parody his role (Law 1982: 63), foreshadowing in turn the techniques of defamiliarization which Bertolt Brecht would soon present and make famous.[12] A grotesque juxtaposition could also be achieved on an emotional level. A case in point was evident in *Earth Rampant* (1923), when an actor carrying a used urinal across the auditorium was followed by the death of the hero. Leach describes this moment as offering a 'contradiction in utilizing carnival-like farce and sublime tragedy in the same production' (Leach 1989: 133). The grotesque could also play on the spectators' memories, creating a juxtaposition with how they remembered key moments of their recent past. For instance, in his review of the production of Ilya Selvinsky's *Commander of the Second Army* (1929), the critic Boris Alpers contrasted the image of Red Army soldiers as passionate revolutionary fighters, 'still warm and living in our memory and our life', with their motionless and sculptural depiction rendered on the stage (in Symons 1971: 183).

More than a style that might be linked to what today we would refer to as 'physical theatre', the grotesque was developed by Meyerhold as a compositional principle to organize performance material. While Meyerhold's pre-revolutionary essays tended to appraise the grotesque in a positive manner (see above), post-revolutionary interventions evidence a negative sense to the word. Thus, for example, within the context of *The Government Inspector*, the grotesque was linked to 'a kind of exoticism' – an indulgent fascination with the eccentricities of a past theatre tradition (Meierkhold 1968 Vol. 2: 119). In a speech dated 24 January 1927 he mentioned how the grotesque (and the vaudeville) had to be brushed aside to make way for realism (Meierkhold 1968 Vol. 2: 140).[13] In the same speech Meyerhold even called the grotesque 'a colossal temptation' for the actor to leave the carefully created score and 'splash out into a rollicking, anarchic, unorganised spectacle' (142). As a compositional principle, the grotesque however links with stylization or the understanding that performance is not a reproduction of life but a weave, a composition of carefully selected and contrasting elements, of heroism and satire, seriousness and buffoonery. Through stylization, theatre practitioners become authors of performance rather than imitators of everyday milieus. In *The Fairground Booth* essay, Meyerhold used stylization as a way of distancing his practice from naturalism, which he believed puts on the stage all the minute details comprising a reality in an all-too-blatant attempt at recreation. Meyerhold's was particularly critical of naturalism's zeal for detailed reconstruction: 'The impossibility of embracing the totality of reality justifies the schematization of the real (*in particular by means of stylisation*)' (Braun 1969: 137; emphasis in the original). It is this separation between an indiscriminating naturalism and the grotesque, the latter seen not as an aesthetics but as a compositional principle based on the selectivity and weaving together of contrasts, which recurred in Meyerhold's career.

The grotesque also extends forwards to realities that superseded Meyerhold. A case in point is the staging of a version of Meyerhold's *The Government Inspector*, produced in 1997 and 1999 by a group of actors from the Yale School of Drama and the St Petersburg Academy of Theatre Arts in Russia. Initially, the project aimed at 'a complete reconstruction' of *The Government Inspector*, but as the process developed participants became more interested in capturing 'the spirit of Meyerhold'. The grotesque was seen as embodying this spirit, not only in the conscious infusion of contrasting elements in the mise-en-scène but also in the contrasting reactions of the spectators: 'The show was repeatedly interrupted by confederated cascades of laughter, followed by lengthy lacunae of ghastly silence: exactly the admixture of grotesque delirium and portentous alarm that Meyerhold had always sought' (Chambers and Pesochinsky 2000: 111).

We readily speak of the Stanislavsky acting tradition, identifying as its bearings the System, truth, believability and the work of the actor upon himself, but then fall short of talking about Meyerhold in a similarly embracing way. The grotesque as a connective thread can do much to conceive a parallel Meyerhold performance tradition, bringing in turn separate theatre realities together and offering a common basis on which the transmission of technique, including the technique of composition, can take place.

Meyerhold's rediscovery of past traditions

The grotesque was Meyerhold's bias through which he differentiated his practice from many of his contemporaries. It was also his way of identifying a recurrence between what he was doing and other theatre traditions from the past. Through his research in the past Meyerhold was asserting that his own experiments were not isolated endeavours without a context, but the latest, i.e. modern, manifestation of a particular lineage. His research in past traditions underscored the grotesque as fundamental to the very nature of theatre, as one of its core principles. Because of this recurrence, the grotesque became the lever that synthesized the past with modernism. It was, in other words, the lens through which Meyerhold read theatre history, the sifter to scrutinize past theatre practices.

Meyerhold looked at the past for models to use in the creation of the theatre of the future. This meant a research into past realities like Ancient Greece, *commedia dell'arte*, Spanish and French sixteenth- and seventeenth-century theatres, and Japanese and Chinese performance genres, up to even 'the Russian theatre of the 1830s with Gogol at its head' (Meierkhold 1968 Vol. 1: 129). In the ways he referred to these theatres Meyerhold underscored a number of qualities necessary for the renewal of theatre. He referred to past theatres in different ways. In a 1911 article he underlined their theatricality, describing them as 'truly theatrical eras' (*podlinno teatral'nykh epokh*; Meierkhold 1968 Vol. 1: 145).[14] A 1918 lecture saw him use the rather colloquial wording of 'old stages' or 'old theatres', exemplars of extreme simplicity (*chrezvychaynoy uproshchennost'yu*) and primitiveness (*primitivnosti*). These references were not derogatory. They are rather to be understood in the Grotowskian sense of 'poor theatre', i.e. a theatre that sheds seemingly unnecessary elements to focus on what is essential and essentially theatre (Grotowski 2002: 19). For Meyerhold, a simplistic theatre meant an aesthetics that does not seek to fabricate illusion. He suggested the minimalism of old theatres as a model for a more modern simplicity, 'for it is only in this direction that one has to look for opportunities to perfect the theatre' (Meierkhold 2001: 39).

Such simplicity defined Meyerhold's 'chamber pieces' at the Interlude House and at Vyacheslav Ivanov's Tower Theatre. The latter was no more than Ivanov's own private apartment, where Meyerhold produced in April 1910 an adaptation of Calderon's *Adoration of the Cross*. Braun argues that 'Meyerhold's aim in this production was not to depict thirteenth-century Siena as prescribed in the text, but rather to evoke the *primitive* theatre of Calderon's day' (Braun 1969: 112; emphasis added). This primitive and simplistic quality was achieved by restricting the set to some hangings and having the actors perform on the same level as the spectators. The production values of the performance might therefore have been minimalist and simple, in line with the way he understood Spanish theatre, but Meyerhold's was a calculated and conscious simplicity. It was directed, in terms again reflective of Grotowski's theatre, towards strengthening the bond between the actors and the spectators.

Past theatre traditions exhibited a number of recurrent features. They were certainly different from one another, but these differences were balanced by what Meyerhold felt was a sense of recurrence. He argued that when comparing past theatre traditions 'we see that each has its own features, their own details, but then they also have the same principles' (Meierkhold 2001: 344). In a very concrete way Meyerhold predated the objectives which Eugenio Barba would set for himself when developing his research in Theatre Anthropology. Both Meyerhold and Barba looked, in fact, at discerning 'recurrent principles' (Barba in Barba and Savarese, 2006: 6) or 'axioms which hold good for the actor, regardless of the type of theatre in which he is performing' (Braun 1969: 148). The theatre realities that Meyerhold researched were distant traditions, in historical, geographical, linguistic and cultural terms. As Nicola Savarese writes, they 'were culturally prestigious examples, technically perfect and [...] sufficiently foreign [...] without the anxieties that more familiar models induce' (Savarese in Barba and Savarese 2006: 185). The recurrent principles these past traditions exhibited included spatial elements, such as the openness on all sides of the performance space, meaning that a stage could be approached not only from the front but also from the sides. Meyerhold argued that past theatre traditions deployed little or no scenery, using only what could be placed at the back of the acting area. They did not use concealing devices like wings to cover the artifice behind stage illusion but exposed their theatricality instead. As a result, past theatre traditions could foreground the work of the actor, revealing in turn the self-sufficiency of the actor's work through an application of stylized pantomime and movement.

In what ways did Meyerhold seek to rediscover past theatre traditions? How did he seek the transmission into modern theatre of their salient characteristics? What were his methods? Four methods can be discerned, namely through (i) the academic approach, (ii) an ethics of selectivity, (iii) the exercise of fantasy and (iv) studio work. The academic approach towards rediscovering the past is evidenced, almost in a throwaway fashion, in the essay *The Fairground Booth*. I am using the term 'academic' to describe that process of 'delving into long-forgotten theories of dramatic art, old theatrical records and iconography' (in Braun 1969: 126). Meyerhold collaborated with several experts, like F. F. Zelinsky, who specialized in classical scholarship and accompanied Meyerhold on his European study visits of 1910. On this tour Zelinsky delivered several lectures on Athenian and Byzantine art. Another expert, Vladimir Solovyov, specialized in *commedia dell'arte*.[15] Vyacheslav Ivanov was another noted figure, especially through his theories about Dionysian ritual. A strong print culture fuelled several translations of key sources, thereby enriching Russian modernism with a broad range of materials from disparate cultural traditions (Wachtel 2011: 5). In turn, these translations gave rise to critical essays on foreign writers, artists and traditions and their relevance to the contemporary scene.

In tackling the past, Meyerhold evidenced no particular indulgence towards the traditions he was researching. He moved on to other realities once he exhausted what it could offer him. In other words, Meyerhold research of the past was a pragmatic one. It was directed towards the development and validation of his own work. Consequently, he worked on constructing a functional and practical past for himself, and in doing so his earlier, i.e. symbolist, fascination with the 'intoxication' of Greek tragedy, for instance, quickly gave way to technical devices sourced from popular theatre.[16] This self-interested pragmatism made Meyerhold steer away from an attempted reconstruction of a tradition to focus instead on selecting specific techniques which he deemed relevant. Transmission in his work gained the upper hand over reconstruction.

The ethics of selectivity was Meyerhold's second methodology when working on the past. To us, the attempt to reconstruct the past must look foolhardy, but Meyerhold had to qualify his discerning approach vis-a-vis other practitioners who were attempting just that. The most notable example was Nikolai Evreinov's Ancient Theatre. In his staging of a season of medieval (1907) and Spanish drama (1911), Evreinov adopted a method known as 'artistic reconstruction' which 'involved the recreation of the *whole* theatrical and dramatic event, including the contemporary audience. It was essential to the experiment that actors dressed and behaved as spectators' (Leach 1994: 11; emphasis added). Meyerhold, on his part, focused on a much freer composition based on a study and selection of techniques from past theatre traditions. He was, in other words, critically processing the past theatre traditions, using some elements but discarding others (see Chapter 4). His ethics of selectivity can be read as 'theft', a term which Thomas Richards links again to Grotowski. Richards described Grotowski as a 'good thief' who did not negate the techniques of those who came before him but who could analyse 'critically their value, [...] stealing what might work for himself' (Richards 1995: 4). Like bias, theft is not to be treated as a pejorative word, but one that denotes a necessary process of selection.[17] The *commedia dell'arte* actor, for instance, served Meyerhold as a paradigm for a physically agile

Figure 10 Meyerhold's actors training in the 1920s. Sueddeutsche Zeitung Photo/Alamy Stock Photo.

and flexible performer, subsequently developed via Biomechanics, but the mask failed to make any noteworthy presence in any of his performances. The whole idea of what a mask is was in fact processed, shifted from the actual, tangible and leather mask to its embodied conception, a definition of 'a character in terms of its external characteristics' (Pitches 2003: 58).

Selecting bits and pieces from a variety of sources is only the first step to realize a modern application of a traditional theatre source. The next step involves wielding these disparate elements together. The performance of *Don Juan*, staged in 1910 at the Alexandrinsky Theatre, was a case in point. Visually, the production was conceived 'in the manner' of the nineteenth-century French artist Honoré Daumier, especially in the composition of costumes, make-up, gestures and so on (Tian 2016: 338). To this I would like to suggest the contribution of the visuals and colours which Meyerhold experienced during his study trip to Greece. In fact, his letters of the time to Alexander Golovin, the stage designer with whom Meyerhold often worked at the Imperial Theatres, referred a number of times to the mise-en-scène of *Don Juan* (Volkov 1929 Vol. 2: 107, 111, 116). To this nineteenth-century and Greek flavouring, Meyerhold also added the property man or proscenium servants modelled on the *kurago*, the stagehands wearing black of the Japanese theatre (Braun 1998: 106).[18] In Oriental Theatre these prop men are tasked with the decidedly non-artistic work of moving scenery and props on the stage, aiding the performers with costume changes and so on.

Here Meyerhold's selective processing rather than reconstruction is again clear. In Japanese theatre, the *kurago* do not contribute anything significant to the unfolding of the dramatic arch. Their significance resides in being both present onstage but absent from the unravelling of the performance. In *Don Juan*, however, they were spectacularly costumed to become important signifiers of the lavishness of Versailles. They also served as anti-illusionistic devices by organizing the space in full view of the audience. Mirella Schino notes that in *Don Juan* Meyerhold 'wanted to recreate the feel of those times but not produce a historical recreation' (Schino 2018: 86). This feel or spirit of seventeenth-century France was thus created through a composition of elements from several sources, including one, the processed *kurago*, which ironically did not even feature in the original epoch.

Meyerhold was often criticized for not giving enough attention to the presumed indivisibility between form and content, especially during his final years when predicating form over content – formalism – meant political persecution.[19] However, within the research environment (see below) that he developed in relation to past theatre traditions, the possible separation between form and content supported his ethics of selectivity and processing. This was the case when Meyerhold's Borodin Studio published in its journal a version of Gozzi's *Love of Three Oranges*. The original version made several references to Gozzi's clashes with his contemporaries. This content, irrelevant to a Russian audience, was removed from the studio's version, to underscore (i.e. select) 'Gozzi technical methods of scenario composition' (Meyerhold, Soloviev and Vogak in Posner 2015: 372). The concept of the type was also embraced in such productions like *Mystery-Bouffe* (1918 and 1921) but altered to reflect new social realities like the Russian Merchant, a Priest, a Diplomat, a Soldier of the Red Army, a Locomotive Engineer and so on. In the case of his 1910 production of *Columbine's Scarf* at the Interlude House, the processing of the original's play from three acts into fourteen episodes transformed the content and presentation of the play from 'a gentle and intelligent revisiting of commedia dell'arte' to 'a chilling grotesque in the manner of ETA Hoffman' (Schino 2018: 89; Braun 1969: 113).

Favouring transmission over reconstruction also allowed Meyerhold plenty of space to exercise his creative fantasy, i.e. the third methodology through which he reimagined anew past theatre practices. In other words, the act of remembrance leads towards reinvention not excavation. It was not Meyerhold's aim to reposition the past in an unalloyed state within the modern landscape. As Clare Cavanagh writes, '[t]he very act of remembering the past changes it irreparably' (1995: 7–8). In imagining the past anew, a healthy dose of imagination or fantasy helps to complete the missing details. Meyerhold's creative fantasy as a director was certainly a key factor that made his name; it comes as no surprise to also note its application when he treated the past. Posner describes this as a process of refraction or 'the artist's deep engagement with a source via the prism of untrammelled fantasy' (Posner 2015: 365). Consequently, a stage direction in Calderon's *Doctor of His Own Honour* like 'Enter Don Gutierre, as though jumping over a fence' is helpful to the director because it does not describe the entrance in exhaustive detail. Rather, the 'as though' formulation plays a similar role as Stanislavsky's use of the magic 'if', or as a lever that shifts the performer or director onto the plane of creative fantasy. It allows the modern practitioner to come up with his own solutions to the stage task, but informed by his understanding of the past. An inventory of a 1598 company 'collected by scholars' and reproduced by Meyerhold in *The Fairground Booth* essay is similarly sketchy, allowing the reader plenty of space to picture scenes involving 'three heads of Cerberus, snakes from *Faustus*, one line, two lion's heads, one big horse with legs' (Braun 1969: 126).

The Borodin Studio as an instance of Practice as Research

In this section I will discuss Meyerhold's laboratorial practice, developed at the Borodin Studio, as the fourth way of processing past theatre traditions to render them applicable to modern practice. I devote a whole section to the Borodin Studio to highlight how it fits our own understanding of Practice as Research, in turn developing a transmission line from Meyerhold to contemporary theatre. The studio opened in September 1913 on Troitskaya Street and then moved to Borodin Street a year later, where it stayed until it closed in 1917. It was Meyerhold's most sustained effort to create a space where, shielded from outside pressures, he could carry out research with a group of like-minded actors, practitioners who wished to be there and who voluntarily wanted to work with him. The Borodin Studio was certainly not oriented towards performance. It served as Meyerhold's practical research into the actor of the future, in other words actors who were physically responsive and prepared, who could engage with the materiality of the stage, who were practised in the use of stylized gestures and movement, and who could enter into a direct relationship with the audience. In many ways, it paved the ground for the work on Biomechanics which Meyerhold would carry out after the revolution.

A study of Meyerhold's Borodin Studio as an early example of Practice as Research (PaR) is worth developing for a number of reasons. In a first instance, it helps us broaden our frame of reference about the origins of Practice as Research. This chimes with Simon Murray and John Keefe's own view that the late twentieth-century concept of physical theatre has its roots in practices down the line of two thousand years of theatre history, particularly such examples like *commedia dell'arte* and modernism, including therefore Meyerhold's work (Murray and Keefe 2007: 14). Murray and Keefe argue that these practices might have been labelled as examples of physical theatre had that particular terminology been culturally available. A similar argument can be made about Practice as Research. While the term has been coined only recently, earlier historical instances might be discerned which partake in our understanding of what Practice as Research is. This is, of course, not to say that the Borodin Studio *was* Practice as Research. For one, it did not have the institutional framing that is so typical of PaR. Still, there are enough Practice as Research qualities in the Borodin Studio to draw a line back from this contemporary research methodology to a modern antecedent. Studying the Borodin Studio as Practice as Research is also one way of making Meyerhold's techniques relevant to contemporary theatre, because of the research bias they both shared. In other words, there are several contemporary instances that seek to rediscover Meyerhold today via Practice as Research experiments.[20]

The roots of Practice as Research are often located to the 1960s. It was part of a broader movement in philosophy, arts, science and technology that acknowledged the potential of practical work as a primer for research processes.[21] Robin Nelson describes it as 'a research inquiry based in practice' (Nelson 2013: 6). It has three basic building blocks or pillars. Like all research, Practice as Research rests on a sense for exploration. The research process is initiated by a research question or the initial intuition that serves as the first pillar of Practice as Research (of research in general, really). The articulation and execution of a pertinent methodology (the second pillar) follows on from the research question. Practice plays a key role in the articulation and execution of PaR methodologies, in the sense that the research is carried out through practical techniques that are readily associated with, in this case, theatre performance. These may include body-based techniques, use of voice, partner and ensemble work, spatial exercises and so on. My own PaR exercise carried out in 2018 at the University of Malta was driven by the following research question: *What are the recurrences and differences in the cross-cultural transmission of a specific actor-training component, namely the magic 'if'?* This question was tackled in the practical environment of a series of workshops with practitioners from Italy, the UK and the Czech Republic. The techniques used included improvisation, spatial sensitivity, imagination and play, i.e. practices that are synonymous with theatre and performance (Aquilina 2019).

The third and final Practice as Research building block is the need to disseminate the results emerging from the research exercise. This dissemination helps to connect the research with a broader public. A practical component like a formalized workshop or a performance might again serve as a transmission channel, though this is often supported through other means like more conventional writing, video material, public presentation and so on. The aim of this, say, written component is both analytical, so as to help the practitioner reflect more on his practice, but also applicability, for other researchers to use when generating further knowledge. The latter is crucial if PaR is to become research rather than simply artistic work. Using the example of Swedish director Ingemar Lindh (1945–97) and his work within the group Institutet för Scenkonst (Institute for Scenic Art), Frank Camilleri underlines the emergence of applicable and transferable principles as a moment that defines Practice as Research:

> In Lindh's context, which is characteristic of other laboratories in the 20th century, pedagogy and research are linked in the empirical endeavor to revisit artistic exploration and extract general principles of technique and composition. These principles lend themselves to transmission outside their original context of generation, to others who did not partake of the process. Research's capacity to crystallize its findings thus makes it amenable to separation, dissemination, application, and re-interpretation in different contexts. (Camilleri 2013: 154)

Melissa Trimingham makes a similar argument when she says that one of 'the most basic (and moral) of research intentions [is], put simply, [...] for the benefit of others apart from the researchers themselves' (Trimingham 2002: 54). Likewise, she emphasizes the transmission of research results as a fundamental component of Practice as Research.

Meyerhold's Borodin Studio manifested all three PaR pillars. Its driving research question (Pillar 1) revolved around Meyerhold's desire to integrate elements from past theatre traditions into his own practice. This research question was articulated as follows in the studio's journal *Love of Three Oranges: The Journal of Doctor Dapertutto*:

> [I]t should be noted that this 'articulation of treasures' [from the past] is not done merely to flaunt them in their original form. Once he has learnt to cherish them, the actor should use them for adornment, should come thus 'endowed' on stage and know how to 'come to life' theatrically.
>
> How do we aim to restore the traditions of the past in the present? (in Braun 1969: 148; emphasis added)

Vladimir Solovyov, Meyerhold's fundamental collaborator and in charge of the *commedia* classes, articulated the research question in very similar terms, establishing the studio as 'a scenic laboratory intended to verify, mathematically, the theatre's past and to prepare the material that the stage master will use in the future with his pupils' (in Schino 2010: 123).

This research question was processed via the work, practical mainly but not only, that was carried out during the sessions. This processing equates with the second PaR pillar, i.e. the methodological level. Apart from the more academic research (see above) that Meyerhold did not shun, the studio exhibited great rigour in its practical work. The research process was not left to its devices but directed towards very particular paths. For example, studio members were divided into groups according to 'their styles and predilections [i.e. bias] for a particular theatrical genre or method of production' (Braun 1969: 146). It is for this reason that an 'Actor's Class', a 'Grotesque Group' and an 'Eighteenth-Century Group' came to be formed. Auditions for new entrants were organized.[22] Students were asked to think about their past work and create a curriculum vitae of sorts that would help to establish the student's emploi. Periodic evaluations were carried out (Braun 1998: 155). There was a sense of continuity to the research, that contrasted with an approach wherein exercises would be done once and 'archived'. A case in point was the work which the studio did on Ophelia's mad scene from *Hamlet*. The group worked on this scenario in 1914 and again in September and December 1915 (Braun 1969: 151). The studio therefore manifested a recursive process of going back to previous experiments and practices but seen anew through freshly accumulated knowledge. Like the early phase of the First Studio of the MAT, the research work at the Borodin Studio also blurred the boundaries between the rigid transmission categories of transmitter and receiver. Alexandra Smirnova, one of the students, described the general atmosphere of the studio as follows:

> We [studio participants] had the opportunity to become acquainted with the great theatrical traditions of the past. We clearly saw how much one could draw from the treasury of various theatrical eras [...].
>
> We realized that the knowledge of this treasury requires a different, new, more advanced acting technique, which is extremely exciting to master, but very difficult.
>
> The studio in those years was creatively needed by Meyerhold himself. Together with us students, with the same joy and interest, he plunged into the theatrical past. For him, the studio was a kind of laboratory. Here he made discoveries in the field of theatrical forms and acting methods and technologies. All this informed the work of the studio in a

peculiar, not at all student-like character. Although Meyerhold was for us a teacher, and we called him 'master', we, being present and participating in his work, interfered boldly, often offered amendments and changes, and Meyerhold accepted or rejected them with a fervour that was not inferior to ours. (in Valentei et al. 1967: 86)

The curriculum of the studio was also extensive. It included lectures and practical sessions in the lazzi of *commedia dell'arte*, improvisation on existing and newly composed scenarios, and the study of popular techniques of the seventeenth and eighteenth centuries. Leach describes the programme as 'an extraordinarily comprehensive and progressive package for its time, one which few of today's higher institutions of drama can match' (Leach 1989: 58). Meyerhold's class was called 'stage movement', in which he researched two key principles, namely the relation of movement to the stage area and its embodiment in the grotesque. The contents of Meyerhold's classes are readily available (Braun 1998: 128), so there is hardly any reason to reproduce them here again.[23] I would only like to remark that Meyerhold's principles were articulated with a precision that one would expect to find in any serious research project, taking the form, in fact, of clear aims, objectives and work outcomes.

The studio functioned as a space that predicated laboratory research over audience engagement via performance. This does not mean that the studio was a closed entity, as its research still found different ways to project outwards (Pillar 3). On occasion the students did perform, including a presentation to soldiers recuperating from the war (Braun 1998: 127). More important on a technical level was the practical demonstration which the studio gave of its work in February 1915. The presentation consisted of études and pantomimes performed on the lines of past theatre traditions and styles (Valentei et al. 1967: 90).[24] Meyerhold himself on occasion discussed his laboratorial work in public debates and lectures.[25] The studio's journal *Love of Three Oranges: The Journal of Doctor Dapertutto* was another key dissemination outlet. While exhibiting the contentious and very one-sided tone of other contemporary journals and manifestos, the studio journal still served as 'a record and instigator of [the studio's] ideas and experiments' (Posner 2015: 370). Future Latvian director Anna (Asja) Lācis confirms the journal's circulation, saying that it was 'passed from one person to another amongst us [university] students' (Lācis 1971: 13). An example of the work principles researched at the studio and applied in other contexts is provided by Sergei Radlov. Even though apparently short-lived, Radlov's experience at the studio exposed him to the dynamism, slapstick and improvisational technique of popular theatre which he subsequently applied at his own Theatre of Popular Comedy (Mokulsky in Radlov 1929: 7–8).

In underscoring the dissemination and applicability of research results, Meyerhold was foreshadowing one of the fundamental PaR questions: how is Practice as Research different from the 'research' that any practitioner carries out when creating a work of art? To avoid confusion, Camilleri refers to the latter as 'search':

> '[S]earch' indicates a specific artistic quality or aesthetic choice as an objective and is dependent on the artist's quest for expression, renewal, or development. It should not be confused with 'research,' which focuses on the identification and definition of principles in the creative process and is not bound to specific artistic results or choices. (Camilleri 2013: 153)

In other words, the search for performance material, added to an exploration of the best means to embody this material on the stage, does not qualify as Practice as Research. This is important to keep in mind if PaR is to delimit its reach and therefore the specific and unique contribution which it can make to academia. Meyerhold's work is helpful to exemplify the distinction between search and research. Thus, when he was working on *Sister Beatrice*, his artistic process led him to search for performance material in the paintings of the Primitives, which he then used as the basis on which to compose his stage groupings (Braun 1998: 59). The process was in function of the performance that opened on 22 November 1906. At the studio, however, and as I have already discussed above, his practical investigation in past theatre traditions was not an end in itself. It was rather directed towards the extraction of practical techniques that could be subsequently used and applied in a variety of other contexts, including after the revolution when his research in acting processes came to be referred to with the more industrially sounding term of Biomechanics.

The studio also embodied many of the contradictions of modernism. It was a space of discovery but also of transmission, a space where past traditions fuelled present practices and a locus to prepare for a theatre of the future. As a lab it did not create a school – understood in the artistic scene of 'a picture that belongs to a particular school' (Crino 1975: 66). The studio encouraged ensemble and group work, but then never developed into a company or production house. It was both formalized, with a programme, a space and a journal, but at the same time highly exploratory and open to what the research was suggesting. Its contribution to theatre histories is that it joins other efforts – like the early phase of Stanislavsky's First Studio and Copeau's Vieux-Colombier School – in establishing research as a valid form of creative practice.

The Meyerhold Theatre's foreign tour of 1930

Like Stanislavsky (see Chapter 2), Meyerhold's reach was not limited to the Russian borders, even if his internationalism was more convoluted than Stanislavsky's. The 1930 tour of the Meyerhold Theatre to Germany and Paris speaks about Meyerhold's own internationalism but also about the internationalism of theatre at the turn of the twentieth century. Historians often refer to this turn as having produced a first-phase globalization, when the conceptual size of the world was diminishing as a result of improved transportation, imperialism, contact between nations and general advancements of technology. As Christopher Balme says, the result was 'a compression of time and space, movement towards standardisation and a growing sensation of being part of an interconnected world' (Balme 2015: 20). Theatre touring was one manifestation of this heightened globalization, with theatre companies leaving their home base in search of new audiences and profits. Like the metaphor used by George Oswell, wherein culture 'finds its way into different places over different times' because it is carried in a traveller's suitcase, with the people taking a flight, or across a telephone conversation (Oswell 2006: 3), in and through the train wagons and the steam boats the transmission of theatre practice was also taking place.

Meyerhold's reasons to tour abroad mirrored those of Stanislavsky almost a decade before. Like Stanislavsky, Meyerhold felt the need to distance himself temporarily from the Soviet context, in his case to overcome a crisis with the Glaviskusstvo, the state body that controlled the arts. He also hoped that a tour in the West would alleviate his theatre's precarious financial position (Picon-Vallin 1992: 127). The Meyerhold Theatre performed for six weeks in Germany during the first part of the year. Compared to the stop in Paris, where the company only presented ten performances of *The Government Inspector* and *The Forest*, the German visit was a substantially heavier engagement. Performances in nine cities were given, including Berlin and Cologne (Braun 1998: 260). Apart from *The Government Inspector* and *The Forest*, the Theatre also performed *Roar China!*, *The Secondary Army Commander* and *The Magnanimous Cuckold*. Originally, an even longer tour had been planned, and visits to Czechoslovakia and Sweden tabled (Picon-Vallin 1992: 127). A visit to England had been floated as early as 1926, possibly followed by a visit to America. These never came to fruition, and difficulties to acquire the necessary visas immediately expected (*New Castle News*, 6 October 1926: 10).

The tour was intertwined with the broader contexts that were surrounding Meyerhold as well as Russian arts in general. An analysis of the tour reveals the porous nature of theatre contextualization, where economic, political, cultural, artistic, logistical and institutional contexts operate not in isolation but in tension with one another. Contextualization becomes even denser in transmission activity, considering that transmission works in relation to two contexts, as a creative collision between that of the transmitter and the receiver's, the latter construed, in the case of Meyerhold's tour, as the receiving landscapes of the German and Parisian cultural scenes. In plainer words, his performances in Germany and especially in Paris became embroiled with the hosting conditions, as I will make evident below. The tour was also in no way detached from what was happening to Meyerhold at home. Nor was it divorced from his persona as it was developing abroad (see next section).

Russian authorities were cautious of the tour. Igor Ilinsky, one of Meyerhold's leading actors and an important chronicler of the trip, wrote how their foreign hosts saw the Meyerhold Theatre as a representative of Soviet artistic accomplishment. He expressed worry about this, as the theatre establishment back home did not want Soviet art to be represented by Meyerhold, or for his Theatre to be seen as the latest achievement of Soviet art.[26] Consequently, the image of an unsuccessful tour was constructed and disseminated in Moscow to support that particular bias:

> The negative attitude towards the Meyerhold Theatre and its foreign tour was also reflected in the fact that the Moscow printed press almost did not react to that tour. One could think – and there were rumours about it based on ill-wishers' words – that the Meyerhold Theatre had failed in Paris. This created an absolutely wrong idea of the tour. […] In Moscow the reaction to this tour was extremely reserved, perhaps because the negative reviews in the foreign press outnumbered the positive ones. (Ilinsky 1962: 301 and 306)

Ilinsky's final assertion in this quote is revealing of the potential which newspapers have in shaping public and private opinions. There is evidence here of Meyerhold's association abroad with bad press which, as I will argue in the next section, contributed to his problems in the 1930s.

Ilinsky's description is a valuable source because it constructs a methodology to evaluate a performance reality like a tour. From the point of view of Soviet criticism, the tour was a failure because it failed to create unanimous or at least generally positive press. Ilinsky, on the other hand, argued that unanimous praise was not a necessarily accurate yardstick to evaluate the success or otherwise of a tour. Newspapers in Berlin[27] were grouped in three distinct clusters of the communist, royalist and fascist factions, meaning that unanimous press on such an acrimonious personality like Meyerhold was not only impossible but also, from his own point of view, unwanted. What Ilinsky took as a yardstick to evaluate the tour's accomplishments was the reach and impact of the visit. What gratified the actor was the magnitude of the tour's coverage rather than its content, coupled with the good old-fashioned criteria that the tour was successful because most of the performances were sold out. He mentioned how even tiny provincial newspapers covered the tour and that he had met ordinary people, such as a 'German provincial man [...] [who] expressed great interest in the Russian theatre' (Ilinsky 1962: 302). He considered the tour a success because it had reached the deeper echelons of mainstream consciousness.

Ilinsky was especially gratified that the audience followed the complex text of *The Magnanimous Cuckold*. He felt that the audience accepted not only the unconventional form of the performance but also its plot (Ilinsky 1962: 304). The same happened with *The Forest* where to his 'surprise not a single funny line was left unnoticed, and during the special night-time performance for the artistic community the audience responded to literary every word' (302). It was precisely the reaction of the audiences that Ilinsky chose as the second criteria against which to evaluate the tour. This comes as no surprise considering that Ilinsky seems to have been particularly adapt as a performer to feel the mood of an audience. His skill as an actor, for example, appears to have given him the ability to read the presence of different groups in the auditorium, on the basis of their political maturity, and to adjust his performance to those who were ideologically prepared:

> In the auditorium there are always spectators who happen to be at the theatre quite by chance. They bring with them their lack of taste. From all that which takes place on the stage they only note whatever satisfies this lack of taste. However, there is another type of spectator, who at the theatre seems to find place next to the actor and the director, and who, like the actor himself, makes use of all the expressive means at his disposal. There are actors who become involved with that part of the audience who have no taste. Other actors [like Ilinsky], on the other hand, establish a tight connection with that spectator who is formed ideologically and who is theatrically better prepared. This is the spectator who year in year out tries to improve his skill of watching performance.
> (Meyerhold in Malcovati 1977: 71)

Ilinsky in fact raised an eyebrow at how in Germany, which he described as a bourgeois country, the critics had missed on the very principle of conventionalism which Meyerhold's theatre was constructed on (Ilinsky 1962: 305). Meyerhold's principle of so-called populism was also misread. This involved the use of popular techniques synonymous with street performance.

These techniques were not understood as a deliberate choice by Meyerhold but as a sign of aesthetic weakness on his part, as a presentation of incomplete work. What the German press did on the other hand was to contextualize Meyerhold within a broader anti-naturalistic effort. Meyerhold's work on its own was not considered to have opened any new artistic avenues. However, in parallel with the efforts of Alexander Tairov and Alexis Granowsky, 'the composition of the movement groups, which were both acrobatic and highly-stylised and clearly revealing the influence of ballet', gained in relief as a production approach (Ilinsky 1962: 305).

The Parisian stop of the tour presented its own challenges. In my introduction to the European section of *Stanislavsky in the World*, I argued that in touring Paris in 1922 and 1923, the Moscow Art Theatre brought with it more than its own repertoire and set of interpretations. They rather carried on their shoulders the weight of the Russian tradition of psychological realism. In Paris this tradition contrasted with its French counterpart, a parallel tradition defined by a rational and artifice-based approach to the construction of theatre (Aquilina in Pitches and Aquilina 2017: 28).[28] Meyerhold was certainly not a representative of psychological realism, but his theatre similarly put him at loggerheads with the established French tradition, what Beatrice Picon-Vallin referred to as 'the French theatrical tradition *requiring faithfulness to the author's text*' (1992: 132; emphasis added). Meyerhold's tour was received through that particular point of view, his productions read from a text-based bias. French criticism was therefore directed towards the liberties which Meyerhold took with the text of *The Government Inspector*. Picon-Vallin summarizes the text-centred criticism received by Meyerhold in Paris in the following way:

> *The Government Inspector* by Gogol/Meyerhold [...] provoked heated discussions, just like it did in Moscow. Aesthetic demands were mixed with political arguments, and voices were raised in defence of the integrity of an author's text. [...] The main reproach on which the opponents of the performance built their argument was the impudence and shamelessness of the director who 'claimed to take the place of the author'; the director who received, corrected, and added to the text. (Picon-Vallin 1992: 132)[29]

Support arrived from theatre people, on occasion from rather surprising places. Meyerhold's visit was backed by the Cartel de Quatres, the informal grouping of Louis Jouvet, Gaston Baty, Charles Dullin and Georges Pitoëff. They were brought together by a shared commitment 'to a policy of respect for the text, simple staging and a serious approach to the poetic function of drama' (Evans 2006: 31). This was of course a far cry from Meyerhold's own approach, but the Cartel still found much to appreciate in Meyerhold's work. Jouvet was particularly taken by Meyerhold's staging practices, seeing these as being powerful and in-your-face productions that disdain theatre as an entertainment (Abensour 1976: 235). The set of *The Forest* was favourably seen by Dullin because it integrated well with the drama (Picon-Vallin 1992: 130). A particularly positive report was given by J. Défini, writing on 16 June 1930 issue of *Comœdia*. This comes as less of a surprise given the newspaper's progressive leanings and bias towards modernism, as evidenced by the fact that Guillaume Apollinaire and André Rouveyre were regular contributors.[30] Défini lauded Meyerhold as 'an enemy of any school, of any abstract system, of abstract theory; he wants to make theatre a superior and meticulously regulated entertainment. He works a lot on a piece' (*Comœdia*, 16 June 1930: 2).

The tour also became entwined with the Parisian scene. To be more precise, it served as a means to comment on or even critique theatre in Paris. For example, Jean-Pierre Liasu reported that as close as ten days before the tour's opening night the company were still without a theatre. Liasu used this to criticize the local scene:

> So generous, so liberal as it is to foreign artists who wish to perform in France or whom we invite, it is not without surprise that we learn that the Meyerhold Theatre of Moscow is arriving in Paris in the absolute ignorance of where it will present its art. [...] The director does not know which theatre will host his work. [...] In which country do fifty foreign artists arrive with their sets and costumes to find similar conditions? Not in Soviet Russia, surely, or in Germany, Italy, or England. (*Comœdia*, 10 June 1930: 2)

This reference paved the way for further criticism which Liasu directed towards the lack of support given to French actors and the rising figures of unemployment.

It is worth remembering that Paris was already an important destination for theatre touring. Meyerhold's tour that year was not the only visit by a foreign company, and he had to compete for exposure and visibility with many other companies. Visits by foreign theatres were not necessarily seen in a positive way by French critics. The matter of the contamination of French theatre with imported values was raised.[31] The following extract gives a flavour of both the large influx of foreign touring companies and the resistance which they encountered:

It may seem strange to ask this question [the article is titled 'Are We Waterproof?'] when, for ten years, our theatre seems open to all kinds of foreign influences. Never, at any time, has France been so invaded. It would seem that wide breaches have been made on all our frontiers, through which we freely let pass works, authors, and arts from the North, East, South, and West.

[...] The season that is coming to an end has seen an unexpected flourishing of foreign works. One of the finest came from England (The Great Journey), and we also had several adaptations of Shakespeare.

America continues to flood us with its operettas, its Negro music, and dreams of colonizing us with its movies, with dreams of collaboration with our authors and our actors, who are expected to kneel in front of the dollar. [...] The Germans began making a few appearances [...]. Finally, several Russian troupes appeared, the last one being Meyerhold's, who wanted to conquer us with his productions. What becomes of the French spirit in this cage with all these exotic birds? [...] In the presence of such an assault, can we defend ourselves? (*Comœdia*, 6 August 1930: 2).

Certainly, however, the stir created by the opening night of *The Government Inspector* chimed with the local propensity to enjoy a bit of theatre commotion, what Thomas Postlewait might have seen as forming part of 'the French theatre['s] [...] heritage of theatrical turmoil beginning with the seventeenth-century controversy over Corneille's *Le Cid*' (2009: 69; see also 73). Coverage of the tour was always given on the second page of the *Comœdia*, but the noisy reactions that met *The Government Inspector*'s opening night were promoted to front-page news and reported in the following manner:

> Coming from afar to the Théâtre de la Gaîté-Montparnasse, which was offered by its new director Mr. Baty, the official Soviet troupe of Mr. Meyerhold gave its first performance yesterday evening.
>
> There was a vibrant crowd made of different people, a large number of critics, and a certain amount of theatre personalities such as Messrs Emile Fabre and Gabriel Astruc. Directors and actors who abandoned the general rehearsal at the Mathurins Theatre joined the Russian spectators, made up of a mixture of White and Red Russians, who had rushed to watch.
>
> There was tension in the air and during the interval, after the fifth Tableau, various Russians who, during the performance had protested against the messing around with Gogol's text, were attacked by their compatriots, supporters who backed Meyerhold's actors. Among others,

M. Balieff protested vehemently against these actors, or rather, against what in his eyes was a mutilation. A fight almost broke out.

A gentleman, who seemed to be speaking on behalf of France, cried: 'We have clapped enough. Silence!'

To which, Mr. Balieff answered pertinently that this was not an exchange of pleasantries but of art. Some spoke of calling the guards. The actors came on stage (because there is no curtain for Meyerhold) and the play continued, a tight performance, sometimes caricatural, but very often too sketchy. (*Comœdia*, 17 June 1930: 1)

In the end, the tour did little to generate an international persona that could have shielded Meyerhold from further attacks back home. What the tour did generate was a wider knowledge of Meyerhold's techniques and contextualization within European modernism.

Meyerhold's internationalism discerned from Western newspapers

In this final exposition, I will develop further the discussion about Meyerhold's internationalism started in the previous section about his 1930 tour, with reference to what newspapers in the West were writing about him and his work. These newspapers emerge as a rich source to add to our range of materials about Meyerhold. The amount of references to Meyerhold in American newspapers between 1920 and 1940 is substantial. The online platform newspapers.com raises seven hundred entries across these years, of which I consulted perhaps a quarter to draw attention to the range of materials which can be excavated. Using entries about Meyerhold in newspapers published in the West evidences the following three points: (i) that Meyerhold was an international figure worth reporting on, (ii) that several typical understandings and evaluations of Meyerhold which today we take for granted were already in place in the West by the 1920s and 1930s, and (iii) the emergence of an occasional name, event or work-related detail which has not, at least to my knowledge, been referred to before. This is particularly important as it opens further research avenues.

Newspapers published in the West did much to chronicle the transmission of Meyerhold's name and general practices outside Russia, in the process making him known to a broad public outside of theatre environments. *The Sydney Morning Herald* of 11 January 1938, for example, described Meyerhold as a practitioner 'whose ideas until recently were held up to the world as the boldest and most brilliant development of revolutionary theatrical art.

[His] theatre earned a high reputation abroad' (12). Just the year before South Dakota's *Daily Argus-Leader* described him as 'internationally famous for his modernistic and futuristic stage technique' (25 June 1939: 9). In this section I will untangle these statements, not only by clarifying what such an international reputation amounted to, but also by drawing attention to possible shortcomings which a newspapers-based research approach entails. Newspapers might be seen as a controversial source to use in academic research, given the subjective nature as well as partiality with which they typically report events or interpret ideas. Still, their potential to represent and articulate public thought is not to be underestimated.

What did Meyerhold's internationalism amount to? Several entries report his deteriorating political situation. In July 1928, Meyerhold and his wife and actress in his theatre Zinaida Raikh left the Soviet Union on holiday and stayed for five months in France (Braun 1998: 248). The government feared that Meyerhold might not return, a concern which leaked into the international press. The North Carolina newspaper *The Sunday Citizen*, in fact, reported that while convalescing in Southern France Meyerhold had sent a telegraph to Moscow saying that his deteriorating health needed a longer stay abroad. This was supported by another telegram, sent by French directors Louis Jouvet and Firmin Gémier, confirming that Meyerhold was unwell (Picon-Vallin 1992: 128). Meyerhold's telegram was understood 'as a gentle way of breaking the news that [he] is not prepared to work in Moscow under present conditions' (*The Sunday Citizen*, 28 October 1928: 5). These conditions included a lack of financial support and materials to produce theatre with, bad leadership and a rigid censorship. One can, of course, understand more from this entry the escalation in Meyerhold's sidelining at home and eventual closure of his theatre, if his name was getting associated in the foreign press with a negative picture of Soviet arts. He became, to use a contemporary phrase, bad press.

Meyerhold's political troubles were chronicled in newspapers abroad as they were taking place. His political life was being reported on in the Western press, underlining in turn the international reach of his name. An entry in *The Guardian* dated 23 December 1937 described a politically troubled Meyerhold as 'the stormy petrel of the Soviet Theatre' (18). His theatre was closed soon after, on 8 January 1938 in fact (Braun 1998: 290). The closing of the theatre was reported three days later in *The Baltimore Sun* (11 January 1938: 8), revealingly in the context of a piece that was again commenting on the declining standards of Soviet art. The anonymous writer underlined the role which censorship played in this decline, an opinion which he or she contrasted to an article in *Pravda* which was putting the blame on 'the foe from within'. Again, Meyerhold's association abroad with the problems

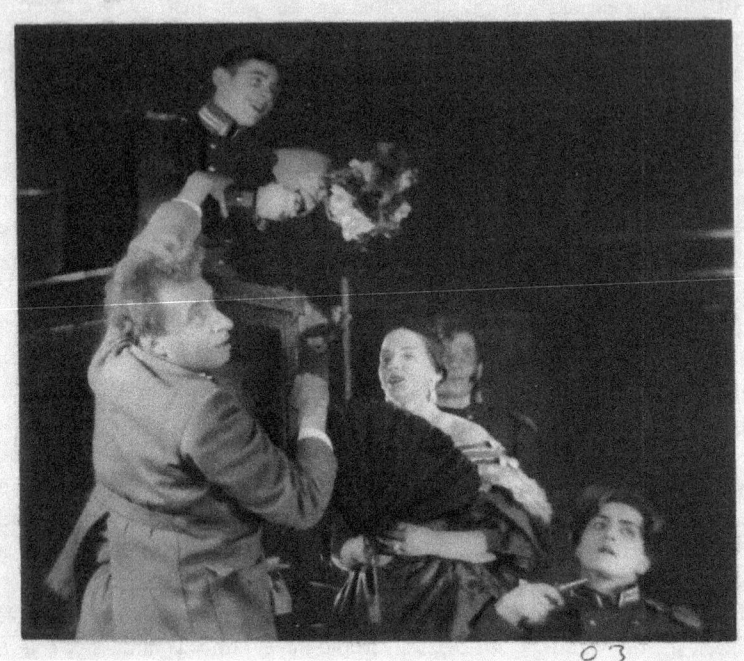

Figure 11 Vsevolod Meyerhold working with Zinaida Raikh during the rehearsals of *The Government Inspector*, 1926. Courtesy Laurence Senelick Collection.

in Soviet arts would have done him no favours with the powers-to-be, and a rapid increase in his persecution was seen around this time. Platon Kerzhentsev's notorious article 'An Alien Theatre', published in *Pravda* on 17 December 1937, was also reported on in Western newspapers and, in the case of Montreal's *The Gazette*, just one day after it appeared in the Russian press. Correspondents writing in the West were certainly following what was happening in Meyerhold's world. *The Gazette* article, titled 'Noted Theatre Doomed. Soviet Attacks Hint End of Famed Russian Producer', reproduced Kerzhentsev's charges to Meyerhold on grounds of 'formalism, conventionalism and mysticism' (18 December 1937: 13). His arrest in June 1939 was widely reported in newspapers based in Miami, Cincinnati, Baltimore, Pennsylvania, North Dakota, Texas and Arizona.[32]

Other reports included reviews of Meyerhold's Parisian tour (*The Guardian*, 20 June 1930: 12), plans to build a new theatre, including a detailed description of the building (*The Manchester Guardian*, 10 January 1936: 7), as well as his appointment in 1938 as a director at the Stanislavsky's Opera

Theatre. The latter, reported in Minnesota's *St. Cloud Times*, was described as a comeback, an 'amazing [...] return to public life', one which had braved, as the title suggested, the 'Kremlin's ire to come back'. The author, a certain Norman B. Deuel, described the criticism that had engulfed Meyerhold in 1937 and 1938, spearheaded by Zhadanov, 'a member of the all-powerful polit-bureau, [who] denounced the Meyerhold Theatre from the tribune of the Supreme Soviet as decadent and anti-Soviet' (14 December 1938: 4).

Beyond politics, how did the West see Meyerhold? The most typical accolades given him today were already evident in the 1920s and 1930s. For example, North Carolina's *The Sunday Citizen* referred to Meyerhold as 'the dynamic leader of revolutionary drama' (28 October 1928: 5). The criticisms typically associated with his practice were also already in place. A particularly critical article was written by one St John Ervine for *The Hartford Daily Courant*. It appeared on 17 March 1929 (69). In this article Ervine manifested a clear anti-Russian bias. Cheekily, he argued that 'Meyerhold, apparently, has revolutionized the Russian theater. Somebody is always revolutionizing something in Russia. One of these days a Russian will cause a frightful sensation by leaving something alone'. He took a direct dig at Meyerhold, describing a pamphlet by the New Playwrights' group on him as a pretentious joke.

On an aesthetic level, Meyerhold's penchant to put disparate theatre elements together in performance was already taken as his signature practice. His aesthetics proved a particularly divisive point, even to Western eyes, hinting that to a certain extent Western newspapers were mimicking what their Russian counterparts were writing. The writer A. W., writing in *The Guardian* on 20 June 1930, remarked that Meyerhold had been called both a genius and a madman. People loved him and loathed him in equal measure as he 'arouse[s] in most people either wildest enthusiasm or the deepest annoyance [for his] [...] piling [of] eccentricities upon eccentricities' (12). The *Des Moines Register*, Iowa, contrasted Meyerhold to Stanislavsky in an article published on 17 August 1938. The anonymous writer remarked that while Stanislavsky's productions had won unanimous praise – an exaggeration certainly – Meyerhold's 'showy' productions, on the other hand, all too often displayed 'a certain freakishness', by using 'bizarre experiments with [the] mechanics of staging in "jazzing up" the classics' (4). More positively, *The Courier* equated Meyerhold's modernism as a 'blending of comedy, operetta, the screen, drama and vaudeville – all in one' (22 June 1928: 3). The references to operetta and vaudeville are worth highlighting as particular biases which the writer put in motion to construct his understanding of Meyerhold's work; both genres were by the late 1920s close to being eradicated from the Soviet stage. In any case, Meyerhold's name had by then become synonymous with unconventional theatre, as evidenced in a 12 April 1936 entry in *The Brooklyn Daily Eagle*. The article in question, written by B. H. Haggin, described a production of the opera *Lucia di Lammermoor* at La Scala. What is revealing is that the author argued that this production was not a modern restaging 'like that of Meyerhold and Appia' (45), underlining the Russian director's use as a signpost of international modernism, even at a time when his position at home was being destabilized.

Other entries juxtapose Meyerhold to realism in order for his non-representational theatre to gain in relief. One of the most detailed of these entries is an article in Ohio's *Dayton Daily News Magazine* dated 6 May 1923. This article used Meyerhold's work to question the artistic credentials of realism. For the author Meyerhold was the main exponent of a 'non-representational and theater-theatrical' theatre (103). He defined non-representational theatre through the example where someone hangs ten stars to the ceiling to depict a sky full of stars. Reflecting theories which Meyerhold had expounded upon some twenty years before about the creative and imaginative participation of the audience, as one where each spectator is given the space to complete missing details in a mise-en-scène, the author of the *Dayton Daily News* expressed his criticism of the 'realistic theatre [as] a trick for the unimaginative and is by way of being an insult to persons of high imagination' (103).

Research in Western newspapers is particularly valuable when it unearths some previously untapped aspect in Meyerhold's work. These findings may at times be minor, reflecting Jonathan Pitches's argument that it is hard today to discover material of such a paradigm-shift quality as the milestone publication in the late 1960s of *Meyerhold on Theatre*. Instead, we have to be content with 'small evolutionary offerings' (Pitches 2016: 2). On occasion, however, some research gems are unearthed which open a whole new chapter in Meyerhold studies. A case in point is a reference to a certain Vadim Uraneff from the same 6 May 1923 issue of the *Dayton Daily News Magazine* just mentioned. We know, of course, how Richard Boleslavsky had moved to the United States in 1922 and became a kind of self-appointed spokesperson of Stanislavsky and American authority on his System. Hints of a similar process taking place for the transmission of Meyerhold in the United States can be discerned from the newspapers, even if perhaps on a smaller scale, a process of transmission in which Uraneff played a central role.

In an earlier report in the *New York Tribune* (7 March 1920), Uraneff was described as a former associate of Stanislavsky at the Moscow Art Theatre and of Meyerhold at the Imperial Theatres. At the time of writing he was producing a play called *Musk* at the Punch and Judy Theatre (37). Three years later he underlined his studies with Meyerhold of past theatre traditions: 'I have studied the Italian Commedia dell'arte, the old Japanese, French and English [theatres]' (*Dayton Daily News* Magazine, 6 May 1923: 103). Uraneff is described as 'the chief exponent of this new [non-representational and theatrical] art in America', a direct interpretation of Meyerhold's work where the audience never forgets that what it is seeing is a play in a theatre and not a slice of life. Uraneff's statement of allegiance to a Meyerhold-informed theatre was made via two productions. One was the production on Broadway of *The Song of Songs*, possibly the same play written by Edward Sheldon and which had already played on Broadway in the 1914–15 season.[33] The other was the decidedly atypical for Broadway *The Show Booth*, an alternative title for Blok's *The Fairground Booth*:

> We have read these words 'Meyerhold', 'non-representational' and 'theater-theatrical' in connection with the ultra-modern in Russian drama and they have been merely words. But the other day when one of Meyerhold's disciples introduced the new movement to Broadway, the words became something more than words. [The productions were intended to] […] fluster the shock-proof serenity of Broadway. (*Dayton Daily News Magazine*, 6 May 1923: 103)

Like the decidedly American interpretation which the Group Theatre gave to Stanislavsky's System (Carnicke 2009: 45–7), Uraneff was quick to assert the American, i.e. contemporary, relevance of his interpretation of Meyerhold: 'Oh, it is American, all American. […] [W]hat we do here is with American actors and the production is essentially American.' The author does not go into any depth to describe what this 'Americaness' might have amounted to, though he did optimistically remark that the productions signalled 'the birth of a new movement in America' (103).

Other instances sourced from the newspapers open further research avenues. Uraneff was not the only among Meyerhold's former collaborators who found work and position abroad. Another example is that of Marlon Gering, a screen director working in Canada and the United States in the 1930s. *The Ottawa Journal* dated 6 January 1934 reported that Gering's first encounter with theatre was in the city of Rostov. Subsequently, he attracted Meyerhold's interest, then described as 'Russia's greatest director, whose influence in the theatre is now a dominating note in European production' (9). Gering, *The Ottawa Journal* reported, studied Meyerhold's techniques and became an actor under him. He was quoted as saying the following: 'In considering his theatre shop, where promising talent can enter upon a four-year post-graduate course in theatrical technique, Meyerhold insures his students' acting experience' (19). Gering suggested that American actor training should adopt such a model. From the newspapers we also get to know that Meyerhold's 1930 tour had been planned for quite some time – it was already announced in October 1926 to take place in spring 1927 (*New Castle News*, 6 October 1926: 10) – and that in 1928 he had taken part in a movie produced by the State Motion Picture of Sovkino. He was criticized for his involvement, on grounds of the nerve he had to take a large salary for the part. His answer, that he must have been good to receive a good payment, was also reported (*Shamokin News-Dispatch*, 23 June 1928: 2).

Using mainstream newspapers published in the West as a research source does not come without its own set of problems. In the case of studying Meyerhold from Western newspapers 'the tyranny of distance' (see Chapter 1) or the very real distance between Moscow, London, New York and the United States as a whole meant that on occasion the discussion (rather than the headline item) could be rather out of date. News do travel fast, but the transmission of more analytical material transpired to be slower. A case in point is provided by St John Ervine's article in *The Hartford Daily Courant* referred to above. As an example of Meyerhold's lack of subtlety in tackling texts, Ervine, himself a playwright, made reference to *The Dawn*, a production that was staged almost a decade before: 'I find myself wondering what poor Varhearan […] would have thought had he lived to see that the exuberant, and, I fear, partially demented Meyerhold was doing with *The Dawn*' (17 March 1929: 69). In another instance, the writer J. Défini writing in 16 June 1930 issue of the *Comœdia* underlined, as one of Meyerhold's greatest theories, the commitment to 'bring to the fore the communion that must exist between the spectators and the actors' (2), even if Meyerhold's clearest articulations about this communion harked back to the 1906–8 period.

The terminology used could also be reflective of the time and now considered obsolete. One instance referred to Meyerhold's theatre as 'mechanical theatre' in lieu of its 'emphasis on stage effects, trick lighting, uneven stage effects, and technical apparatus' (*The Baltimore Sun*, 2 September 1938: 5). In reality mechanical theatre is a colloquial term that never had much currency, nor is it in use today. Factual mistakes – such as Meyerhold being called a playwright (*The Daily Argus-Leader*, 25 June 1939: 9) or his Sohn theatre described as one of the largest in Moscow (*The Guardian England*, 23 December 1937: 18) – also emerge on occasion. A superficial understanding of the contextual complexities at work is also apparent at times. For instance, an entry in *Comœdia* dated 21 January 1930 made reference to the Five Year Plan and the stringing censorship of the time. It reported that Mikhail Bulgakov's 'satirical comedies' had been banned. Unrealistically, Meyerhold was described as 'being quite at ease in this atmosphere' because of the recent production of Ilya Selvinsky's *The Second Army Commander* (2). The newspaper piece, however, completely sidesteps all the difficulties that Meyerhold was encountering at the time to get any new material passed by the censors. At other times the writing was particularly contentious and one sided, typical of newspapers' opinion pieces, hinting at the specific agendas and biases of the writers.[34] As with any source, the background, intention and bias of the author also need to be contended with. This is problematic, as the authors are often anonymized or only the initials of their names given. Especially in these cases of anonymity, the question whether the writers were white émigrés or supporters is raised.

Suggestions for practice

Introducing Meyerhold's theatricality

This is an exercise which I have used several times to introduce Meyerhold and his aesthetics to students. The session revolves around the bribe scene in *The Government Inspector*. You might wish to find the famous picture of this scene as produced by Meyerhold, with Khlestakov in the middle of the stage and the hands or figures coming out of the doors behind him. The image is reproduced in Braun (1998: 232), apart from being easily found online.

1. Outline the plot

- Introduce the story of *The Government Inspector* in general terms, making reference to the provincial town and the consternation of the people when they hear that a government inspector is coming from St Petersburg to investigate operations.
- Make reference to Khlestakov, what the folk think of him, but also who he really is.
- Draw attention to the role of the scene within the broader arch of the play.

2. Divide roles

- Each participant takes one of the following characters: Khlestakov, Mayor, Mayor's Wife, School Director, Judge, Warden of the Hospital, Postmaster, a Merchant, Police Superintendent and Doctor.

3. Improvise: Realistically

- Improvise a scene along the following lines. It is important that the improvisation is devised in a realistic manner, with people behaving as they do in everyday life, without therefore accentuating any of the actions.

- The scene is Khlestakov's room. Each participant enters the room as the character and introduces himself or herself to Khlestakov.
- Khlestakov 'invents' an excuse and asks for a loan. Each role consents, gives the money and leaves.
- Khlestakov's excuses include: I ran in unexpected expenses while travelling; I seem to have forgotten my subsistence to pay for the hotel; On my way, the train was attacked by a group of thieves, and I was the only one who had some money on; I need to purchase my return ticket: don't worry, the central government will reimburse you with interest.
- At the end of the scene, Khlestakov is alone and reacts to all these collected loans. End the improvisation.
- Discuss the scene with the students. Was the scene repetitive? How different were the stage solutions of the various characters?

4. Improvise: As a type and/or animal

- Repeat the scene, but this time assign a type and/or animal to the various characters.
- Possible types include a loud child, a miser, a flirtatious woman, a fat man, an old man, a sly/suspicious person, a wise man and so on.
- Typical animals include a cat, a hyena, a loud dog, a lion, an eagle, a hippopotamus, a horse, a snake, etc.
- Participants are to support their improvisation either by improvising their lines or by using any fragments from the text or from the previous improvisation.
- Consider having the actor playing Khlestakov choose a type/animal for himself. Otherwise, he may be played realistically along the lines of the first improvisation.
- Discuss the scene with the students. How was it different from the first draft? Are the types/animals clear to an audience? What defines a type or animal? Any patterns of behaviour stand out? How different from each other were the stage solutions of the various types/animals?
- As a director or outside eye, your role can be that of highlighting and accentuating parts of the improvisation. Which parts did you choose to highlight? Why? How? By enlarging the size (magnitude) of the movement? Through repetition?

5. Improvise: Pantomime

- Now attempt a more unconventional presentation of the scene, relying on movement and pantomime rather than text.

- You can recall material from previous improvisations, and invent new solutions to the stage tasks. For example: how do you enter the room? Can you create an alternative way to a conventional 'knock on the door and enter' action? How do you hand the money? Are the money bills of a conventional size or larger? How does Khlestakov collect the money? Experiment with using larger-than-life objects (e.g. a one-metre pencil) or changing their nature and use (e.g. using a book as a hat).
- Introduce the picture of the way Meyerhold staged this scene. You might wish to draw the participants' attention to this general description of Meyerhold's aesthetics:

> In Meyerhold the structures break apart, and the grotesque medley of heterogeneous antics and devices takes over, for he sees the world as fragmenting, or perhaps experience as fragmentary. He takes a script and breaks it up, and the performance teases us. It debunks those who even seek coherence [...]. It throws up allusions and associations [...]. In Meyerhold's production, peals of bells rang out, evoking all sorts of associations [...]. This is a theatre which revels in implication, creates a unique mix of violence and clowning, and draws strength from metaphors. (Leach 2004: 99)

How does your final version fit within this description of Meyerhold's aesthetics? Are there any parallels? How would you describe the scene? Stylized? Pantomimic? Theatrical? Unconventional? Why? How does it compare to more realistic interpretations of the scene? What kinds of training would the actors need to perform the scene 'the Meyerhold way'? (This is also a good place to introduce Biomechanics to the students.)

'Expressing thoughts spatially'

In her memoirs about theatre in pre-revolutionary St Petersburg, Asja Lācis shows a strong affiliation with the work that Meyerhold was doing on both the Imperial stages and his studio experiments (see Chapter 6). She gives evidence of his many activities, even calling him a jack of all trades. Central to his research was the fact that 'he also led the scenic movement in his studio. This was not a coincidence – he was searching for a way to express thoughts *spatially*' (Lācis 1971: 13; emphasis in original). This exercise unpicks such a statement.

- Create a short physical routine. There are several ways of doing this – see for instance the suggestions for practice at the end of Chapter 1, which had elaborated on the use of images. An important aspect of this routine

is that the participants do not remain fixed in one spot, but rather include an element of moving around the space. The routine is to be practised and performed as a loop.
- Start with the whole group performing their routines together at the same time and in the same studio space. Explore moments when participants cross each other while moving in the space or when they make any kind of contact. This could be a fleeting moment like eye contact or an instance when two or more participants perform their separate routines in close physical proximity. In what ways do you 'explore' these moments? Do you pause? Do you use the moment as a trigger to change the rhythm? Do you mirror briefly the other participant?
- Using four cones, reduce the size of the space, say, by about 20 per cent. How does a smaller space impact the performance of the routine? How does it impact the moments of contact?
- Repeat, each time reducing the size of the space, until the participants are performing their routines very close to each other.
- Introduce the following level of meaning, what Lācis referred to as 'expressing thoughts spatially'. Underpin a moment of contact with another participant, whether it is fleeting or otherwise, with a basic intention of 'acceptance' or 'rejection'. Do you give yourself to the encounter? Or do you refuse it? How clear do you make your decision? What levels are there to the encounter? Could one part of the body accept the encounter while another reject it?
- As always, encourage participants to reflect on their work, starting with the questions above.

6

Lesser-known names: Rediscovering female voices

The status of women in early Soviet Russia

As it should be clear by now, much of the research going into the writing of this book was guided by the principle that there is material about lesser-known realities across the landscape of Russian modernism that is worth engaging in. It is for this reason that I tackled in substantial length Valentin Smyshlaev's work in Chapter 3 and argued that more than a misinterpretation of the System his practice constituted a hybrid between a Stanislavsky-informed technique and the post-revolutionary thrust towards collective work. Similarly, the exposition in Chapter 4 about amateur and proletarian theatre depicted a workers-based theatre not as inferior to its professional counterpart, but as a reality that had ample potential for the transmission and processing of acting techniques. Even when discussing the two canonical names of Stanislavsky (Chapter 2) and Meyerhold (Chapter 5), particular attention was given to uncover sidelined documents and instances of practices, like the former's relationship with German actor Ludwig Barnay (an example of Scenic Transmission) or his rehearsal work on the 1933 production of Ostrovsky's *Artists and Admirers* (referred to as Rehearsal Transmission). In Meyerhold's case, examples of transmission practice tackled in some detail included the 1930 European tour and his international persona as discerned from newspapers published in the West. As I move towards concluding the book, I would like to stress further this endeavour that sheds light on marginal names and their practices. I will do so by discussing a number of female figures and their contribution to the theatrical experimentation of the 1920s. Studies about early Soviet culture from the point of view of women are currently flourishing, as evidenced by the many sources that tackle the position, status and achievements of women during those years.[1] These studies often adopt a multidisciplinary approach, with Melanie Ilic's extensive work, for instance, drawing from the fields of history, sociology, political science, geography, cultural theory, economy, literature and linguistics (Ilic 2018: 1–2). Theatre and Performance Studies are missing from this list, and hopefully my short intervention will encourage others to delve deeper in the subject. The work of Asja Lācis (1891–1979), a Latvian-born theatre practitioner and Walter Benjamin's one-time love interest, will serve as the main case study, seeing how her theatre work with children, though known in certain research milieus, still has to find a place in mainstream theatre scholarship. As Patty Lee Parmalee argued, 'it is [Lācis'] sex that condemns her to obscurity' (quoted in Ingram 2002: 170), an obscurity that I will seek to partly untangle below by underlining the implications to transmission which her practice gives rise to.

Life for women in pre-revolutionary Russia was particularly disadvantageous. Strong traditions tied women to a life of domestic servitude and gave males near-complete control over their wives and families. Formal laws made divorce extremely difficult, and a husband could restrict his wife's movement and potential to get a job (Ilic 2018: 61). In brief, early Soviet reformers understood that women had undergone a particular form of oppression because of their gender, which necessitated focused political retraining if they were to participate in a more public life. Reflective of this thinking is the popular poster, reproduced as the cover image of the book *Everyday Life in Early Soviet Russia* (Kiaer and Naiman 2006), which depicts a woman sweeping away pots and pans, symbols of a life at home engaged in domestic duties, while longingly pointing towards a workers' club, canteen and factory. The message is, of course, unequivocal: the revolution will sweep away former restrictions and oppressions. Educational and work opportunities for women were promised, as was the realization of a more emancipated life where they would be on a par with men. Post-revolutionary life would also hand women the highest accolade possible, that of contributors in the creation of a new Soviet life.

After the revolution and Civil War, the Bolsheviks certainly trumpeted all the right words about the emancipation of women. These efforts were consonant with the image of the hopeful 1920s. As Macelline Hutton underlined, life for many women and their families did improve in the mid-1920s, not in the least because millions of peasant women were able to have their own households independently of their in-laws. On the labour front, women found work not only in factories, but also as teachers, doctors, engineers and pilots, possibilities, in other words, that were near impossible to achieve before (Hutton 2015: 9–14). Moreover, clear efforts to tackle the 'women issue' were made at governmental level. As early as 1919, the party founded a special section, the Zhenotdel or Women's Department, which, under the leadership of Aleksandra Kollontai, Inessa Armand and others, looked 'to create institutions that could liberate women. [...] [They] sought to make the department a refuge and official "support group" for working-class and peasant women and an intellectual inspiration' (Evans Clements 1992: 486). Efforts in the direction of women's emancipation were therefore real and not inconsequential. In their most extreme forms, these efforts suggested the eradication of the family as the basic societal unit, for its place to be taken by communes where monogamy was a thing of the past. Men would thus lose control over their wives. This position was enthusiastically argued for by Kollontai. Lenin, crucially, had a much more conservative view on the subject, very consonant in fact with his favouring of realism as a theatre style instead of experimentation. As a result of disparate viewpoints, Bolshevik treatment of women in the 1920s treaded a fine line between fulfilling the early promise of emancipation but safeguarding women's traditional roles of reproduction and home builders, which certainly remained important issues:

> The Soviet woman was expected to be an exemplary worker, and to develop the qualities and traits which were appropriate to the work place; yet she was also supposed to have certain 'natural' traits and behavioural patterns which made her innately suited to domesticity and child-care. (Atwood 1999: 3-4)

These two factors, a balance between new rights and conservative duties, came to be known as women's 'double burden'.

The belief that it was possible to construct a new kind of individual, what Leon Trotsky described as 'an improved edition of mankind' (Hellbeck 2006: 5), was a fundamental principle in the Bolshevik's vision for the new state. Part of this project also involved the construction of the 'New Soviet Woman', a 'type' or a collection of qualities which ordinary women could strive for. The New Soviet Woman attended lectures and training to raise her intellectual capabilities. She was confident, self-reliant, and had the means to be financially independent. The New Soviet Woman was also politically active by voting in elections and by participating in trade union business. Kollontai's words are helpful to depict this image and its various characteristics:

> Self-discipline instead of emotionality; the ability to value her freedom and independence, instead of being submissive and lacking in personality; the affirmation of her individuality, instead of a naïve attempt to absorb and reflect someone else's cast of mind, that of the 'beloved'. Before us is no mere wife, no shadow of a man: before us is an individual, a woman who is above all a person. (Kollontai quoted in Attwood 1999: 10-11)

The New Soviet Woman exemplified the transformative power of the revolution as a new figure coming out of bourgeois oppression. This image was fine-tuned in relation to shifting times, but the needs for self-worth and value independence, and balance between public life and family responsibilities remained constant even when the promising 1920s turned into the collectivism of the 1930s.

In the end, the promise of emancipation was a difficult one to implement. As post-revolutionary life showed over and over again, deep-seated mentalities were hard to change. Everyday culture remained inherently patriarchal.[2] What resulted was an expansion in the public roles which women could take and more visibility. The work of the Leningrad Theatre of Working-Class Youth (TRAM) exemplified this.[3] TRAM opened in 1922 as an amateur company devoted to staging productions relevant to Soviet youth. It eventually turned professional and instigated the development of several other national cells. Actresses played key roles on the TRAM stage but still remain marginal in discussion at management and policy level. More exposure was gained by the actresses, without this necessarily translating into leadership (Mally 1996: especially 82). The unhappy denouement of the Bolshevik's first efforts to create gender equality was therefore a persistence in male-dominant hierarchies and what Brovkin described as 'false promises, dashed hopes, and the pretense of emancipation' (1998: 218).

Contributions of female artists

Within this ambivalent context, marked by revolutionary and transformative fervour, propagandistic articulations about the New Soviet Woman, and the grim realization that everyday cultures of gender inequality were hard to dislocate, theatre became not only a vehicle for women and pertinent issues to achieve public visibility, through on-stage depictions for example, but also a terrain where female theatre practitioners – actresses, directors, set designers – could carve a place alongside their male colleagues. Simon Karlinsky describes this upsurge of female artists as follows:

> The period between 1908 and ca. 1925 saw the mass emergence of talented, creative women in many branches of Russian artistic life: Zinaida Gippius, Anna Akhmatova, Elena Guro, Maria Tsvetaeva, and [Natalia] Goncharova, [Alexandra] Exter, Liubov Popova, Varvara Stepanova, Olga Rozanova, Nadezhda Udaltsova, and numerous others in painting and stage design. The production style devised by Meyerhold and Tairov and later called *constructivist* suited the talents

of such artists as Exter, Popova, and Stepanova. Like a number of male colleagues, however, some of the most important women writers and artists (Gippius, Tsvetaeva, Goncharova, and Exter, for example), chose to emigrate to the West in the 1920s because of the lack of personal and artistic freedom under the Bolshevik regime. (in Van Norman Baer 1992: 30–2)

The Silver Age of Russian theatre had already elevated the status of actresses like Maria Savina, Glikeriya Fedotova, Anna Brenko and Vera Komissarzhevskaya into bona fide stars (Schuler 1996). Soviet times similarly bequeathed many well-known actresses like Maria Babanova and Alla Tarasova, and cinema also proved a fertile ground for actresses to gain public and political recognition. Actresses were often awarded prestigious titles like People's Artist of the USSR and Hero of Socialist Labour, cementing their position in mainstream culture.

One such figure was Serafima Birman (1890–1976).[4] Birman's description of her own theatre formation is worth noting, as it flags an interesting tug of war between formal and informal training grounds (see below). In Chapter 1 the point was raised that the transmission of acting techniques evidences that transmission belts or channels rarely operate in isolation. Rather, transmission activity is strengthened when it calls upon the use of different channels and their respective qualities, when, so to speak, the transmission of a technique is carried out through different approaches and in different ways. This diversity was evident in Berman's development. In her writings, she in turn manifested the strengths and weaknesses of these various channels.

On a formal level, Birman started her theatre life as a member of the school run by Alexander Adashev. She enrolled at this school in 1908 and graduated three years later. Adashev was an actor of the Moscow Art Theatre, with one of his roles being that of Grandpa in *Blue Bird*. Other actors from the Moscow Art Theatre like Kachalov, Leonidov and Luzhsky also taught at the school and both Sulerzhitsky and Stanislavsky were known visitors. The school thus developed a close connection with the MAT and a reputation of being a preliminary formation ground for actors wanting to join the Theatre. Birman wrote that these professional actors 'brought with them the spirit of the Art Theatre', of which the young students were in complete awe (Birman 1962: 27). In her memories she also described the classes on stage mastery led by Adashev. These classes revolved around the performance of dramatic scenarios, similar to short plays, which exposed the students to a concrete stage task. They were called 'monodrama', possibly because of the single task, within a single dramatic genre, which students were exposed to. In Birman's description, these scenarios amounted to an early version of using études for training purposes. One such étude involved a guest entering an inn. He interests himself in the paintings on the wall, looks in the mirror, casually takes a book, sits down next to the stove and falls asleep. The owner of the inn subsequently enters the scene, notes the sleeping guest and wakes him up. They both laugh heartily and for a long time. This scenario examined the students' ability to easily and contagiously laugh on the stage, what Birman described as a particularly difficult task to carry out in performance. The group also developed another monodrama to offer training in dramatic tragedy, revolving around finding a note of treason and deceit from a loved one. These études took place in the first year of study, while more developed performance work in front of an audience took place in the second and third years (Birman 1962: 27–8).

At the end of the three years Birman had no delusions about what she had learned. She understood her position as a budding actress with little technical knowledge. In a way, she spoke of her training at Adashev's school as a missed opportunity, because she was never properly casted.[5] She still felt unable to control her stage temperament and often confused it with 'goose bumps'. On graduating her skill was very rudimentary but at least she felt she 'had a better understanding of the main issues involved in the profession' (33). It was on tour with other young actors just before joining the MAT that she informally acquired a more concrete acting knowledge, such as the implications of working with an exacting director, the demands which a big stage puts on an actor, and the discipline needed to overcome difficult work conditions. During this tour Birman also felt that for the first time she was creating her own roles rather than simply imitating what other actors had created (41–2).[6]

Apart from touring, Birman's participation in the mass scenes of the Moscow Art Theatre proved to be another informal training ground. In this case, the young actors learned by being in close proximity with the more seasoned performers:

> Participation in the mass scenes made it possible for us the young to see the brilliant actors [of the MAT]. We stood with them on the same stage. Watching them play on the stage, their attitude to the work, their behaviour behind the scenes, we passed our acting university. (Birman 1962: 52)

It is interesting that Birman referred to the word 'attitudes' (*otnosheniye*), delineating an aspect of work that underlines and supports technical mastery (see Chapter 4). In this case, an attitude is the mindset brought in when carrying out an activity, whether in one's professional life or everyday environments. How is work looked at, as a chore or as an instance of character-building? With what predisposition does one fulfil his or her duties? For instance, Birman felt that when performing mass scenes, the older generation had instilled (transmitted) in them the value of being on the stage irrespective of the number of lines. This is an attitude towards work which she felt her own generation would then fail to transmit to the younger actors working with them (85).

Birman remained a member of the First Studio even when it was reconstituted as the Second Moscow Art Theatre, until in fact it was forced to close in 1936. It was at the Second MAT that Birman developed her practice both as an actress and as a director. With Sofia Giatsintova and Lidia Deikun, she directed in 1929 *The Women (Baby)*, a combination of Carlo Goldoni's *The Curious Women* and *Women's Gossip*; Rose Whyman identifies this production as 'the first distinctive women's theatre project' (Whyman 2018: 347). Birman was also a member of the Trade Unions Theatre (1936–8) and, immediately afterwards, the Lenin Komsomol Theatre, where she continued acting and directing until 1958. Laurence Senelick highlights her directing 'for its intellectual clarity, especially in political plays' (Senelick 2007: 46). She received the title of People's Artist of the RSFSR in 1946.

Names of female set designers also stand out. One of these was Alexandra Exter (1882–1949). Exter is not exactly an unknown artist, given the visibility and fame which she achieved by working as set designer for three of Alexander Tairov's productions at the Kamerny Theatre.[7] Born in the city of Bialystok (modern Poland), Exter lived and worked in various places, most notably Kiev, Paris and Moscow. In Paris, she became acquainted with such luminaries like Pablo Picasso, Gertrude Stein, Marcel Duchamp and others. In 1914 she exhibited her works at the Salon des Indépendants in Paris, at the International Futurist Exhibition in Rome and in various other places in the USSR (Kovtun 2007: 149). On her return to Moscow she became associated with Cubo-Futurism. A contemporary essay documenting her work indicates the gender-biased environment in which she and other female artists operated. Exter's talent, her undoubted 'extraordinary experiments' and 'creative power', shone in spite of the prevalent 'female dilettantism' with which female artists were associated (Tugendhold 1922: 5 and 6). She exhibited a rigour in her work which, while typical of male artists, was seen as uncharacteristic of their female colleagues:

> As a woman she gives herself up to the all-absorbing charm of art with passionate enthusiasm. I remember how for whole days she worked during the bombardments of Kieff and Odessa – so frequent

in contemporary Russia, the shells hissing and bursting. And the artist shuddered for what was taking place in the streets troubled her. But life's emotions were overcome by voluntary and *very masculine self-discipline in work.*

[...]

And in all that she does one feels the dry brightness of a flame which never dies out but is ever regulated: some peculiar pathos of the mind. In that sense Alexandra Exter is near to some others among the best of Russia's feminine artists: these are few but distinguished by the circumstance that in their creation *there was more of masculine originality of force than of sentimentalism so proper to female artists.* (Tugendhold 1922: 6; emphasis added)

I draw attention to Exter's work to underline her contribution to the development of a theatre style where movement was a central component of the overall scenic design. She was attributed 'the ability to transcend the confines of the pictorial surface and to organize forms in their interaction with space' (in Bowlt 2014: 176), which is what experimental directors like Meyerhold, Tairov and Sergei Eisenstein were attempting in their work. Exter's theatre work is in fact closely linked with Tairov and the Kamerny Theatre in Moscow. The Kamerny opened in 1914 as director-driven but actor-centred theatre;[8] it also developed as 'a laboratory for new ways to design for the stage' (Kolesnikov in Van Norman Baer 1992: 87). This experimentation was possible because of the influx of painters which joined the theatre's ranks, often for specific productions. Tairov's objective was to obliterate naturalism from his productions by elevating in importance stage movement, generated by both performers and set, and combined with a 'symphonic melding of voices' (Senelick in Rzhevsky 2002: 273). His theatre was aptly titled 'synthetic theatre'. Artists became important allies of this theatre, considering that art had already made strong inroads in non-naturalistic expression which even Stanislavsky conceded (Stanislavski 2008a: 242–5). In Chapter 2 the argument was developed that an application of improvisation at the MAT's First Studio nourished a democratic levelling between actor, director and playwright. A similar levelling can be noted at the Kamerny, but with the addition of the artist. Hints of this democratic levelling can be found in the description which Mikhail Kolesnikov gives of *Famira Kifored*, a play by Innokenty Annensky which the Kamerny staged in 1916. The production was Exter's first commission for the Kamerny: 'it was *Famira Kifored* that the principle of volumetric stage design as it related to directing and performing was first realized on the Russian stage at its most consistent and complete level' (in Van Norman Baer 1992: 88).[9] Instead of framing the performance along the lines expected from a proscenium stage, where the frame is used to heighten the action, Exter's set operated on equal terms with the action emanating from the stage. It was perceived as an intrinsic element of the synthetic performance. The contribution of the performer in this democratic levelling, as best exemplified by the company's star actress Alisa Koonen, was that of finding her own creative individuality within the milieus generated by the director and stage designer.

Another of Exter's notable contribution was her pedagogical work between 1921 and 1922 at the Higher Art and Technical Studios (VKhUTEMAS) in Moscow. Set up in 1920 by a decree issued by Lenin, the studios aimed at the training of 'highly qualified master artists for industry' (quoted in Ioffe and White 2012: 230). It developed as a dynamic institution, with course programmes changing not only in reaction to industrial needs, but also as a consequence of changes in the leadership. Initially, a basic course for all students was introduced, followed by specialization in one of the various faculties, namely painting, sculpture, textiles, ceramics, architecture, woodwork and metalwork (Lodder 1983: 112–15). At VKhUTEMAS, Exter taught the application of colour in space. She was joined by Lyubov Popova, another artist whose work in constructivism allowed her to crossover to the world of theatre, most notably as the designer of Meyerhold's *The Magnanimous Cuckold* (1922) and *Earth Rampant* (1923).[10] Popova's intention with these two productions was to create a 'machine for acting', i.e. a platform which the actor could use to defy realistic representation and daily corporeal representations. Even Meyerhold agreed that much of the directorial invention that characterized *The Magnanimous Cuckold* had been stimulated by the set (Rudnitsky 1988: 92), thus creating another democratic levelling between the actor's work, the director's mise-en-scène and the designer's set:

> Popova constructed with Meyerhold an appropriate space for the new actor, who she had seen developing at his laboratory. Biomechanics transformed the actor into the space of performance, while the training in the relationship between the actors, and between each actor and the space, developed the performers' spatial and kinetic thought. The scenic construction [of *The Magnanimous Cuckold*] therefore became both an instrument-object for the actor as well as the spatial projection of his thoughts and emotions. It was analogous to the actor, and a 'machine' that was his 'double'. (Cruciani 1998: 149)

Within this milieu, it is unsurprising to see that the playwright's text lost the ground that it conventionally held within the Russian theatre tradition

Figure 12 A scene from *The Magnanimous Cuckold*, directed by Vsevolod Meyerhold, set by Lyubov Popova, 1922. The set is often described as a 'machine' or 'platform' for acting. Courtesy Laurence Senelick Collection.

(Chapter 1). It is perhaps here, in the collaboration between Meyerhold, Popova and the constructivists, that the attack on the hegemony of the text was strongest.

The case of Asja Lācis

The obscure place which Asja Lācis has within the broader landscape of modern theatre is certainly underserving. Her main written output is *Revolutionär im Beruf: Berichte über proletarisches Theater, über Meyerhold, Brecht, Benjamin und Piscator* (1971; *A Revolutionary by Profession: Reports on Proletarian Theatre, on Meyerhold, Brecht, Benjamin and Piscator*).[11] A 1975 review of this book described Lācis as a practitioner who was 'unjustly forgotten' and one who was cast aside by both the Left and the Right (Parmalee 1975: 163). At the turn of the twenty-first century this position remained largely unresolved. She is discussed in some secondary sources, while two of her essays are reproduced in English translation and can be found on the online portal of the journal *South as a State of Mind*.[12] In the introduction to this collection, Andris Brinkmanis underlined Lācis's oblivious state in current scholarship:

Lācis's name was rarely encountered in official historiographies of twentieth-century European political theatre. [...] The legacy of this revolutionary female director [...] is still largely unexplored and unfamiliar, except to a small community of scholars and academics. [...] Her work remains underrated and unknown. (Lācis, Benjamin and Brinkmanis 2017)

There are political but also historiographical reasons for this obscurity. As I will discuss below, her imprisonment for ten years in a Siberian prison 'stained' her name and limited the natural progression and transmission of her practice. Very much like Meyerhold, she needed a rehabilitation. Moreover, her amorous relationship with Walter Benjamin overshadowed the substantial impact which she had on his writing and development.[13] The two, for example, co-wrote together the essay 'Naples', but then again only Benjamin's name appeared in print when the essay was republished in 1955. The Lācis myth constructed as a result of such historiographical tampering was that of 'the femme fatale [who was] responsible for seducing him [Benjamin] with Marxist materialism away from his Jewish heritage and faithful wife' (Ingram 2002: 159).[14] However, Lācis was very much embroiled in the scene and in many ways reflected it, becoming a micro embodiment of the macro context at large. Through her theatre work with children she also did enough to forerun theatre developments emerging in the mid-to-late twentieth century, such as applied performance and therapeutic uses of theatre.

Far more than mere entertainment, theatre processes with children were seen by Lācis as a therapeutic tool to combat the calamitous effects which war, poverty and aversion had on children. Theatre was seen as a way of developing their creative potential. These contributions to a children's theatre are certainly important, but Lācis's relevance does not stop there. She, for instance, personified many of the characteristics that came to define modernism. In a first instance, Lācis showed a penchant for contact-building that was so representative of the times and partook in the movement of ideas generated by such networking.[15] She was the one who introduced Benjamin to both Brecht and Meyerhold (Eaton 1985: 18).[16] Lācis was also the in-between person between Benjamin, Brecht and actress Margarete Steffin when in 1935 Benjamin needed to review some of Brecht's work (Benjamin 1994: 395). Lācis, Benjamin wrote, was also instrumental for him to receive the work of the writer F. Panferov, which he was also to review (345). These are only a few examples of what Latvian writer Arvīds Grigulis described as her 'ability to strike up an acquaintance with exceptional people. Whether in Berlin, Paris, or Riga, Lācis was always able to get to know those whose work best expressed the essence of the cultural life of their times' (in Ingram 2002: 173–4).

As a result of her networking Lācis became a link between the experimental theatre in Russia and the theatre of the Weimar Republic. In modernism, ideas, techniques, staging examples and values migrated because of the acquaintances between people or, in other words, depending on who knew whom. Eaton captures the essence of this movement as follows:

> The Kamerny Theatre, Vakhtangov Theatre, Blue Blouse, and the Meyerhold troupe exemplify the relatively free passage of dramatic art from Russia to the West. Among the important individual transmitters were Anna Lācis, Bernhard Reich, Anatoly Lunacharsky, Sergei Tretiakov, and Sergei Eisenstein. German artists and intellectuals (such as Brecht, Piscator, Ernst Toller, Johannes B. Recher, Hugo Huppert, and Walter Benjamin) travelled to the Soviet Union to experience for themselves the tenor of art and life in what was heralded as a new and more humane society. Brecht made four trips. (Eaton 1985: 14–15)

Like many of her contemporaries, and as a result of the changing world in which she lived, Lācis moved between different contexts and experienced different realities. She was born in 1891 in the Latvian town of Līgatne but then gravitated away from the fringes towards bigger metropolitan centres to receive a formal education. As a result of this move she immersed herself, so to speak, in the thick of things, namely the artistic and theatrical life of St Petersburg. In 1912, she joined the renowned Psychoneurological Institute in St Petersburg, founded and led by the pioneer psychologist V. M. Bekhterev. The scholars that taught there were expelled from other universities, especially because of their Marxist affiliations. The backgrounds of the students were also diverse, and they included anarchists, nationalists and Marxists. At this institute Lācis developed a love for Dostoevsky, with material from his novels often serving as the basis for discussions. German philosopher Friedrich Nietzsche was another area of study. She valued his philosophy as an alternative and criticism of religion (Lācis 1971: 11).

Lācis's observation of St Petersburg's theatre proved a formative ground for her future artistic work. It became an informal transmission channel, one that contrasted with more formal training spaces like the Bekhterev's institute itself and the studio of Fyodor Komissarzhevsky, which she would eventually join (see below). I use the term 'informal training' to postulate a space which does not make technical transmission its defining principle, but through which the transmission of technique still occurs because of the prior formation and bias of the receiver. To Lācis, watching performances became a training ground because of her cultural bias as an educated woman who was open to the arts. She was what today we might refer to as an 'informed spectator', that is the spectator who does not view performances passively, but who has the critical ability to distil the creative mechanics behind a production. Of the Moscow Art Theatre productions, for example, she valued, like others, the actors' ensemble playing. The Imperial Theatres, in contrast, appeared stagnant, and 'drowning in an atmosphere of bureaucracy and academism' (Lācis 1971: 12). The yardstick she adopted in her criticism was that of Meyerhold, whom she regarded as a model and described as an 'indefatigable experimenter' (Lācis, Benjamin and Brinkmanis 2017). She credited him with infusing creative energy in the Theatres' academicism. In her memories Lācis also described Meyerhold's production of Fyodor Sologub's *Die Geiseln des Lebens*. This seems a rather obscure reference, given the difficulty I had to trace this production in other sources about Meyerhold. In any case, the unconventional setting for this production stood out. The proscenium was covered in a blue fabric, and several doors were put on the stage, a precursor perhaps of the famous set of *The Government Inspector*. Through these doors characters entered, left, appeared and disappeared, thus serving as 'a symbol for the absurd muddle of life' (Lācis 1971: 12). A production of Arthur Wing Pinero's *Mid-Channel* is also described as an avant-garde achievement. The set, constructed by Alexander Golovin, was built of different cubes. The play caused a scandal, even if Edward Braun in his account placed *Mid-Channel* among a group of safe productions devoid of Meyerhold's experimental signature (Braun 1998: 139).

Lācis's informal training through the observation of performance worked in conjunction with her formal attendance at the theatre studio of Fyodor Komissarzhevsky (1916–17). The studio, Jonathan Pitches and Claire Warden argue, was Komissarzhevsky's way of honouring the memory of his sister Vera. It encouraged students to situate theatre within broader cultural contexts and to develop the ability of articulating reasoned arguments (Pitches 2019: 95). Lācis commented on the work from a first-hand perspective. She attended the studio at night, after teaching at a Latvian refugee school in Moscow during the day.[17] She described the three-pronged training programme adopted at the studio. A substantial number of theoretical classes were given. Subjects covered in these classes included the history of medieval theatre, the theory of literature, and that of stagecraft. Practical training was led by Komissarzhevsky and the actor Pevzov. Lācis noted that this training used improvisations on pre-existing texts to develop imagination. 'Komissarzhevsky', Lācis wrote, 'wanted a thinking actor' (Lācis 1971: 18). The studio was also connected to his theatre, where students performed bit-parts and supernumeraries in mass scenes. The October Revolution left an undeniable impact on this studio, very much along the same lines of the First Studio (see Chapter 3). Clusters were formed among the students depending on their political allegiance. An 'immediate change of the repertoire and the curriculum was demanded' (Lācis, Benjamin and Brinkmanis 2017), presumably with the students wanting to produce more politically oriented work. Similar to Smyshlaev, Lācis's support of the revolution was immediate and unequivocal: 'I wanted to be a good soldier of the revolution and to change my life in line with it' (Lācis, Benjamin and Brinkmanis 2017). It was as a committed political player, therefore, that in 1918 she moved to Orel, a relatively small town, ostensibly as a director of the municipal theatre, but soon shifting a lot of her creative energies to developing a theatre for and with children.

With her Lācis took a multi-layered and mixed baggage. One layer comprised the formal training with Bekhterev and Komissarzhevsky, and their heightening of process, theoretical underpinning, discussion and an open-minded attitude towards criticism. Her experiences as a spectator of professional theatre, on the other hand, made her realize the importance of artistic standards in performance-oriented work. She valued the ensemble playing of the MAT and, through Meyerhold, the need to defy tradition through experimentation. In her writings Lācis also referred to theories about theatre production that were developing at the time, showing her exposure to the cultural debates that soared after the revolution. Like others, she argued that theatre is a synthesis of all arts and a form of collective creativity. She also appraised amateurism as a vehicle for theatre renewal. The revolution played a further role in her formation, providing her theatre with a political underpinning that made it relevant to the contemporary world. In other words, it was through theatre that she sought to play a public life and contribute to the transformative energy of the revolution. She paid allegiance to theatre as a school, which squarely placed her within the Russian tradition where theatre was seen as a tool for moral improvement.

It was this holistic baggage – formed by studio processes, theoretical verification, openness to experimentation and political relevance – that informed Lācis's work with children in Orel. She took on very difficult cases, like war orphans living in governmental institutions and the homeless gangs roaming the streets. The former were relatively well taken care of, but they carried with them the most defeated of looks: 'Nothing interested them. Children without a childhood' (Lācis, Benjamin and Brinkmanis 2017). The gangs living on the streets were in an even worse state, clearly at the beginning of a life of crime. On seeing the children, she reacted as follows:

You couldn't remain indifferent when confronted with all of this. I felt I had to do something, and I knew that children's songs and nursery rhymes would not be enough here. In order to get them to break out of their lethargy, a task was needed which would completely take hold of them and set their traumatized abilities free. I knew how great the power of making theatre was and what it might do for these children. (Lācis, Benjamin and Brinkmanis 2017)

Had Lācis moved to Orel in the late 1920s, she would have most certainly been asked to work on a more ideologically driven programme, perhaps presenting children with pre-planned material already vetted by the authorities. This material would have extolled the successes of the Soviet regime, types of performances which agitprop brigades specialized in.[18] The more open, at least for the arts, first years after the revolution, when concepts of proletarian culture were at their most fluid, and when artistic paths were not yet restricted to canonized models, allowed Lācis to carry out process-based work with the children. Instead of the transmission of ideology she focused on the transmission of what today we might refer to as 'life-skills' or what James McFarland describes, when discussing her work, as a formative experience underscored by 'spontaneity and reactivity, [as ways] to emancipate the children's abilities' (McFarland 2012: 300).

In doing so Lācis's work drew close to a variety of sources. She referred to Platon Kerzhentsev's theories on collective creativity as another important model. Lācis's approach paralleled Kerzhentsev's, whose own theories critiqued the political theatre underscored by tendentious and ideological content (Chapter 4): 'ideology was not forced upon them [the children], nor was it drilled into them' (Lācis, Benjamin and Brinkmanis 2017). Her work also chimed with the tradition of progressive education that was developing from the late nineteenth century onwards. Representatives of this progressive education include John Dewey and Maria Montessori, who argued for an experiential rather than fact-based approach to education. The aim of this education was, and still is, to develop fully rounded human individuals who can think critically, who are proactive and who can work in a group. I could find no mention of these theories and names in Lācis's writings, but this is not a lacuna. Rather, it evidences that modernism and turn-of-the-twentieth-century culture can be construed as a positive tension between localized and culturally specific concerns and more overarching and cross-cultural issues that recurred between and across fields and disciplines. In line with progressive education, Lācis's theatre with children offered substantial potential for transformation, detaching its participants from the streets and occupying their time with creative work. 'My goal', Lācis wrote, '[was] their aesthetic education, the development of their aesthetic and moral capabilities' (Lācis, Benjamin and Brinkmanis 2017).

Kerzhentsev's critiqued bourgeois theatre for its drive for product over process, glittery spectacle and dominance of the director (Keržencev 1979: 5–25). This criticism was realigned by Lācis. Her own criticism of bourgeois education became a starting point for her theatre practice. This was a vestige of her years at Bekhterev's institute, which is where she expressed an early criticism of the bourgeoisie as a strata 'where words and actions do not align' (Lācis 1971: 11). She argued that performance and the appearance in front of an audience become the objective 'when children play theatre according to bourgeois rules'. In such a context, the educator equates with the director-dictator as the agent of the mise-en-scène. Moreover, with an educator who 'drills the children [...] the joy in playfull producing is lost' (Lācis, Benjamin and Brinkmanis 2017). Benjamin, who wrote a well-known theoretical programme for Lācis's theatre, argued very much along the same lines. For him bourgeois education was unsystematic, open as it was to the latest trends of psychology which find a place in the curriculum out of fashion rather than need. It lacked a taught-out framework that was to be implemented over a prolonged period of time. Like its professional model, children's theatre within the context of bourgeois culture was read as product- and performance-oriented:

> In the view of the bourgeoisie, nothing presents a greater danger to children than the theatre. [...] What we find expressed is the fear that the theatre will unleash in children the most powerful energies of the future. And this fear causes bourgeois education theory to anathematize the theatre. [...] Fully rounded performances that people torment children to produce can never compete in authenticity with improvisation. (Lācis, Benjamin and Brinkmanis 2017)

It does not mean that performance did not feature in Benjamin's framework and Lācis's activity, but that it was treated like a kind of barometer that indicates where the children are within their formative process.

In practical terms, Lācis's work with children revolved around classes in observation and improvisation. Her emphasis on the observation of visuals, colours and sounds comes as no surprise given what was her own developed sense of reactivity to life and scrutiny of its details. Her memoirs, for example, recall the youthful memories of icy landscapes, busy train stations and 'the sound of the siren and the ringing of the horsecar' (Lācis 1971: 9). These recollections were not taken in, in an unalloyed state, but rather processed through her artistic imagination. Observations of St Petersburg, for instance, stirred her imagination. They became another informal training ground and formation channel:

> In retrospective, I see that the time in Petersburg stimulated me in a way that influenced my life. I remember the effect the city had on me. When I passed by the Pushkin memorial, with its expressive dynamic, stood beneath the rearing horses next to the Neva, and walked over the Fontanka through the nebulous white blue nights, which made even the dead feel restless, there they flashed by: the heroes of Pushkin, Lermontov, Gogol, and Dostoevsky – struggling with the weariness of the world, disappearing in the white fog, searching for a way out. I can still see the stone casemates of the Shlisselburg fortress in front of me. (Lācis 1971: 14)

Observation classes were often carried out outdoors. Children observed objects and their relations. They also paid attention to the people around them and how these reacted to the objects. The observations were not treated as an end in themselves, but as a means to study how elements in everyday life connect with one another, a crucial transferable skill to performance. An emphasis was made on how these connections change depending on the variables at hand. For instance, Lācis exposed students to how colour is contingent to distance and the time of the day. She also made students aware of the differences in the sounds throughout the day and that silence is not necessarily the opposite of sound. These sessions were supported by drawing and music sessions (Lācis, Benjamin and Brinkmanis 2017). Other classes included diction, rhythm, gymnastics and the creation of props.

From Stanislavsky to Smyshlaev, amateur theatre and Meyerhold, improvisation resurfaces here again as a practical tool to engender a collective attitude, develop initiative, harness theatrical skills and generate performance material. Lācis selected a play for children written by Meyerhold, titled *Alinur*, which was itself based on a fairy tale by Oscar Wilde. Out of the improvisations carried out on this play a public performance took shape. The work proceeded as follows. She gave the children a scene from the play on which to improvise. In the scenario, robbers were sitting in a forest around a fire, talking and boasting about their deeds. Lācis hints that the children returned regularly to this scene, in the process of fine-tuning the theatrical material. This particular scene was important for the street children to join the group. They interpreted the scene in a realistic manner, drawing from their own experiences. Lācis described what the improvisations meant to the group:

The improvised play meant luck and adventure to the children. They understood a great deal, and their interest was aroused. They worked seriously: cut things out, glued, danced, and sang. Texts were learned. And gradually the figure of the evil Tartar boy 'Alinur,' who insulted his mother and terrorized other children, took shape. When the different sections of the work moved toward a synthesis, we began to discuss the public performance. Then a demand for collective action arose – moral-political education in a socialist sense – and they wanted to present the play to the other children of the city. The public performance became a festival. The children of our studio went to the city's open-air theater in a kind of Mardi Gras parade. They carried animals, masks, theatre props, and parts of decorations through the streets, and sang as well. Big and little spectators joined in. (Lācis, Benjamin and Brinkmanis 2017)

Several implications emerge from this anecdote. First, it shows the potential which improvisation has to obliterate differences between practitioners. Lācis recounts that the orphans were terrified of the street children when these first joined the group. However, the two groups integrated when they worked together. Second, a balanced teacher–student relationship was formed. Lācis's position as an educator did not simply vanish. She was important for the transmission of the technical skills (e.g. observation) and was also the one to suggest the themes for improvisation and to make the choice of the Alinur story. However, the public performance developed from the material which the students suggested and developed: 'The children believed that they had done everything themselves – and they did it through play' (Lācis, Benjamin and Brinkmanis 2017). Even the decision to perform for the other children of the city was taken by the children. Third, collective work was not forced on the children as an ideology but rather presented through practical means, in turn transforming the sessions into an experiential form of education. Lācis again saw this kind of work as harking back to the theories on collective practice developed by Kerzhentsev (she also mentioned Meyerhold in this context). Her own unique contribution was in detaching collective practices from their working-class origins and realigning them in a different, educational environment. In the end, improvisations at Orel were meant 'to set free the children's hidden powers' (Lācis, Benjamin and Brinkmanis 2017). As a consequence, the play performed 'originated as children performing for children', another spin-off of Kerzhentsev's theatre of the workers.

Lācis's theatre work did not end in Orel. Between 1920 and 1922 she was affiliated to the People's University in Riga, who wanted her to open and lead a theatre studio. This studio had a clear outreach dimension. Lācis invited workers to come and take part in improvisations organized around revolutionary themes.[19] Her penchant towards mixing elements together was also clear here, especially when 'linking socially explicit characteristic with a grotesque acting style' (Lācis 1971: 32). The actors only wore their work overalls because they had no costumes, while the stage was constructivist in form. The studio also contributed to outdoor mass performances, which at the time were reaching the height of their popularity in Moscow. With these performances, Lācis confirms the transmission of performance practices outside the capital. One such production, Leon Paegle's *Face the Centuries*, showed her ability to use tactical ploys to elude the censorship and vigilant eye of the police. I use tactical ploy in the sense suggested by the everyday-life theorist Michel de Certeau, who argued in favour of subliminal, silent and often invisible actions that are carried out to elude the controlling hand of a power-based entity (de Certeau et al. 1980: 5–10). The play depicted the struggle between oppressors and oppressed in Egypt, Greece and the Middle Ages, up to the more recent revolutions. The play passed the censorship only because it was presented as a historical piece. The censor cut the singing of the Internationale from the concluding scene, which Lācis substituted with a parade of the actors around the city. Sections of the city applauded while others derided them. The performance ended when a crowd of workers met the actors in a public park and themselves sang the Internationale (Lācis 1971: 33–4). Lācis was again tactical in her approach to theatre making when, following an invitation by Leon Paegle, she returned to Riga in 1925 to lead a political theatre group at the club of the left-oriented unions. The police were vigilant again, and she 'had to be really inventive with the choice of the repertoire in order to keep the police away' (Lācis 1971: 52). To divert the attention of the police, the group used charades and riddles as a way of covering the political content of their work.

These examples notwithstanding, it was with children that Lācis worked most consistently. She developed other theatres for children both in Riga and Moscow. Ultimately, this work, with its unclear ideological allegiance, defined her fate as a political outcast. Like so many of her generation, Lācis was a daughter of the revolution whose work reached maturity in the 1920s, only to be then arrested and politically repressed in the late 1930s. In her article 'New Tendencies in Theatre', she just falls short from expressing her support of do-it-yourself, *samodeiatel'nost'* theatre (see Chapter 4):

> We may work on the construction of proletarian theater at the theater workshops, encouraging (inviting) people of the working classes to join in and help. What should such theater workshops look like? These workshops must unite people who share common interests. The main value should be assigned to the collective action in order to establish a

solid bond, which would then serve the common cause: to inspire the need for the creative self-expression in the pupils, to locate their creative instincts, and to allow their personalities to blossom. This work must be conducted in freely accessible workshops, and the masses should be encouraged to participate, even if only as observers and critics. (Lācis, Benjamin and Brinkmanis 2017)

Like other adherents of *samodeiatel'nost'*, these statements, so liberating and positive-sounding to any democratic ears, conflicted with the more regulatory 1930s. If the history of amateur theatre is read as the government's drive to control and subjugate *samodeiatel'nost'*, then Lācis's theatre processes with children had little chance to survive within such a context. These processes can, however, be treated as an early instance of Applied Theatre and of the use of theatre practices outside conventional theatre spaces in order to improve the life of its participants.

Conclusion

It is time to draw some concluding remarks. What does modern theatre in Russia tell us about tradition building? Can a number of axioms be identified from this particular scene that speak about transmission processes as they pertain to theatre? As I conclude this book, I would like to attempt such a summation. My attempt equates to a series of pointers rather than a tight-fitting definition, since using a series of strict formulas to measure a dynamic phenomenon like modern theatre will always end up being a limiting affair. I also offer some organizational guidelines to consider when planning transmission workshops. These guidelines are in line with the 'Suggestions for practice' sections of the book. They are formulated directly from my own experience of running transmission workshops and further supported by many of the modern instances of practice discussed in this book. However, they are again far from a complete methodology. Any reader and trainer is, of course, very welcome to consider these and others guidelines.

Axioms about modern theatre in Russia

1. **Theatre traditions can be construed as a positive tension between recurrence and difference.** They exhibit both localized and culturally specific factors and more overarching and cross-cultural issues that recur

between and across practices. The latter also help to connect theatre and performance to other fields and disciplines.
2. **A transmission line from the nineteenth to the twentieth century contributed to the transformation and survival of the Russian theatre tradition.** While the most radical avant-garde practitioners and theoreticians called for a fundamental break with the past, modernists were more inclined to learn from the past and to adopt practices from previous theatre traditions which benefitted their work. Theatre traditions, including the Russian manifestation, thus produce transmission content.
3. **Transmission activity is never simply about the transference and dissemination of theatre and acting techniques.** Other issues, including economic, political, artistic and social considerations, need to be factored in not only when unpicking transmission activity as a scholarly endeavour, but also whenever practical transmission is attempted.
4. **Transmission is a multifarious activity.** Its contents are diverse and include acting techniques, directing approaches, staging ideas and work attitudes. Transmission belts are also numerous. The channels through which transmission content moves can be formal (studios, schools, workshops, printed acting manuals, published mises-en-scène) or informal (watching performance, observing everyday life, being onstage with seasoned actors). Transmission belts and channels do not negate each other as practice often shows their interchangeable use. Improvisation repeatedly resurfaces in Russian modernism as a transmission tool to engender a collective attitude, harness acting skills and generate performance material.
5. **Transmission processes blur boundaries between seemingly steadfast categories.** Within transmission processes, the role of the transmitter and the receiver may become interchangeable, especially within environments where the former is engaged in a learning experience as much as the receiver or when transmission is treated as knowledge exchange. The receiver impacts actively on the transmission activity through the transmission bias that he brings into the proceedings. Bias serves as a potent processing filter.
6. **Transmission gives rise to hybrid phenomena**. It necessarily implies the processing of a source technique. A distrust of reproduction, coupled to a process of selection and natural openness to a variety of sources, allows different practices to engage creatively with one another. This gives rise to unexpected combinations of techniques and ideas.

7. **Transmission joins other characteristics to become a hallmark of modernism.** Modern theatre revelled in experimentation and a tug of war between realistic and theatrical reconstructions. It generated the rise of the figure of the director and elevated the status of theatre as a distinct art form. Transmission joins these markers to become an important reference point for a number of practitioners who, at the turn of the twentieth century, started forging cross-cultural connections.

Organizational principles when running transmission workshops[20]

- Consider the **conditions** of transmission, starting from the duration of the workshop. What are the immediate implications arising from the workshop duration?
- Identify with clarity the technical skills (i.e. the transmission **content**) that you want to transmit. Make sure this content is articulated precisely both for yourself as the transmitter and for the participants.
- Which exercises or transmission **channels** are best suited for the transmission of the content?
- What does the identification of technical skills say about your **bias** as a transmitter? Is the bias in any way 'indulgent', or does it support the over-arching learning objectives?
- Who are the participants (**receivers**)? How familiar are they with the workshop environment? Did they have other workshop experiences? Is the transmission of different perspectives, from different teachers, a characteristic of their training?
- To what extent do you need to be aware of the participants' **backgrounds** (political, cultural, religious, ethical, health, etc.)? How do you become aware of these, while at the same time respecting people's privacy?
- What is the participants' **motivation** to join the workshop? Was it a voluntary decision? Are they responding to an open call for participation?
- Have participants worked together before? How well do they know each other? What kinds of **group** projects did they work on before?
- Will participants be given the opportunity to reflect on how the work fits within their **broader training** curve?
- How **adaptable** is the transmitted content to other training and performance scenarios?
- Will participants be encouraged to **document** the process? Which are the possible means of documentation?

- Consider creating formal channels for the participants to offer **feedback** about the work. Which means can be used to gather such feedback?
- What is the **direction** of the transmission? Is it only one way, from transmitter to receiver? How is the transmission helping you to reflect on your teaching practice? Identify these points with clarity.

Notes

Chapter 1

1 See also Leach's description of modernism as being 'usually – and correctly – associated with startling novelty, with art which deliberately shocks or which deliberately – even joyfully – breaks conventions. It is often designed to be partial, contentious, and challenging' (Leach 2004: 1).
2 Selections of Stanislavsky's texts or entries on him are to be found in representative collections about modern theatre such as Bentley (1968), Milling and Graham (2001) and Leach (2004).
3 On the confrontational tone of the avant-garde manifestos, see Innes (1998: 2) and Kleberg (1993: 4 and 23).
4 While conventional scholarship has placed Bogdanov in opposition to pre-revolutionary art, more recent studies tend to give a more balanced view. See, for example, Sochor (1988: 182) and Mally (1990: 130–1).
5 Benedetti even goes as far as (incorrectly) saying that Stanislavsky was born on the same day that Shchepkin died (Benedetti 1989: 11).
6 For Stanislavsky's commentary on Shchepkin, with particular reference to his teaching methods, see Stanislavski (2008a: 56–9). See also Senelick (1984: 249–50).
7 Meyerhold's production of *The Government Inspector* is well known and documented, but it is not the only example of modern practitioners staging this classic text. For example, see Komissarzhevsky (1926) production in England, which a local critic described as 'an admirable entertainment […] [rich in] logic and skill with which this amazing producer has brought off this *tour de force*' (in Borovsky 2001: 368). Another key production was Stanislavsky's (1921), with Mikhail Chekhov playing the lead role of Khlestakov. Gogol's name also appeared regularly in the repertoire lists suggested at the time by, for example, Kerzhentsev (1918b: 6). Meyerhold, on his part, had already included Gogol in his programme of study of the Borodin Study, under the title of 'Styles of Theatrical Presentation (and the peculiarities of theatres which develop from the peculiarities of playwrights)' (in Leach 1989: 51).
8 On an in-depth study of Ostrovsky's continuity into the early Soviet era, see Gunn (2012).
9 The major sources in English that tackle Bolshevik mass spectacles and festivals are von Geldern (1993) and Malte (2013).
10 On the influence, albeit in 'a modernised form', of Ivanov's theories on post-revolutionary theatre, see also Rudnitsky (1988: 9 and 89).

11 This incident repeated itself in Stanislavsky's (1902) production of Tolstoy's *The Power of Darkness*. During the rehearsals a peasant woman included in the cast failed to differentiate between the real life with which she was familiar and its stage reproduction. Her temperamental outbursts 'would throw aside Tolstoi's lines and replace them with her own, which included such foul language it would never pass the censor' (Stanislavski 2008a: 227). In the end, Stanislavsky did not use her in the production, but the experience did throw light on the realism-naturalism debate in which the theatre was engulfed.
12 *The Forest* remained in the repertoire for fourteen years, during which the number of episodes was on occasion whittled down (Malcovati 1977: 201).
13 Sayler makes a similar comment in relation to The Bat, a 'super-cabaret' theatre run by the clown N. F. Baliev. According to him, '[i]t is difficult, almost impossible to conceive of him [Baliev] in a serious part, until you remember that every Russian player takes his work, whether it be in comedy or tragedy, with the utmost seriousness. Balieff is most serious as artist when he is most ludicrous as entertainer' (Sayler 1920: 196).
14 Skinner especially makes the point on the 'perceived avant-garde/socialist binary' which, she argues, 'conceals a more fluid relationship between these two cultural moments' (Skinner 2016: 259).
15 One exception is my own co-edited volume with Jonathan Pitches on the transmission of Stanislavsky's System across the world (Pitches and Aquilina 2017).
16 The city was named Petrograd in 1914 and Leningrad in 1924.
17 This exercise is an adaptation of the reconstruction activity found in Pitches 2003: 149.

Chapter 2

1 That Stanislavsky's influence reached much further than the American theatre scene is the central idea of *Stanislavsky in the World: The System and Its Transformation across Continents* (Pitches and Aquilina 2017). This volume presents case studies of Stanislavskian transmission sourced from Europe, Asia, Australasia, Africa and Latin America.
2 The tug of war between the French and Russian theatre traditions is a point that I reappraise in Pitches and Aquilina (2017: 27–8).
3 This collection of post-revolutionary speeches is very rich in that it tackles a diverse range of topics and areas, including aesthetics, the pull of theatre on its audiences, the collective nature of theatre production, studio culture and the educational role of performance. Benedetti uses these articles to argue how Stanislavsky's role at the Moscow Art Theatre was, at the time, a peripheral one (Benedetti 1999: 246–8). I myself have previously used these texts to argue a different point, that Stanislavsky might not have been as detached from revolutionary developments as conventionally thought (Aquilina

2012a). These post-revolutionary texts are: 'Appeal project to the Moscow Actors' Union' (which includes 'About Actors' Charity', 'About public aesthetic education' and 'About organizing the Studio of the Actors' Union') (1917), 'About Theatre Pantheon' (1918), 'Appeal to Participants of the Meeting of Workers of Theatre Arts' (1919) and 'Theatre for the Starving' (1922).

4   See the discussion below on Stanislavsky's internationalism and compare with that of Meyerhold in Chapter 5.
5   During this tour Barnay's repertoire included *Hamlet, Othello, King Lear, Richard III, Kean* and *Uriel Acosta* (Vinogradskaia Vol. 1 2003: 190).
6   Detailed descriptions of the production can be found in Stanislavski (2008a: 128–30) and Benedetti (1999: 47–50).
7   I make reference to this periodization because the First Studio was especially defined by the respective talents and character of its directors. In fact, what had begun as a research space under Sulerzhitsky became more of a production house under Yevgeny Vakhtangov and a personal vehicle for parts under Mikhail Chekhov.
8   This hierarchy could, of course, be extended to include other contributors of the production process, like the designer and the musical composer. Indeed, designers like Viktor Simov and musical composers like Ilya Satz contributed in no small measure to Stanislavsky's work as well as the MAT's success. However, I will focus here on the triumvirate of the actor, director and playwright because of their recurrent presence in Stanislavsky's work.
9   He also quotes Inna Solovieva, who in her leading scholarship on Nemirovich-Danchenko underlines the two founders' sense that 'theater was somehow embarrassing and questionable for both; it needed to be justified' (Rzhevsky 2016: 30).
10 This newspaper report carries no signature, though Vinogradskaia believes that in all probability it was written by Nikolai Efros, a respected critic of the MAT, but based on Stanislavsky's own words (Vinogradskaia Vol. 2 2003: 381).
11 These scenarios are reproduced in the Suggestions for Practice of this chapter.
12 Gorky writes: 'With these characters [that are suggested in the letter] you already have not only the material but also the inevitability of drama. Put these characters against each other and they will immediately begin to act, i.e. live. […] If there are firmly defined characters then their collisions are inevitable' (Gorkii 1955: 269).
13 Meyerhold's negative assessment is to be set against his own thinly veiled wish to work with Ignatov, who however had already expressed interest in collaborating with Stanislavsky's First Studio.
14 See Pitches and Aquilina (2017: 64, 75, 81, 91, 96, 129, 201, 248, 348) for some examples.
15 On the practice of improvisation in Active Analysis, see Merlin's exposition in White (2014: 325–40).

16 I am here somehow conflating together Stanislavsky's final searches of the Method of Physical Action and Active Analysis. For a more nuanced reading, see Carnicke (2009: 192) and Merlin (2003: 33).
17 One clear similarity between the two accounts relates to Stanislavsky's treatment of emotional work. When Toporkov, while rehearsing *Dead Souls* (1933), was about to describe how his character Chichikov feels in a particular moment of the play, Stanislavsky quickly stopped him: 'Don't think of that, think of how he acts' (Toporkov 1979: 85). Compare to the rehearsal of *Artists and Admirers* when Stanislavsky remarked: '*Do not speak and think about feelings and moods. Search for action*' (Vinogradskaia 2000: 214; emphasis in the original).
18 Tarasova also played the role of Negina.
19 Contrast to Meyerhold's approach found in the rehearsal notes of *The Government Inspector*, where the actors are asking questions for him to answer (Braun 1969: 229–30).
20 Elsewhere, I use theories developed by Michel de Certeau to discuss how these images carried significant political implications, in that they shielded elements of Stanislavsky's practice from political appropriation (Aquilina 2013).
21 Note that the applicable nature of the acting technique discerned here is emphasized through the use of the words 'always' and 'forever'. Compare to another instance when the use of the actor's own life and behaviour 'applies to every role' (Vinogradskaia 2000: 215).
22 Zon described such accessories as 'little plusses' to an actor's characterization, which Stanislavsky removed (Vinogradskaia 2000: 249).
23 Zon writes: 'The mises-en-scène cannot be decided upon in a rehearsal room. Till then everything was done in relation to that environment, to that room in which the rehearsals were held. And since Stanislavsky demanded that everything has to be worked out as it is right now on the stage, with those exact decorations, the mises-en-scène are kind of found again' (Vinogradskaia 2000: 247).
24 Symptomatic of this idealization is Vilar's description of Stanislavsky as a very ethical man where '[t]hroughout his long career at the head of his theatre he has not committed a single imbecile act, let alone a discourtesy with regard to a fellow-actor. No, Stanislavsky does not yell at people, he does not insult anyone, he does not roll on the floor and break porcelain vases' (in Stanislavski 1963: 206). See also Antoine's description of Stanislavsky's 'triumphs' (176–7).
25 The only production on this tour without a straightforward Russian content was *An Enemy of the People*.
26 For a reference of Stanislavsky's impact on Kvapil, especially when the latter staged *Three Sisters* in 1907, see Autant-Mathieu in White (2014: 158–9).
27 Recurrence and difference is a framework that I also call on in my analysis of Meyerhold and his appropriation of past theatre traditions. See Chapter 5.

28　The Second Studio was particularly Russian as an institution, because it wanted to draw from but also contribute to its immediate revolutionary surroundings. For example, it performed for the workers in local factories. These performances served the actors not only to hone their skills, but also contributed to 'Lunacharsky's call for active participation in the education of the masses' (Gauss 1999: 65).

29　This text is reproduced here: https://www.theguardian.com/news/1917/jul/07/mainsection.fromthearchive (Accessed on 23 June 2018).

30　See also Morgan (1961: 28): 'Undoubtedly, he [Granville Barker] and the great Russian producer, faced with similar dramatic material, had been moving in rather similar directions before direct influence of one on the other was possible.'

Chapter 3

1　For short references about Smyshlaev, see Benedetti (1999: 251–2); Senelick (2007: 361); Mally (1990: 216–17).

2　I am using 'romantic' in a conversational sense here, with no connection to Romanticism.

3　The depiction of the sensitive type is fuelled with a good old-fashioned love triangle, to which Smyshlaev makes reference a number of times (Anrusenko 2004: 56–8).

4　The following is another example of his romantic tone: 'Faith is the basis of life's actions. If I do not believe in success, I will not act. Belief makes me act. Desire wakes up faith, faith feeds the passion, and invites one to move. Faith is the strongest lever in our inner life. Faith plays a great role in Art: almost miraculously faith becomes suffering when you fail, and suffering becomes faith again if you have even a little chance to satisfy the will' (Anrusenko 2004: 55).

5　A discussion about the organic laws of nature is a central discussion in Stanislavsky studies. For representative material see Pitches (2006) and Whyman (2008: 1–37).

6　On the eve of the Duma election of September 1917, Smyshlaev asserted: 'I heartily wish them good luck. Because only the Bolsheviks judge reality sensibly. Because only their tactic deserves to be the tactics of the future. Never mind that the opponents hiss, Bolsheviks will win, they are already winning! […] It is hard for me to realize how little I can do for this party – I am too busy! At the MAT Studio and at the Theatre. I wish that the forces which I do not have tomorrow still help the B[olsheviks]! I wish their victory would be great! Long live the Bolsheviks!' (Anrusenko 2004: 74–5).

7　He was, for example, given the cold shoulder by his music teacher on discovering his Bolshevik sympathies (Anrusenko 2004: 88).

8　The tone which Smyshlaev uses here to speak about the First Studio as a production house is to be noted: the First Studio was thus steadily losing

the laboratorial dimension which Stanislavsky had initially desired. In the end, the production of *Twelfth Night* was a resounding success. It featured Stanislavsky's full involvement in what Benedetti's describes as 'an overt display of "theatricality"' (Benedetti 1999: 261).
9 On one occasion, Smyshlaev overheard a member of the Second Studio saying that 'the union between First and Second Studio is impracticable because the First Studio is zero' (93).
10 The same can be said about Fyodor Komissarzhevsky's own book about Stanislavsky's System, which Stanislavsky was equally dismissive of (Benedetti 1999: 260).
11 Historical contextualization is a historiographical methodology that I use on occasion to unpick historical material. See Aquilina (2017).
12 See, for example, Stanislavsky's statement during the *Tartuffe* rehearsals: 'Art begins when there is no role, when there is only the "I" in the given circumstances of the play' (Toporkov 1979: 156).
13 Affective Memory, as opposed to Emotion Memory which Benedetti uses in his translation of *An Actor Work*, is the term suggested by Sharon Carnicke. See Carnicke (2009: 213–14).
14 Compare to Mikhail Chekhov's famous anecdote when he created the image of a son lamenting his dying father not by relieving the past emotion but by projecting forwards towards an imaginary and future event (Gordon 1988: 120).
15 This is an adaptation of Mikhail Chekhov's exercise known as 'Crossing the Threshold' (Chamberlain 2014: 16). The exercise is presented here as an icebreaker, but it has a lot of potential for development. The leader can for example create group sequences or montages from the actions which the students suggest.
16 I experienced the last three layers when participating in a workshop on Stanislavsky's, Meyerhold's and M. Chekhov's actor training techniques, led by Sergei Ostrenko of the International University Global Theatre Experience, in March 2007 at the Retzhof Castle in Leitring bei Leibnitz, Austria. For more information see http://www.iugte.com/.
17 This is an exercise Bharatanatyam dancer Mavin Khoo used in the initial stages of work on the performance *L-Imħalla*, staged during the official opening of the School of Performing Arts (University of Malta) in February 2012. The exercise was used as a way of bringing together students from the Departments of Theatre and Dance. *L-Imħalla* was directed by Khoo; assistant director Stefan Aquilina.

Chapter 4

1 Between 1918 and 1923, Kerzhentsev's book went through five editions. For this chapter I used the Italian translation of the fourth edition (1922). This translation came out in 1979, which explains my referencing. Kerzhentsev's name in Italian is transliterated as Keržencev.

2   The fullest source in English about post-revolutionary amateur theatre remains Lynn Mally's *Revolutionary Acts – Amateur Theatre and the Soviet State* (2000). For an extensive list of sources in Russian, see her bibliography.
3   For an exposition on the pre-revolutionary amateur theatre scene, see Swift (2002: 181–204).
4   On accounts explaining the upsurge in post-revolutionary amateur theatre, see Leach (1994: 36–41); von Geldern (1993: xxii–xxiii); Evreinoff (1927: 34–6); and Gorchakov (1957: 119–22).
5   See also Gorchakov (1957: 120–1) and Mally (2000: 18).
6   Other references and examples of the crude nature of amateur theatrics can be found in Gorchakov (1957: 131); Russell (1988: 153–4); and Leach (1994: 38–42).
7   For fuller descriptions of these two productions, compare and contrast Nina Gourfinkel's account (1979: 131) with Stanislavsky's (2008a: 145).
8   For example, see Dorita Hannah's work on the performativity of space, which she labels as 'space-event' (in Pitches and Popat 2011: 55–9).
9   Proletkult, in fact, is an abbreviation of the words Proletarian Culture.
10 It is worth noting that the early Proletkult received exceptional and substantial government funding in a way that other entities did not. On the government's funding of the Proletkult and how this went on to be reduced and then altogether cancelled, see Mally (1990: 44, 48, 158 and 209).
11 Leningrad from January 1924.
12 Professionals associated with the Proletkult included Valentin Smyshlaev in Moscow and Alexander Mgebrov in Petrograd. The latter had cut his teeth in the symbolist approach developed at Vera Komissarzhevskaya theatre, which he sought to then implement with the workers (see Mally 1990: 88, 103, 148; Gorchakov 1957: 159–60). Other professionals associated with the Proletkult included Meyerhold, Nikolai Foregger, Mikhail Chekhov, Sergei Tretyakov and Sergei Eisenstein.
13 *Samodeiatel'nost'* is also the term which Kerzhentsev uses in a central essay (1918c) and which I am currently planning to include in a collection of primary sources about proletarian theatre. In the translated version of the essay I will also opt to use 'the amateur theatre' term.
14 Kerzhentsev was equally critical of those dilettantes 'who threat the problems of theatre art lightly, superficially, and carelessly' (Keržencev 1979: 61).
15 It is no surprise that Kerzhentsev is described as the doyen for amateur theatre (Mally 2000: 36), as his support to amateurism in *The Creative Theatre* is unabashed. Typical quotations include: 'The collective of actors is to be made of amateurs who are workers within that particular context [where theatre is being produced]' (Keržencev 1979: 57). And: 'I am of the opinion that the principle of amateurism need to be safeguarded as much as possible. The real and only creators of the new theatre are those actor-workers who will also remain at their lathe' (58). I quote from Kerzhentsev not only because his work remains untranslated in English, but especially to counter the negative image, developed in the 1930s, of a hardened and

dangerous critic of the arts. His theories on amateur theatre and collective practices have a lot to commend them for. See also Chapter 3 above and, for more detail, Aquilina (2014).
16 Elsewhere I suggest the application of critical theories, specifically those on 'everyday life', as a way of countering this lack of documentation, in order to support, for example, certain conclusions which Mally makes on the reactionary potential of amateur theatre (Aquilina 2020).
17 See, for example, the heated debate between Viktor Shklovsky and Adrian Piotrovsky aired in the cultural journal *Zhizn' Iskusstva* (*The Life of Art*). The former only saw amateur theatre as a necessary evil which had little to go for it. The latter, on the other, took an opposite stance, saying that amateur theatre was a manifestation of the transformative energy generated by the revolution. The debate remained unresolved (Mally 2000: 45).
18 See Chapter 6.
19 The New Economic Policy (NEP) was devised by Lenin and launched in 1921. It allowed small businesses to open for personal profit while the state still controlled the large industries, banks and foreign trade. The aim of the NEP was to revive the economy, which had suffered severely since the beginning of the First World War. It was not without its critics, with Lenin himself seeing it as a necessary concession, a 'retreat from socialism'. Literature on the NEP is extensive, including Brovkin (1998) and Fitzpatrick et al. (1991). Of particular importance for theatre was the fact that state subsidy was cut off for the majority of the theatres which now needed to show a profit (Rudnitsky 1988: 89).
20 Kerzhentsev's three-phase programme to nationalize the theatre involved: (i) the transference of all theatre spaces to the Soviets, (ii) an auditing of all theatrical companies and their inventories and (iii) the severing of all contracts between the artists and the companies so that the former enter into the service of the Soviets.
21 Kerzhentsev was adamant against the workers leaving their day jobs to turn professional, showing how conflicting the debates surrounding proletarian theatre could be, even between its leaders at the centre. By turning professional, the worker would lose contact with the masses (Keržencev 1979: 66). Kerzhentsev did concede that some workers would be lost to the professional world, but this was to be seen as an exception and a dangerous rather than desirable one (1979: 58). See also Mally (1990: 153–4).
22 Even on the issue of skill and technique, Kerzhentsev would exhibit a different opinion. He argued that whereas technical skill was indeed necessary, one 'should not overestimate the importance of technical formation'. The 'right guidelines for the theatre are more important, as are the right keywords, and the immediate enthusiasm for that being carried out' (Keržencev 1979: 59). He does, however, show a degree of inconsistency on the matter. In another instance of *The Creative Theatre*, for example, he asserted that '[i]t is heard sometimes that technique is not necessary for the workers, that technique is a bourgeois prejudice, and that it is only necessary to develop the revolutionary temperament of the workers. All the rest will

emerge on its own. A coherent application of this point of view would only plunge the nascent theatre of the proletariat in the abyss of the deadliest dilettantism. This thinking is adhered to by many of the dramatic circles that corrupt the masses of workers with superficial and inconsiderate amateur theatre. We have to fight against this contempt towards the school, the study, and serious work' (Keržencev 1979: 70).

23 Compare now rather than contrast to Kerzhentsev's words expressed the year before: 'It is clear then that both the proletarian theatre and the proletarian theatre school must develop their own special technique. Right now we do borrow the most necessary tools from the arsenal of the bourgeois theatre technique, but we must critique them and strive to find new paths for ourselves' (Kerzhentsev 1918a: 23).

24 Further discussion on the repertoire crisis can be found in sources like Stanislavski (2008a: 336); Gourfinkel (1979: 103–36); Keržencev (1979: 17–18). See also Mally (2000: 45). It is because of the repertoire problem that official competitions were set up to encourage new political writing (in Russell and Barratt 1990: 153–4), and why alternative forms of performance like the Living Newspapers and Agit-Trials were developed.

25 The debate about the form and content of proletarian theatre typically showed disparate views. Was proletarian theatre to be content with staging proletarian-friendly themes, or was it to extend its remit to the discovery of new forms? Mally argued that many Proletkult participants 'seemed to believe that art with a revolutionary content [...] was a sufficient expression of the proletarian spirit' (1990: 146). A vocal minority who had access to the newspapers 'was [however] convinced that revolutionary messages needed innovative modes of expression' (Mally 1990: 147). Kerzhentsev was among the latter faction (1918a: 33). Typically, Pletnev's views are among the most developed, underlining how form and content need to create a unity and that new forms can only arise from the proletarian content (Pletnev 1919: 33–4).

26 See also Kerzhentsev (1918a: 23).

27 For Meyerhold's practical reworking of *commedia dell'arte* and other past theatre traditions, see Chapter 5.

28 Sources on Bolshevik mass spectacles include von Geldern (1993); Malte (2013); and Fischer-Lichte (2005: 97–121).

29 It is interesting to underline the value given to collective criticism, when the group would be given the chance to express its views on a piece. Smyshlaev, for example, opens his essay on the staging of Verhaeren's *Insurrection* by asserting its importance 'in all our [i.e. the Proletkult's] achievements and the ways to reach them' (Smyshlaev 1919: 89).

30 The Introduction only gives the surnames of the authors in the following note: 'The parts [of the book] are worked as following: Theatre – by comrades Kravchunovsky, Neznamov, Zlatov, and Strekalov; Art – by comrades Zhmudsky and Tarabukin; Literature – comrades Sillov and Vinokur' (Pletnev 1924: 3).

31 It is for this editorial accreditation that I am referencing the volume as Pletnev (1924).
32 For a selection of these official State decrees, see Matthews 1974.
33 See also the contrast made between the Russian *byt*, as in 'the material, repetitive, unchanging and therefore deeply conservative activities associated with the domestic sphere and the body', and *bytie*, i.e. activities that are 'progressive, inventive, emotional, spiritual, and transcendental' (Kiaer and Naiman 2006: 10).
34 The integration together of the various arts forms within the medium of theatre is the theme of Kerzhentsev's article 'Strife between the arts', in which he argued the following: 'The art of theatre takes an exclusive and fortunate place in relation to a number of other arts because it is in theatre that the they can combine creatively. [...] A true and genuine theatre always unites the poet and the actor, the artist and the musician, the architect and the dancer. The majority of the arts live separately outside the theatre. Painting sometimes (though not often) combines with architecture but never with music. Music shuns architecture. Poetry does not communicate with painting. With no scene or theatre, and if the art of spectacle did not exist (the same as theatre art), the entire family of the arts would not meet. It would stay without communication, without connection. [...]. Theatre art is unique in its form and methods, because it synthesizes all other arts' (Kerzhentsev 1919a: 2).

Chapter 5

1 Elsewhere I use Henri Lefebvre's theories about everyday life to discuss Meyerhold's encounter with the revolution and to argue that some actions of his supported the emerging regime while others exhibited the seed of resistance (Aquilina 2018).
2 Much is made of the *Ubu Roi* riot as the moment that signalled the birth of modern theatre, but Thomas Postlewait, for instance, shows how this event has acquired the image of a larger-than-life moment that is shrouded in myth-making and obfuscated by superlatives. The riot, which the documents of the time do not really support, however, 'is the narrative that most commentators insist upon. It's the story we want to tell' (Postlewait 2009: 69), because a scandal and a riot have appeal. Another myth, that modernism was not only a rapture with the past but also a milieu that produced artefacts that were culturally and aesthetically superior to popular art forms, is discredited by Jeff Wallace (2011: 6).
3 One instance sees her saying that '[t]he masters were great artists but also strange artists' (Schino 2018: 15).
4 Contrast to Amy Skinner's more balanced evaluation of Meyerhold's work with actors, wherein his overarching directorial vision for a particular

production did not necessarily offset the emergence of an acting ensemble (in Britton 2013: 68–9).
5 A denouncement of Stalinism was, in reality, the same bias of another émigré, Nicholai Gorchakov. See, for example, Gorchakov (1957: vii–x).
6 For a short summary of Meyerhold's rediscovery in Russia, see Leach (1989: 173).
7 In my work on this chapter I used several of these published efforts, often in the form of collected primary sources. They include Braun (1969); Crino (1975); Malcovati (1977, 2002, 2011). For other sources on and by Meyerhold, see the Bibliography.
8 Krizhanskaya, for example, notes the following: 'Persuaded by Meyerhold's own declarations, Western scholars frequently forget that Soviet historical documents should not be taken at face value, even if they come from the recently opened post-Communist archives' (2000: 158).
9 Recurrence and difference are evident when Patrice Pavis identifies a text (or an action), an actor's body, a stage and a spectator as 'the necessary sequence of all theatre communication [i.e. as recurrences], even though '[e]ach link in the chain […] can take very different forms [thus signalling epochal stylistic differences]' (Pavis 1998: 388). The body of the performer thus recurs, whether through the embodied presence of an actor, a puppet or as a virtual presence.
10 As expected, a substantial amount of sources about Meyerhold contain entries about the grotesque. The following are just a few examples: Tian (2016: 238–9); Posner (2015, especially 363); Braun (1998: 67–8); Symons (1971: 65–70); Pitches (2003: 61–6).
11 The example which Meyerhold gives of the grotesque in everyday life is that of the funeral march, a solemn and tragic moment which, however, still embraced the more comic instance of a man whose hat had been blown away by a gust of wind (Braun 1969: 138).
12 On the links between Meyerhold and Brecht, see Zazzalli (2008) and Eaton (1985).
13 This change of heart is undoubtedly a reaction to the shifting times and steady movement towards socialist realism.
14 The appellation 'theatrical traditions' is commonly used, in both translation (e.g. Braun 1969: 146) and in scholarship (see Picon-Vallin in Schino 2010: 126).
15 On this trip Meyerhold wrote: 'I am going to Greece under the guidance of Prof. Zelinsky. […] I will see Greece through the prism of Zelinsky. […] There I will not only see, but also learn' (in Volkov 1929 Vol. 2: 102).
16 Meyerhold argued that the New Drama should be modelled on ancient Greek tragedies so as 'to intoxicate the spectator with the Dionysian cup of eternal sacrifice' (Braun 1969: 60). Devices from popular performance held in high esteem by Meyerhold included sudden switches in the mood, knowing disruption of illusion, asides to the audience and physical tricks. These were recurrent features of his productions.

17 Theft is evidenced even by great poets like Dante when they 'pile up all the excellences they can beg, borrow, or steal from their predecessors and contemporaries' (Ezra Pound in Cavanagh 1995: 16).
18 Min Tian's all-together more detailed account of Meyerhold's use of the prop man also links to the Chinese performance form of *xiqu* (Tian 2016: especially 244).
19 For a detailed reconstruction, through primary sources, of the 'anti-formalist campaign', see Clark and Dobrenko (2007: 229–48).
20 Practice as Research has already been adopted as a means of rediscovering Meyerhold for twenty-first-century performance. A case in point is Katie Normington's work as movement director on the Red Shift Theatre Company's adaptation of Herman Melville's short story *Bartleby*. Normington's study looked at integrating Meyerhold's techniques like *rakurs* and *tormoz*, at integrating training with rehearsal, which she considered as 'essentially two very different activities' (Normington 2005: 120). Another practical investigation involving Meyerhold's practice was carried out by Jonathan Pitches (2010). His study in Meyerhold's object work is explicitly presented as a PaR exercise. Pitches argued that there are many vivid accounts of Meyerhold's productions, which however 'avoid one nagging question: how did actors realize [his] vision? [...] How can one trace [his] training back into the practice? And what is the best mechanism to do so?' (Pitches 2010: 97–8). Pitches's answer is via object work, researched through practical workshops with sticks and conveyed as a series of four exercises titled 'Stick Balance', 'Stick Throw', 'Extension to Stick Throw' and the 'Stab to the Chest étude' (99–102). These exercises, Pitches concluded, offer 'one possible channel into Meyerhold's training and performance work'. For more examples of practice-based research in Meyerhold's work and its applicability today, see Baldwin (1995) and Whitehead (2017).
21 On the origins of Practice as Research, see Baz Kershaw's exposition in Kershaw and Nicholson (2011: 63–4).
22 One such audition, based on a pantomimic étude of a lady making fun of her two suitors, is described by Smirnova in her account of the work at the Borodin Studio (in Valentei et al. 1967: 86).
23 For another extended description of the work of the Borodin Studio, see Leach (2003: 110–29).
24 See also Leach (1989: 48–9).
25 See, for example, Picon-Vallain in Schino (2010: 123).
26 Ilinsky also mentioned that the actors were excited at the prospect of touring abroad, as the memory of previous triumphant tours by the Moscow Art Theatre, the Kamerny Theatre and the Vakhtangov Theatre had by then sedimented into the consciousness of theatre makers (Ilinsky 1962: 300).
27 Ilinsky only participated in the German leg of the tour. He wished his wife to join him in Paris, but permission to travel was not granted her. He thus returned to Moscow before the rest of the company (Ilinsky 1962: 301).

28 For a discussion of the Moscow Art Theatre's tours of Paris, see Marie-Christine Autant-Mathieu in Pitches and Aquilina (2017: 71–8).
29 Jean Tarvel, reporting in Paris but on the Berlin's performance of *The Government Inspector*, showed that Meyerhold was vilified on daring to transform the piece into an 'eccentric puppet parade' (*Comœdia*, 20 April 1930: 2). Comparably, a review in *The Guardian* of the dress rehearsal of *The Government Inspector* also says that 'what [Meyerhold] gave us on Monday night was hardly Gogol at all. Gogol was merely the raw material with which Meyerhold had manufactured his pantomime. The brilliance of Gogol's dialogue, the glorious comedy of the situations, the subtlety of Khlestakov's character – these are sacrificed in Meyerhold's production' (*The Guardian*, 20 June 1930: 12).
30 During the Nazi occupation the *Comœdia* also featured contributions by Jean Cocteau, Paul Valery, Paul Claudel, Jean-Louis Barrault and Jean-Paul Sartre, among others. See https://fr.wikipedia.org/wiki/Com%C5%93dia_(journal), accessed 1 April 2019.
31 Compare to what André Antoine said about the Russian-born George Pitoëff, who, even though based in Paris, was still treated as a foreigner: 'He is not one of us and he in no way represents our spirit or traditions' (in Whitton 1989: 97).
32 See *The Miami News*, 24 June 1939: 5; *The Cincinnati Enquirer*, 24 June 1939: 22; *The Wilkes-Barre Road*, 24 June 1939: 2; *The Baltimore Sun*, 24 June 1939: 1; *The Herald-Press*, 24 June 1939: 6; *The Abilene Reporter-News*, 25 June 1939: 21; *Arizona Daily Star*, 25 June 1939: 7.
33 See https://www.ibdb.com/broadway-production/the-song-of-songs-8107, accessed 15 April 2019.
34 Ervine even described constructivism and Biomechanics as 'pretension flapdoodle' (*The Hartford Daily Courant*, 17 March 1929: 69). Conversely, see how the author of the article announcing Meyerhold's possible tour of 1927 took an all-positive appraisal of his work, unsurprisingly considering this text was promoting the tour (*New Castle News*, 6 October 1926: 10).

Chapter 6

1 In my brief exposition I make use of the following sources: Evans Clements (1992); Atwood (1999); Hutton (2015); and Ilic (2018).
2 Vladimir Brovkin debunks the Bolshevik's project for the emancipation of women, by describing the 'clash between official promises of emancipation and the reality of Soviet existence for women' (1998: 18). See especially 133–54.
3 For an in-depth analysis of the group, see Mally (2000: 109–45) and Mally (1996).
4 Rose Whyman has recently published an essay on Birman, describing her and the context in which she worked as follows: 'Birman's work as an

actress and director is hardly known outside Russia, nor is that of other actresses of the Moscow Art Theatre (MAT) Studios who remained in the Soviet Union after the Revolution. These include Sofia Giatsintova and Lidia Deikun, founder members of the MAT First Studio in 1912, as well as Maria Durasova, Nadezhda Bromlei, and Olga Pyzhova, who joined the First Studio a little later. […] [T]he contribution of this generation of actresses to the development of Stanislavsky's System and other acting practices remains under-researched' (Whyman 2018: 339).

5 Birman wrote: 'In all my school years I did not have a passage [from a play] that corresponded in any way with my inclinations and possibilities' (Birman 162: 34).

6 More generally, Birman's criticism of training institutions ran as follows: 'No matter how good a drama school, a studio, or a theatre institute is, they cannot prevent the state of spiritual shock that a graduate receives when placed in a theatre, on its stage and in front of an auditorium' (1962: 43).

7 For an extended introduction of Tairov's work, see Worrall (1989: 15–75).

8 Konstantin Rudnitsky remarks, when introducing the Kamerny Theatre, that the driving principle was that '[t]he stage is the stage: an arena for the actor's performance' (Rudnitsky 1988: 15).

9 The two other collaborations between Tairov and Exter were *Salomé* (1917) and *Romeo and Juliet* (1921). These productions developed further the experiments which the two carried out in *Famira Kifored*. The set of *Romeo and Juliet* was particularly innovative in its use of the vertical plane, and its criss-crossing of platforms, horizontal levels and mirrors to serve 'as a brilliant metaphor for the tangled intrigues of Shakespeare's tragedy' (in Van Norman Baer 1992: 44). The set was not an all-together successful realization, however, and disappointed by this relative failure, Exter ceased working for the Kamerny.

10 Both Exter and Popova featured their constructivist work in the influential 1921 exhibition in Moscow titled '5 x 5 = 25'. Amy Skinner argued that it was after seeing this exhibition that Meyerhold made up his mind to work with Popova (Skinner 2015: 31). The other exhibiting artists were Alexander Vesnin, Alexander Rodchenko and Varvara Stepanova.

11 This source remains untranslated in English, and I will therefore refer to the German original. Another source of hers is called *Krasnaya Grozdika* (The Red Curtain).

12 For more information, see https://www.documenta14.de/en/south/. More sources about Lācis can be found in the Bibliography (accessed 14 July 2019).

13 Justine McGill in fact argues that Benjamin's style of writing changed considerably after he met Lācis in 1924 (2008: 59–60).

14 Brinkmanis adds: 'Her depiction by the Frankfurt School scholars as a "Bolshevik girlfriend" who brought on Benjamin's turn toward Marxism and his "downfall" was made possible through inaccurate interpretation and a lack of research materials, especially published writings by Lācis herself, which would immediately have dismissed such stereotypes' (Lācis, Benjamin and Brinkmanis 2017).

15 An example of networking in modernism is the way that Isadora Duncan connected together Stanislavsky and Craig, and the resultant collaboration which, though fraught, still generated the production at the Moscow Art Theatre of the 1911 version of *Hamlet*.
16 Lācis also worked with Brecht in 1923, as an actress playing the role of the young king in *Edward II* (Eaton 1985: 17–18).
17 It was at this school that Lācis started introducing dramatics as a teaching tool, improvising a short play about animals as a metaphor for the biblical story of Christ and Judas (Lācis 1971: 17).
18 Agitprop brigades were mobile troupes that coerced their audiences in accepting government programmes and state messages (Mally 2000: 146–7).
19 One scenario tackled the imprisonment of some workers in a Riga prison. It developed as follows: '[I]mprisoned workers, the door opens, prison guards enter with a list and call names, the called ones are brought out, the rest are left inside, after a while you hear shooting. Afterwards there is a conversation between the prisoners, anger and hate, the fight continues' (Lācis 1971: 33).
20 These principles have already appeared in a previous publication of mine on cultural transmission (Aquilina 2019). Reproduced by kind permission of Taylor and Francis.

References

Abensour, G. (1976), 'Art et politique. La tournée du théâtre Meyerhold à Paris en 1930', *Cahiers du Monde russe et soviétique*, XVII (2–3): 213–48.
Allen, D. H. (2013), *Directed Culture: The Spectator and Dialogues of Power in Early Soviet Theater*, unpublished PhD, University of California.
Anrusenko, S., ed. (2004), *The Moscow Art Theatre in Diaries and Notes*, Moscow: Avantitul.
Aquilina, S. (2012a), 'Stanislavski's Encounter with the Revolution', *Studies in Theatre and Performance*, 32 (1): 79–91.
Aquilina, S. (2012b), 'Stanislavski's Accumulative Practice in *Artists and Admirers* Rehearsals (1932–33)', *Stanislavski Studies*, 2: 3–20.
Aquilina, S. (2012c), 'Stanislavsky and the Impact of Studio Ethics on Everyday Life', *Theatre, Dance and Performance Training*, 3 (3): 302–14.
Aquilina, S. (2013), 'Stanislavski and the Tactical Potential of Everyday Images', *Theatre Research International*, 38 (3): 229–39.
Aquilina, S. (2014), 'Platon Kerzhentsev and His Theories on Collective Creation', *Journal of Dramatic Theory and Criticism*, 28 (2): 29–48.
Aquilina, S. (2016), 'As Simple but as Complex as Everyday Cooking: Stanislavski's Use of Physical Action in the Recreation of Nature', *Stanislavski Studies*, 4 (2): 111–24.
Aquilina, S. (2017), 'It Is Less about the System and More about the Attitudes: Stanislavsky's Lesser Known Essays about Actor Training', *Theatre, Dance and Performance Training*, 8 (1): 19–32.
Aquilina, S. (2018), 'Meyerhold and the Revolution: A Reading through Henri Lefebvre's Theories about "Everyday Life"', *Theatre History Studies*, 37: 7–26.
Aquilina, S. (2019), 'Cultural Transmission of Actor Training Techniques: A Research Project', *Theatre, Dance and Performance Training*, 10 (1): 4–20.
Aquilina, S. (2020), 'Communal Solidarity and Amateur Theatre in Post-Revolutionary Russia: Theoretical Approaches', in M. Galea and S. Musca (eds), *Redefining Theatre Communities. International Perspectives on Theatre and Communities*, 17–32, London: Intellect.
Artaud, A. (1988), *Antonin Artaud: Selected Writings*, S. Sontag (ed.), California: University of California Press.
Artaud, A. (1993), *The Theatre and Its Double*, trans. V. Corti, London: Calder.
Atwood, L. (1999), *Creating the New Soviet Woman*, London: MacMillan Press.
Balme, C. (2008), *The Cambridge Introduction to Theatre Studies*, Cambridge: Cambridge University Press.
Balme, C. (2015), 'The Bandmann Circuit: Theatrical Networks in the First Age of Globalization', *Theatre Research International*, 40 (1), 19–36.
Balme, C., and T. C. Davis, eds (2017), *A Cultural History of Theatre*, London: Bloomsbury.

Barba, E., and N. Savarese (2006), *A Dictionary of Theatre Anthropology. The Secret Art of the Performer*, trans. R. Fowler, Oxon: Routledge.
Barnay, L. (1913), *Über Theater Und Anderes*, Berlin: Otto Elsner Verlagsges, M.B.H.
Benedetti, J. (1989), *Stanislavski: An Introduction*, London: Methuen.
Benedetti, J., ed. and trans. (1991), *The Moscow Art Theatre Letters*, New York: Theatre Arts/Routledge.
Benedetti, J. (1999), *Stanislavski: His Life and Art*, London: Methuen.
Benjamin, P. (1989), *The Poetic Imagination of Vyacheslav Ivanov*, Cambridge: Cambridge University Press.
Benjamin, W. (1994), *The Correspondence of Walter Benjamin*, ed. G. Scholem and T. W. Adorno, trans. M. R. Jakobsen and E. M. Jakobsen, Chicago: University of Chicago Press.
Bentley, E., ed. (1968), *The Theory of the Modern Stage*, London: Penguin.
Bergan, R. (1999), *Sergei Eisenstein: A Life in Conflict*, New York: Overlook Press.
Biggart, J. (1987), 'Bukharin and the Origins of the "Proletarian Culture" Debate', *Soviet Studies*, 39 (2): 229–46.
Birman, S. (1962), *Put' Aktrisy*, Moscow: VTO.
Baldwin, J. (1995), 'Meyerhold's Theatrical Biomechanics: An Acting Technique for Today', *Theatre Topics*, 5 (2): 181–201.
Bogdanov, A. (1919), 'Ocherki Organizacionnoy Nauki', *Proletarskaia Kul'tura*, 7–8: 8–29.
Borovsky, V. (2001), *A Triptych from the Russian Theatre – An Artistic Biography of the Komissarzhevskys*, London: Hurst.
Bowlt, J. E., ed. (2014), *Russian Avant-Garde: War, Revolution & Design*, London: Nick Hern Books.
Burian, J. M. (2000), *Czech Theatre – Reflector and Conscience of a Nation*, Iowa City: University of Iowa Press.
Bratton, J. (2003), *New Readings in Theatre History*, Cambridge: Cambridge University Press.
Braun, E., ed. and trans. (1969), *Meyerhold on Theatre*, London: Methuen.
Braun, E. (1998), *Meyerhold: A Revolution in Theatre*, London: Methuen.
Britton, J., ed. (2013), *Encountering Ensemble*, London: Methuen.
Brook, P. (1988), *The Shifting Point*, London: Methuen.
Brovkin, V. (1998), *Russia after Lenin: Politics, Culture and Society, 1921–9*, London: Routledge.
Camilleri, F. (2013), 'Between Laboratory and Institution: Practice as Research in No Man's Land', *TDR*, 57 (1): 152–66.
Cardullo, B., ed. (2013), *Theories of the Avant-Garde Theatre – A Casebook from Kleist to Camus*, Lanham, Toronto, Plymouth: The Scarecrow Press.
Carnicke, S. (1993), 'Stanislavski Uncensored and Unabridged', *TDR*, 37 (1): 22–37.
Carnicke, S. (2009), *Stanislavsky in Focus*, 2nd edn, London and New York: Routledge.

Carriere, P. C. (2010), *Reading for the Soul in Stanislavski's* The Work of the Actor on Him/Herself: *Orthodox Mysticism, Mainstream Occultism, Psychology and the System in the Russian Silver Age*, unpublished PhD, University of Kansas.
Carter, H. (1925), *New Theatre and Cinema of Soviet Russia*, New York: International Publishers.
Cavanagh, C. (1995), *Osip Mandelstam and the Modernist Creation of Tradition*, New Jersey: Princeton University Press.
Chamberlain, F. (2014), *Mikhail Chekhov*, London: Routledge.
Chambers, C., and R. Nelson, eds (2017), *Granville Barker on Theatre: Selected Essays*, London: Bloomsbury.
Chambers, D., and N. Pesochinsky (2000), 'The Fall and Rise of Meyerhold', *American Theatre*, 17 (1): 24–8, 110–12.
Chaney, D. (2002), *Cultural Change and Everyday Life*, New York: Palgrave.
Clark, T. (1993), 'The "New Man's" Body: A Motif in Early Soviet Culture', in C. Brown (ed.), *Art of the Soviets. Paintings, Sculpture and Architecture in a One-Party State, 1917–22*, 33–50, Manchester: Manchester University Press.
Clark, K., and E. Dobrenko, with A. Artizov and O. Naumov (2007), *Soviet Culture and Power: A History in Documents*, trans. M. Schwartz, New Haven: Yale University Press.
Craig, E. G. (1957), *On the Art of the Theatre*, London, Melbourne, Toronto: Heinemann.
Crino, G., ed. and trans. (1975), *La rivoluzione teatrale*, Roma: Editori Riuniti.
Cruciani, F. (1998), *Lo Spazio del Teatro*, 6th edn, Roma-Bari: Editori Laterza.
Cuddy-Keane M., A. Hammond, and A. Peat (2014), *Modernism: Keywords*. Oxford: Wiley-Blackwell.
Davidson, P. (1989), *The Poetic Imagination of Vyacheslav Ivanov*, Cambridge: Cambridge University Press.
Davis, J. (2011), 'Research Methods and Methodology', in B. Kershaw and H. Nicholson (eds), *Research Methods in Theatre and Performance*, 89–98, Edinburgh: Edinburgh University Press.
Doyle, C. (2011), *A Dictionary of Marketing*, Oxford: Oxford University Press.
De Certeau, M. (1988), *The Practice of Everyday Life*, trans. S. Rendall, California: University of California.
De Certeau, M., F. Jameson, and C. Lovitt (1980), 'On the Oppositional Practices of Everyday Life', *Social Text*, 3: 3–43.
Dukore, B., ed. (1974), *Dramatic Theory and Criticism – Greeks to Grotowski*, Orlando: Harcourt Brace Jovanovich College Publishers.
During, S. (2005), *Cultural Studies: An Introduction*, Oxon: Routledge.
Eaton, K. B. (1985), *The Theatre of Meyerhold and Brecht*, London: Greenwood Press.
Evans, M. (2006), *Jacques Copeau*, London and New York: Routledge.
Evans Clements, B. (1992), 'The Utopianism of the Zhenotdel', *Slavic Review*, 51 (3): 485–96.

Evreinoff, N. (1927), *The Theatre in Life*, ed. and trans. A. Nazaroff, New York: George G. Harrap.
Eysteinsson, Á., and V. Liska, eds (2007), *Modernism Vol. 1*, Amsterdam/Philadelphia: John Benjamins Publishing.
Fallace, T. D. (2015), *Race and the Origins of Progressive Education, 1880–1929*, New York: Teachers College Press.
Fischer-Lichte, E. (2005), *Theatre, Sacrifice, Ritual – Exploring Forms of Political Theatre*, London and New York: Routledge.
Fitzpatrick, S., A. Rabinowitch, and R. Stites, eds (1991), *Russia in the Era of NEP*, Indiana: Indiana University Press.
Frame, M. (2006), *School for Citizens – Theatre and Civil Society in Imperial Russia*, Yale: Yale University Press.
Gagné, R. M. (1977), *The Conditions of Learning*, 3rd edn, New York: Holt, Rinehart and Winston.
Gale, M. B., and A. Featherstone (2011), 'The Imperative of the Archive: Creative Archive Research', in B. Kershaw and H. Nicholson (eds), *Research Methods in Theatre and Performance*, 17–40, Edinburgh: Edinburgh University Press.
Gardiner, M. (2000), *Critiques of Everyday Life*, New York: Routledge.
Gauss, R. B. (1999), *Lear's Daughters: The Studios of the Moscow Art Theatre 1905–1927*, New York: P. Lang.
Gorchakov, N. (1957), *The Theater in Soviet Russia*, trans. E. Lehrman, New York and London: Columbia University Press/Oxford University Press.
Gordon, M. (1988), *The Stanislavski Technique: Russia – A Workbook for Actors*, New York: Applause Theatre Book Publishers.
Gordon, M. (2010), *Stanislavski in America*, London and New York: Routledge.
Gorkii, M. (1955), *Sobranie Sochinenij v 30 tomah, tom 029*, Moscow.
Gorky, M. (1995), *Untimely Thoughts*, trans. H. Ermolaev, New Haven: Yale University Press.
Gourfinkel, N. (1979), *Teatro Russo Contemporaneo*, trans. M. Turano, Roma: Bulzoni Editore.
Gottlieb, V., and P. Allain, eds (2000), *The Cambridge Companion to Chekhov*, Cambridge: Cambridge University Press.
Grafton, A., and A. Blair, eds (1990), *The Transmission of Culture in Early Modern Europe*, Philadelphia: University of Pennsylvania Press.
Grange, W. (2006), *Historical Dictionary of German Theatre*, Lanham, Maryland, Toronto, Oxford: The Scarecrow Press.
Gunn, W. D. (2012), *Back to Ostrovsky!: Reclaiming Russia's National Playwright on the Early Soviet Stage*, unpublished PhD, University of Southern California.
Grotowski, J. (2002), *Towards a Poor Theatre*, ed. E. Barba, New York: A Theatre Arts Book, republished by Routledge.
Harorimana, D., ed. (2010), *Cultural Implications of Knowledge Sharing, Management and Transfer: Identifying Competitive Advantage*, Hershey and New York: Information Science Reference.

Heddon, D., and J. Milling (2006), *Devising Performance: A Critical History*, Hampshire and New York: Palgrave Macmillan.
Hellbeck, J. (2006), *Revolution on My Mind*, Massachusetts: Harvard University Press.
Heywoord, A. (2013), *Politics*, 4th edn, London: Palgrave.
Highmore, B. (2002), *Everyday Life and Cultural Theory*, London and New York: Routledge.
Hodge, A., ed. (2010), *Actor Training*, 2nd edn, Oxon: Routledge.
Hoover, M. L. (1974), *Meyerhold. The Art of Conscious Theatre*, Amherst: University of Massachusetts Press.
Hutton, M. (2015), *Resilient Russian Women in the 1920s and 1930s*, Lincoln, Nebraska: Zea Books.
Ilic, M., ed. (2018), *The Palgrave Handbook of Women and Gender in Twentieth-Century Russia and the Soviet Union*, London: Palgrave Macmillan.
Ilinsky, I. (1962), *Sam o sebe*, Moscow: Iskusstvo.
Ingram, S. (2002), 'The Writing of Asja Lācis', *New German Critique*, 86: 159–77.
Innes, C. (1998), *Avant-Garde Theatre 1892–1992*, London and New York: Routledge.
Innes, C., and M. Shevtsova (2013), *The Cambridge Introduction to Theatre Directing*, Cambridge: Cambridge University Press.
Ioffe, D. G., and F. H. White, eds (2012), *The Russian Avant-Garde and Radical Modernism: An Introductory Reader*, Brighton: Academic Studies Press.
Jannarone, K. (2012), *Artaud and His Doubles*, Michigan: University of Michigan Press.
Kapsali, M. (2013), 'The Presence of Yoga in Stanislavski's Work and Nineteenth-Century Metaphysical Thought', *Stanislavski Studies*, 2 (1), 149–78.
Kershaw, B. (1992), *The Politics of Performance. Radical Theatre as Cultural Intervention*, London: Routledge.
Kershaw, B., and H. Nicholson, eds (2011), *Research Methods in Theatre and Performance*, Edinburgh: Edinburgh University Press.
Keržencev (Kerzhentsev), P. (1979), *Il Teatro Creativo*, trans. E. Casini Ropa and C. Falletti, Roma: Bulzoni Editori.
Kerzhentsev, P. M. (1918a), *Revoliutsiia i teatr*, Moscow: Dennitsa.
Kerzhentsev, P. M. (1918b), 'Repertuar proletarskogo teatra', *Iskusstvo*, 1 (5): 5–7.
Kerzhentsev, P. M. (1918c), 'Proletkul't' – organizatsiia proletarskoi samodeiatel'nosti', *Proletarskaia kul'tura*, 1: 7–8.
Kerzhentsev, P. M. (1918d), 'Posle prazdnika', *Iskusstvo*, 6: 3–5.
Kerzhentsev, P. M. (1919a), 'Rozn' iskusstva', *Vestnik teatra*, 19: 2.
Kerzhentsev, V. (1919b), 'Kollektivnoe tcorchestvo v teatre', *Proletarskaia kul'tura*, 7–8: 37–41.
Kerzhentsev P. M. (1919c), 'Peredelyvaite p'esy!', *Vestnik teatra*, 36: 6–8.
Kiaer, C., and E. Naiman, eds (2006), *Everyday Life in Early Soviet Russia. Taking the Revolution Inside*, Bloomington: Indiana University Press.
Kleberg, L. (1993), *Theatre as Action – Soviet Russian Avant-Garde Aesthetics*, trans. C. Rougle, Houndmills, Basingstoke, Hampshire and London: Macmillan Press.

Koller, A. M. (1984), *The Theater Duke: Georg II of Saxe-Meiningen and the German Stage*, Stanford, CA: Stanford University Press.

Komisarjevsky, T. (1929), *Myself and the Theatre*, London: William Heinemann.

Kovtun, E. (2007), *Russian Avant-Garde: 1920–1930*, Vietnam: Parkstone International.

Krizhanskaya, D. (2000), 'Meyerhold – "revizor" – revolution', *Theatre History Studies*, 20: 157–70.

Lācis, A. (1971), *Revolutionär im Beruf: Berichte über proletarisches Theater, über Meyerhold, Brecht, Benjamin und Piscator*, ed. H. Brenner, Munich: Rogner and Bernhard.

Lacīs, A., W. Benjamin, and A. Brinkmanis (2017), 'Signals from Another World: Proletarian Theater as a Site for Education Texts by Asja Lācis and Walter Benjamin, with an Introduction by Andris Brinkmanis', *Documenta14*, 9. Available online: http://www.documenta14.de/en/south/25225_signals_from_another_world_proletarian_theater_as_a_site_for_education_texts_by_asja_la_cis_and_walter_benjamin_with_an_introduction_by_andris_brinkmanis, accessed 29 July 2018.

Law, A. (1982), 'Meyerhold's "the magnanimous cuckold"', *The Drama Review*, 26 (1): 61–86.

Law, A., and M. Gordon (1996), *Meyerhold, Eisenstein and Biomechanics – Actor Training in Revolutionary Russia*, North Carolina: McFarland.

Leach, R. (1989), *Directors in Perspectives – Vsevolod Meyerhold*, Cambridge: Cambridge University Press.

Leach, R. (1994), *Revolutionary Theatre*, London and New York: Routledge.

Leach, R. (2003), *Stanislavsky and Meyerhold*, Bern: Peter Lang.

Leach, R. (2004), *Makers of Modern Theatre*, London and New York: Routledge.

Leach, R., and V. Borovsky, eds (1999), *A History of Russian Theatre*, Cambridge: Cambridge University Press.

Lefebvre, H. (2008a), *Critique of Everyday Life Vol. 1*, trans. G. Elliot, London: Verso.

Lefebvre, H. (2008b), *Critique of Everyday Life Vol. 2*, trans. G. Elliot, London: Verso.

Lenin, V. (1974), *Collected Works Vol. 28*, ed. and trans. J. Riordan, Moscow: Progress Publishers.

Lodder, C. (1983), *Russian Constructivism*, New Haven and London: Yale University Press.

Logan, J. (1966), 'Foreword', in S. Moore (ed.), *Stanislavski's System: The Professional Training of an Actor*, London: Victor Gollancz.

Lunacharsky, A. (1919), 'Proletkul't i sovetskaya kul'turnaya rabota', *Proletarskaia Kul'tura*, 7–8: 1–3.

Lvov, N. (1919), 'Tiaga na stsenu', *Vestnik Teatra*, 56: 8.

Malaev-Babel, A. (2013), *Yevgeny Vakhtangov – A Critical Portrait*, Oxon: Routledge.

Malcovati, F., ed. (1977), *L'Ottobre Teatrale 1918/39*, trans. and annotated S. de Vidovich, Milano: Feltrinelli Editore.
Malcovati, F., ed. (2011), *L'Ultimo Atto*, trans. S. de Vidovich and E. Guercetti, Firenze: La Casa Usher.
Malcovati, F., and N. Pesoĉinskij (2002), *Vsevolod Mejerchol'd: L'attore biomeccanico*, trans. M. R. Fasanelli, Milano: Ubulibri.
Mally, L. (1990), *Culture of the Future - The Proletkult Movement in Revolutionary Russia*, Berkeley, Los Angeles, Oxford: University of California Press.
Mally, L. (1993), 'Autonomous Theater and the Origins of Socialist Realism: The 1932 Olympiad of Autonomous Art', *Russia Review*, 52 (2): 198–212.
Mally, L. (1996), 'Performing the New Woman: The Komsomolka as Actress and Image in Soviet Youth Theater', *Journal of Social History*, 30 (1): 79–95.
Mally, L. (2000), *Revolutionary Acts – Amateur Theatre and the Soviet State*, New York: Cornell University Press.
Malte, R. (2013), *Soviet Mass Festivals, 1917–1991*, trans. C. Clohr, Pittsburgh, PA: University of Pittsburgh Press.
Markov, P. (1934), *The Soviet Theatre*, New York: G. P. Putnam's Sons.
Marowitz, C. (2014), 'Getting Stanislavsky Wrong', *New Theatre Quarterly*, 30 (3): 210–12.
Martins, L. J. (2017), 'Recurring Misconceptions in Stanislavski's Translations', *Stanislavski Studies*, 5 (1): 27–35.
Matthews, M., ed. and trans. (1974), *Soviet Government. A Selection of Official Documents on Internal Policies*, London: Jonathan Cape.
Mazer, C. M. (2013), *Great Shakespeareans*, London: Bloomsbury.
McDonald, J. (1986), *The 'New Drama' 1900–1914*, London: Macmillan.
McFarland, J. (2012), 'One-Way Street: Childhood and Improvisation at the Close of the Book', *The Germanic Review: Literature, Culture, Theory*, 87 (3): 293–303.
McGill, J. (2008), 'The Porous Coupling of Walter Benjamin and Asja Lācis', *Angelaki: Journal of Theoretical Humanities*, 13 (2): 59–72.
Mele, G. (1990), *Cultura e Politica in Russia – Il Proletkul't 1917–1921*, Roma: Bulzoni Editore.
Meierkhold, V. E. (1968), *Statyi, pisma, rechi, besedy Tom 2*, Moscow: Iskusstvo.
Meierkhold, V. E. (2001), *Lekcii. 1918–1919*, Moscow: OGI.
Merlin, B. (2003), *Konstantin Stanislavski*, London: Routledge.
Milling, J., and G. Ley (2001), *Modern Theories of Performance – From Stanislavski to Boal*, New York: Palgrave Macmillan.
Morgan, M. (1961), *A Drama of Political Man. A Study in the Plays of Harley Granville Barker*, London: Sidgwick & Jackson.
Murray, S., and J. Keefe (2007), *Physical Theatres. A Critical Introduction*, London: Routledge.

Nelson, R. (2013), *Practice as Research in the Arts: Principles, Protocols, Pedagogies, Resistances*, London: Palgrave.
Nemirovich-Danchenko, V. (1936), *My Life in the Russian Theatre*, trans. J. Cournos, London: Butler and Tanner.
Nonaka, I., and D. J. Teece (2001), *Managing Industrial Knowledge*, London, Thousand Oaks, New Delhi: Sage.
Normington, K. (2005), 'Meyerhold and the New Millennium', *New Theatre Quarterly*, 21 (2): 118–26.
Oddey, A. (1994), *Devising Theatre: A Practical and Theoretical Handbook*, London and New York: Routledge.
Osborne, J. (1988), *The Meiningen Court Theatre 1866–1890*, Cambridge: Cambridge University Press.
Oswell, D. (2006), *Culture and Society*, London, Thousand Oaks, New Delhi: Sage.
Parmalee, P. L. (1975), 'Book Review, Revolutionär im Beruf: Berichte über proletarisches Theater, über Meyerhold, Brecht, Benjamin und Piscator by Asja Lacis and Hildegard Brenner', *New German Critique*, 4: 163–6.
Partridge, E. (1966), *Origins – A Short Etymological Dictionary of Modern English*, London and New York: Routledge.
Pavis, P. (1998), *Dictionary of the Theatre: Terms, Concepts, and Analysis*, trans. C. Shantz, Toronto and Buffalo: University of Toronto Press.
Pavis, P. (2013), *Contemporary mise-en-scène – Staging Theatre Today*, trans. J. Anderson, London and New York: Routledge.
Picon-Vallin, B. (1992), 'Meierkhold glazami Zhuve', in A. Sherel (ed.), *Meierkholdovskiy sbornik tom 2*, 127–34, Moscow: Artistic Centre of Meyerhold.
Pitches, J. (2003), *Vsevolod Meyerhold*, London and New York: Routledge.
Pitches, J. (2006), *Science and the Stanislavsky Tradition of Acting*, London: Routledge.
Pitches, J. (2010), 'Tracing/Training Rebellion: Object Work in Meyerhold's Biomechanics', *Performance Journal*, 12 (4): 97–103.
Pitches, J., ed. (2012), *Russians in Britain*, Oxon: Routledge.
Pitches, J. (2016), 'Introduction', in E. Braun (ed. and trans.), *Meyerhold on Theatre*, 4th edn, 1–18, London: Bloomsbury.
Pitches, J., ed. (2019), *The Great European Stage Directors Volume 3: Copeau, Komisarjevsky, Guthrie*, London and New York: Bloomsbury.
Pitches, J., and S. Aquilina, eds (2017), *Stanislavsky in the World: The System and Its Transformations across Continents*, London: Bloomsbury.
Pitches, J., and S. Popat, eds (2011), *Performance Perspectives: A Critical Introduction*, London: Palgrave.
Pletnev, V. (1919), 'O professionalizme', *Proletarskaia Kul'tura*, 7–8: 31–37.
Pletnev, V. (1924), *Iskusstvo V Rabochem Klube*, Moscow: All-Russian Proletkult.
Posner, D. (2015), 'Baring the Frame: Meyerhold's Refraction of Gozzi's *Love of Three Oranges*', *Theatre Survey*, 56 (3): 363–88.

Postlewait, T. (2009), *The Cambridge Introduction to Theatre Historiography*, Cambridge: Cambridge University Press.
Purdom, C. B. (1955), *Harvey Granville Barker. Man of the Theatre, Dramatist and Scholar*, London: Rockliff.
Radlov, S. (1929), *Desyat' let v teatre*, Leningrad: Surf.
Richards, T. (1995), *At Work with Grotowski on Physical Actions*, London and New York: Routledge.
Ridout, N. (2009), *Theatre and Ethics*, Basingstoke: Palgrave Macmillan.
Rudnitsky, K. (1988), *Russian and Soviet Theatre – Tradition and Avant-Garde*, ed. L. Milne, trans. R. Permar, London: Thames and Hudson.
Russell, R. (1988), *Russian Drama of the Revolutionary Period*, Houndmills, Basingstoke, Hampshire and London: Macmillan Press.
Russell, R., and A. Barratt, eds (1990), *Russian Theatre in the Age of Modernism*, Houndmills, Basingstoke, Hampshire and London: Macmillan Press.
Rzhevsky, N. (2002), *The Cambridge Companion to Modern Russian Culture*, Cambridge: Cambridge University Press.
Rzhevsky, N. (2016), *The Modern Russian Theatre: A Literary and Cultural History*, Oxon: Routledge.
Salmon, E. (1983), *Granville Barker. A Secret Life*, London: Heinemann Educational Books.
Sayler, O. (1920), *The Russian Theatre*, Brentano: Little, Brown and Company.
Schechner, R. (2002), *Performance Studies. An Introduction*, New York: Routledge.
Schino, M. (2010), *Alchemists of the Stage: Theatre Laboratories in Europe*, trans. P. Warrington, Holstebro, Malta and Wroclaw: ICARUS Publishing Enterprise, Routledge.
Schino, M. (2018), *An Indra's Web: The Age of Appia, Craig, Stanislavski, Copeau, Artaud*, trans. V. A. Cremona and M. Galea, Holstebro, Malta and Wroclaw: ICARUS Publishing Enterprise, Routledge.
Schmidt, P. (1977), 'A Director Works with a Playwright: Meyerhold and Mayakovsky', *Educational Theatre Journal*, 29 (2): 214–20.
Schmidt, P. (1978), 'Discovering Meyerhold: Traces of a Search', *October*, 7: 71–82.
Schmidt, P., ed. (1981), *Meyerhold at Work*, New York: Applause Theatre Books Publishers.
Schönpflug, U., ed. (2009), *Cultural Transmission – Psychological, Developmental, Social and Methodological Aspects*, Cambridge: Cambridge University Press.
Schuler, C. A. (1996), *Women in Russian Theatre. The Actress in the Silver Age*, London and New York: Routledge.
Schumacher, C., ed. (1998), *Naturalism and Symbolism in European Theatre 1950–1918*, Cambridge: Cambridge University Press.
Senelick, L., ed. (1981), *Russian Dramatic Theory from Pushkin to the Symbolists: An Anthology*, Austin: University of Texas Press.

Senelick, L. (1984), *Serf Actor – The Life and Art of Mikhail Shchepkin*, Connecticut: Greenwood Press.
Senelick, L. (2000), 'Recovering Repressed Memories: Writing Russian Theatre History', in S. E. Wilmer (ed.), *Writing and Rewriting National Theatre Histories*, 47–64, Iowa: University of Iowa Press.
Senelick, L. (2003), 'The Making of a Martyr: The Legend of Meyerhold's Last Public Appearance, *Theatre Research International*, 28 (2): 157–68.
Senelick, L. (2007), *The A to Z of Russian Theater*, Lanham, Toronto, Plymouth: The Scarecrow Press.
Senelick, L., ed. (2008), *Theatre Arts on Acting*, London and New York: Routledge.
Senelick, L., ed. and trans. (2014), *Stanislavsky – A Life in Letters*, London and New York: Routledge.
Sheperd-Barr, K. (2016), *Modern Drama – A Very Short Introduction*, Oxford: Oxford University Press.
Sheringham, M. (2009), *Everyday Life*, Oxford: Oxford University Press.
Simpson, A. (2008), 'Craving the Whole Essence: The Photograph as Document, Artwork and Framework in the Theatre of Vs. E. Meyerhold', *About Performance*, 8: 111–23.
Skinner, A. (2015), *Meyerhold and the Cubists: Perspectives on Painting and Performance*, London: Intellect.
Skinner, A. (2016), 'Exploring the Hinterlands, Avant-Garde Temporality, Socialist Realism, and Pogodin's *Aristocrats*', *Studies in Theatre and Performance*, 36 (3): 257–68.
Smith, K., M. L. Kalish, T. L. Griffiths, and S. Lewandowsky (2008), 'Introduction. Cultural Transmission and the Evolution of Human Behaviour', *Cultural Transmission and the Evolution of Human Behaviour*, 363 (1509): 3469–76.
Smyshlaev, V. (1918), 'O rabote teatral'nogo otdela Moskovskogo Proletkul'ta', *Gorn*, 1: 54.
Smyshlaev, V. (1919), 'Opyt instsenirovki stikhotvoreniia Verkharna "Vosstanie"', *Gorn*, 2–3: 82–90.
Smyshlaev, V. (1922), *Tekhnika obrabotki Stsenicheskogo zrelishcha*, 2nd edn, Moscow: All-Russian Proletkult.
Sochor, Z. A. (1988), *Revolution and Culture – The Bogdanov-Lenin Controversy*, London and Ithaca: Cornell University Press.
Stanislavski, K. (1984), *Selected Works*, trans. E. Hapgood, Moscow: Raduga Publishers.
Stanislavski, K. (2008a), *My Life in Art*, trans. J. Benedetti, Oxon: Routledge.
Stanislavski, K. (2008b), *An Actor Works*, trans. J. Benedetti, Oxon: Routledge.
Stanislavski, K. (2009), *An Actor's Work on a Role*, trans. J. Benedetti, Oxon: Routledge.

Stanislavsky, K. (1963), *Konstantin Stanislavski 1863–1963, Man and Actor, Stanislavski and the World Theatre, Stanislavski's Letters*, trans. V. Schneierson, Moscow: Progress.
Stanislavskii, K. (1954), *Sobranie Sochinenii v 8 Tomakh, Tom 1*, Moscow: Iskusstvo.
Stanislavskii, K. (1958), *Sobranie Sochinenii v 8 Tomakh, Tom 5*, Moscow: Iskusstvo.
Stanislavskii, K. (1959), *Sobranie Sochinenii v 8 Tomakh, Tom 6*, Moscow: Iskusstvo.
Stanislavskii, K. (1960), *Sobranie Sochinenii v 8 Tomakh, Tom 7*, Moscow: Iskusstvo.
Stourac, R., and K. McCreery (1986), *Theatre as a Weapon*, London and New York: Routledge and Kegan Paul.
Swift, E. A. (2002), *Popular Theater and Society in Tsarist Russia*, California: University of California Press.
Symons, J. M. (1971), *Meyerhold's Theatre of the Grotesque*, Miami: University of Miami Press.
Terras, V., ed. (1985), *A Handbook of Russian Literature*, New Haven and London: Yale University Press.
Thomas, J. (2016), *A Director's Guide to Stanislavsky's Active Analysis. Including the Formative Essay on Active Analysis by Maria Knebel*, London: Bloomsbury.
Tian, M. (2016), 'Authenticity and Usability, or "Welding the Unweldable": Meyerhold's Refraction of Japanese Theatre', *Asian Theatre Journal*, 33 (2): 310–46.
Tillis, S. (2007), 'Remapping Theatre History', *Theatre Topics*, 17 (1): 1–19.
Toporkov, V. (1979), *Stanislavski in Rehearsal*, trans. C. Edwards, New York: Theatre Arts Books.
Trimingham, M. (2002), 'A Methodology for Practice as Research', *Studies in Theatre and Performance*, 22 (1): 54–60.
Tugendhold, J. (1922), *Alexandra Exter*, trans. Count Petrovsky-Petrovo-Solovovo, Berlin: Sarja.
Vago, S. (2004), *Social Change*, New Jersey: Pearson Prentice Hall.
Valentei, M., P. Markov, B. Rostotsky, A. Fevralsky, and N. Chushkin, eds (1967), *Vstrechi s Meierkholdom*, Moscow: Vserossiyskoye Teatral'noye Obshchestvo.
Van Norman Baer, N. (1992), *Theatre in Revolution. Russian Avant-Garde Stage Design 1913–1935*, New York: Thames and Hudson.
Vinogradskaia, I., ed. (2000), *Stanislavski Repetiruiet*, Moscow: Moscow Art Theatre.
Vinogradskaia, I., ed. (2003), *Zhizn I Tvorchestvo K.S. Stanislavskovo*, Moscow: Moscow Art Theatre.
Volkov, N. (1929), *Meierkhold (2 Tomakh)*, Moscow-Leningrad: Academia.

Von Geldern, J. (1993), *Bolshevik Festivals, 1917–1920*, Berkeley, Los Angeles, Oxford: University of California Press.
Wachtel, M. (2011), *Russian Symbolism and Literary Tradition: Goethe, Novalis and the Poetics of Vyacheslav Ivanov*, Wisconsin: University of Wisconsin Press.
Wallace, J. (2011), *Beginning Modernism*, Manchester: Manchester University Press.
White, R. A., ed. (2014), *The Routledge Companion to Stanislavsky*, London and New York: Routledge.
Whitehead, C. (2017), 'An Explanation and Analysis of One Principle of Meyerhold's Biomechanics - *tormos*', *Theatre, Dance and Performance Training*, 8 (1): 89–102.
Whitton, D. (1989), *Stage Directors in Modern France*, Manchester: Manchester University Press.
Whyman, R. (2008), *The Stanislavsky System of Acting: Legacy and Influence in Modern Performance*, Cambridge: Cambridge University Press.
Whyman, R. (2018), 'Serafima Birman: The Path of the Actress from the Moscow Art Theatre to People's Artist of the USSR', *New Theatre Quarterly*, 34 (4): 339–56.
Williams, R. (1983), *Keywords. A Vocabulary of Culture and Society*, New York: Oxford University Press.
Williams, R. C. (1977), *Artists in Revolution – Portraits of the Russian Avant-Garde*, Bloomington, London: Indiana University Press.
Worrall, N. (1989), *Modernism to Realism on the Soviet Stage*, Cambridge: Cambridge University Press.
Worrall, N. (1996), *The Moscow Art Theatre*, London and New York: Routledge.
Zazzali, P. (2008), 'Did Meyerhold Influence Brecht? A Comparison of Their Antirealistic Theatrical Aesthetics', *European Legacy*, 13 (3): 293–305.
Zarrilli, P., B. McConachie, G. J. Williams, and C. F. Sorgenfrei (2010), *Theatre Histories: An Introduction*, New York and London.

Newspaper references

The New York Times, 1882, 22 December: 3.
The New York Times, 1888, 8 March: 8.
New York Amusement Gazette, 1888, 19 March: 9.
The New York Times, 1888, 24 March: 4.
New York Times, 1888, 6 April: 5.
The Guardian, 1917, 7 July. https://www.theguardian.com/news/1917/jul/07/mainsection.fromthearchive, accessed 23 January 2019.
New York Tribune, 1920, 7 March: 37.
Dayton Daily News Magazine, 1923, 6 May: 103.
New Castle News, 1926, 6 October: 10.

The Courier, 1928, 22 June: 3.
Shamokin News-Dispatch, 1928, 23 June: 2.
The Sunday Citizen, 1928, 28 October: 5.
The Hartford Daily Courant, 1929, 17 March: 69.
Comœdia, 1930, 21 January: 2.
Comœdia, 1930, 10 June: 2.
Comœdia, 1930, 16 June: 2.
Comœdia, 1930, 17 June: 1.
The Guardian, 1930, 20 June: 12.
Comœdia, 1930, 6 August: 2.
The Ottawa Journal, 1934, 6 January: 19.
The Manchester Guardian, 1936, 10 January: 7.
The Brooklyn Daily Eagle, 1936, 12 April: 45.
The Gazette, 1937, 18 December: 13.
The Guardian, 1937, 23 December: 18.
The Baltimore Sun, 1938, 11 January: 8.
Des Moines Register, 1938, 17 August: 4.
St. Cloud Times, 1938, 14 December: 4.
The Baltimore Sun, 1939, 24 June: 1.
The Cincinnati Enquirer, 1939, 24 June: 22.
The Herald-Press, 1939, 24 June: 6.
The Miami News, 1939, 24 June: 5.
The Wilkes-Barre Road, 1939, 24 June: 2.
The Abilene Reporter-News, 1939, 25 June: 21.
Arizona Daily Star, 1939, 25 June: 7.
The Daily Argus-Leader, 1939, 25 June: 9.

Index

1905 revolution 4, 6, 127

Academic Theatres 108
Academy of Performing Arts (Prague) 93
Adashev, Alexander 175
Adler, Stella 74
Agit-Trials 112, 122, 202
Aikhenvald, Yury 42
Akhmatova, Anna 174
Alekseev Circle 82
Alexander II 8
Alexandrinsky Theatre 15, 146
Alpers, Boris 141
amateur theatre 23, 40, 46, 71, 77, 83, 89, 97–134, 171, 174, 184, 187, 190, 200, 201, 202
amateur-professional relationships 98, 104, 115, 126
Ancient Theatre 145
Annenkov, P. V. 6
Annensky, Innokenty 178
Antoine, André 36, 54, 206
Apollinaire, Guillaume 158
Appia, Adolphe 2, 136, 164
archives 107, 138–9, 204
Armand, Inessa 172
Artaud, Antonin 2, 60, 136
attitudes 123, 176–7, 187, 191
authorial realism 9–11
avant-garde 3–4, 16, 17, 183, 191, 194, 195

Babanova, Maria 175
The Baltimore Sun 161
Barba, Eugenio 116, 144
Barnay, Ludwig 22, 34–41, 61, 171, 196
Baty, Gaston 157
Bekhterev, V. M. 182, 184, 186

Benjamin, Walter 181, 182, 186; 'Naples' 181
Berger, Henning 59
Besnard, Lucien 31–2, 34
Birman, Serafima 175–7, 206–7
Blok, Alexander 43, 47
Blue Blouse 100, 101, 182
Bogdanov, Alexander 4, 66, 109, 110, 118, 194
Boleslavsky, Richard 30, 70, 73, 164
Bolsheviks 9, 68, 70, 172, 198
Bolshoi Theatre 51, 108
Borodin Studio 23, 147, 148–54, 194, 205; *Love of Three Oranges: The Journal of Doctor Dapertutto* 150, 152
boulevard drama 14
bourgeois theatre 108, 118, 186, 202
Braun, Edward 137, 183
Brecht, Bertolt 2, 141, 181, 182, 204, 208
Brenko, Anna 175
Broadway 165
Brook, Peter 60–1, 65
The Brooklyn Daily Eagle 164
Bryusov, Valery 12
Bulgakov, Mikhail 166

Calderón 1, 143, 148; *Adoration of the Cross* 143
Camilleri, Frank 150, 153
canons 1, 14, 24, 64, 171
Cartel de Quatres 157–8
Carter, H. 99, 106, 111, 115, 119
censorship 137, 161, 166, 189, 195
Chaliapin, Feodor 68
Chekhov, Anton 8, 15; *The Cherry Orchard* 59; *Three Sisters* 55, 59, 197; *Uncle Vania* 55

Chekhov, Mikhail 25, 30, 194, 196, 199, 200
Chinese theatre 143, 205
Civil War 6, 33, 99, 111–12, 119, 132, 134, 172
clowning 66, 169, 195
clubs 16, 22, 98, 100, 102, 121, 130
collective authorship 109, 118
collective creation 43, 44, 46, 74–80, 89, 97, 109, 112, 114–15, 117, 118–25, 184, 185
Comédie Française 31, 32
comedy 14, 43, 44, 141, 163, 195, 206
commedia dell'arte 18, 45, 119–20, 143, 145, 147, 149, 152, 165
composition 10, 32, 44–5, 55, 57, 115–16, 127, 129–30, 133, 134, 140, 142, 145, 146, 147, 150, 157
constructivism 21, 135, 141, 179, 206
contextualization 31, 154–5, 160, 199
continuity 1–14, 15, 21, 151, 194
conventionalism 12, 16, 21, 156, 162
Copeau, Jacques 2, 53, 54, 59, 65, 136; Vieux-Colombier School 153
The Courier 163
Crimean War 8
critical processing 113–18, 120, 127
crowd/mass scenes/performances 7, 39–41, 49, 76, 84, 103, 115, 117, 120, 126–9, 159, 176–7, 183, 189, 202
Cubo-Futurism 177
cultural memory 32, 137, 138
cultural transmission 17–21, 30, 55, 63–6, 74, 78, 89, 135, 208; transmission belts 19–20, 91, 175; transmission bias 20, 23, 78, 135–9, 143, 145, 149, 151, 155, 157, 158, 163, 167, 182, 191, 192, 204; transmission clusters 21, 107

Daily Argus-Leader 161, 166
Daumier, Honoré 146
Davidson, Pamela 88
Dayton Daily News Magazine 164–5

de Certeau, Michel 130–2, 189, 197
de Filippo, Eduardo 54
de Vega, Lope 1
Défini, J. 158, 166
Deikun, Lidia 177, 207; *The Women (Baby)* 177, 207
Demidov, Nikolai 30, 108
Democratic Levelling 22, 34, 41–7, 81, 178–9
Department of Theatre Studies (University of Malta) 93
Des Moines Register 163
Deuel, Norman B. 163
devised theatre 42, 79, 85, 118, 120, 167
Dewey, John 185
diaries 2, 23, 35, 66–74
Dickens, Charles 59
director-auteur 11
Distorting Mirror Theatre 16
Doctor of His Own Honour 148
documentation 2, 17, 35, 37, 137, 192, 201
Dostoevsky, Fyodor 33, 70, 182, 187; *The Village of Stepanchikovo* 33, 70–1
Duchamp, Marcel 177
Dullin, Charles 58, 157
Duncan, Isadora 53, 208

Eisenstein, Sergei 3, 25, 111, 178, 182, 200
Elagin, Yury 137
embodiment 120, 123, 152, 181
Enlightenment 3
ensemble 15, 46, 78, 95, 149, 153, 183, 184, 204
Ervine, St John 163, 166, 206
ethics 1, 8, 11, 55–6, 59–60, 103, 144, 145, 147, 192, 197
eurhythmics 22, 53, 121
everyday life 4, 9, 19, 21, 23, 44, 47, 50, 60, 67, 81–3, 88, 91, 99, 103, 109, 118–25, 130, 132, 141, 142,

167, 172, 174, 177, 187, 191, 201, 203, 204
Evreinov, Nikolai 7, 42, 145; *The Storming of the Winter Palace* 7
experimentation 3, 5, 13, 14, 15, 42, 171, 173, 184, 192
Exter, Alexandra 174, 175, 177–9, 207

February Revolution 6, 33, 68, 115
Fedotova, Glikeriya 175
feudalism 3
First Studio 22, 31, 41–7, 56, 58, 59, 60, 61, 64, 66, 69, 71–3, 76, 81, 123, 151, 153, 177, 178, 184, 196, 198, 199, 207
First World War 6, 23, 58, 68, 136, 201
Five Year Plan 112, 166
Ford, Henri 114
formalism 147, 162
French theatre 1, 14, 32, 57, 143, 157–9, 161, 165, 195
futurism 58, 135

Gagné, Robert M. 19, 123
The Gazette 162
Gémier, Firmin 161
Gering, Marlon 165–6
Giatsintova, Sofia 177, 207: *The Women (Baby)* 177, 207
Gielgud, John 54
Gippius, Zinaida 174, 175
Glaviskusstvo 154
globalization 53, 154
Gogol, Nikolai 5, 6, 7, 10, 14, 15, 61, 143, 157, 159, 187, 194, 206; *The Government Inspector* 6, 12, 141, 142, 154, 157, 159, 162, 167–9, 183, 194, 197, 206
Golden Age 4, 14
Golovin, Alexander 146, 183
Goncharova, Natalia 174, 175
Gorchakov, Nikolai 111, 204
Gorky, Maxim 7, 43–6, 61–2, 76; *The Lower Depths* 7, 55

Gorn 69, 126
Gourfinkel, Nina 134
Gozzi, Carlo 147; *Love of Three Oranges* 147, 150, 152
Granowsky, Alexis 157
Granville Barker, Harley 36, 59–61, 198
Great Terror 112
Greek tragedy 145
Green, William 110
Grigulis, Arvīds 181
Grotowski, Jerzy 60–1, 65, 145
Group Theatre 165
The Guardian 161, 163
Guro, Elena 174

Habima 57
Hamsun, Knut 59
The Hartford Daily Courant 163, 166
Heijermans, Herman 59
hierarchies 32, 41–2, 64–5, 114, 174
Higher Art and Technical Studios (VKhUTEMAS) 179
historiography 23, 24, 63–4, 98, 105–13, 181, 199
Huppert, Hugo 182
hybridity 12, 22, 66, 78, 98, 104, 115, 126, 171, 191

Ibsen, Henrik 59
Ignatov, S. S. 45, 196
Ilic, Melanie 171–2
Ilinsky, Igor 155–7, 205
imagination 12, 31, 42, 45, 56, 80, 81, 99, 127, 128, 133, 147, 149, 164, 183, 187
Imperial Theatres 15, 108, 146, 164, 183
imperialism 154
impressionism 58
improvisation 7, 22, 42–6, 49, 50, 61–2, 73, 79, 80–3, 84, 88, 89, 97, 119–20, 127, 132, 134, 149, 152, 167–8, 178, 186–8, 191, 196
independent action 118–19

Industrial Revolution 3
informal training 175–7, 182, 183, 187
intelligentsia 6, 68, 110
Interlude House 16, 143, 147
International Futurist Exhibition 177
internationalism 53–61, 154, 160–7
Iskusstvo V Rabochem Klube (Art at the Workers' Clubs) 98, 119, 112, 121
Ivanov, Vyacheslav 7, 88, 145; Tower Theatre 143

Jacques-Dalcroze, Emile 53
Japanese theatre 142, 146, 147, 165; *kurago* 146–7
Jarry, Alfred 136: *Ubu Roi* 136, 138, 203
Jouvet, Louis 157, 158, 161

Kalinin, Fedor 110
Kerzhentsev, Platon 7, 22, 66, 76–8, 80, 89, 97–8, 102–3, 105–10, 112, 113, 115–21, 124, 127–8, 129, 132, 162, 185–6, 188, 194, 199, 200, 201, 202, 203; 'An Alien Theatre' 162; *Revoliutsiia i teatr (Revolution and Theatre)* 112; *Tvorchesky Teatr (The Creative Theatre)* 22, 97, 112, 119, 127, 200, 201
Knipper, Olga 60, 74
Kollontai, Aleksandra 172–3
Komissarzhevskaya, Vera 175, 200
Komissarzhevsky, Fyodor 5, 6, 42, 182–3, 184, 194, 199
Komsomol 109
Komsomol Theatre 177
Koonen, Alisa 179
Korčák, Jakub 93
Korenev, Mikhail 138
Korsh Theatre 16
Kristi, G. V. 49
Kvapil, Jaroslav 29, 55, 56, 197

La Scala 164
Laban, Rudolph 2
laboratory 18, 23, 119, 124, 150, 151–2, 178, 179, 199
Lācis, Asja 24, 152, 169–70, 172, 180–90
LAMDA 60
Lan-Fang, Mei 54, 56
le Brun, Charles 18
League of Nations 57
Lebedev-Poliansky, Pavel 110, 113
Lee Parmalee, Patty 172
Lefebvre, Henri 67, 124–5
Left Front of the Arts 103
Lehmann, Hans 120
Lenin, Vladimir 4, 13, 103, 108, 109, 111, 122, 173, 179, 201
Leningrad Theatre of Working-Class Youth (TRAM) 174
Leonidov, Leonid 51, 175
Liasu, Jean-Pierre 158
Lindh, Ingemar 150
literature 42, 106, 111, 117, 121, 122, 124, 129, 172, 183, 202
Litovtseva, Nina 48, 49
Living Newspaper 112, 122, 202
Lord, Jon 90
Lucia di Lammermoor 164
Lunacharsky, Anatoly 4–5, 6, 9, 102, 108, 115, 126, 182, 198
Lvov, Nikolai 99

Maeterlinck, Maurice 36, 59; *The Blue Bird* 36, 59, 175; *Sister Beatrice* 153
Malaev-Babel, Andrei 108
Malevich, Kazimir 3
manifestos 4, 21, 85, 101, 110
Markov, Pavel 43, 99
Maxwell, Ian 54
Mayakovsky, Vladimir 3
mechanical theatre 166
medieval theatre 145, 183
Meinengen theatre 36, 40

melodrama 44, 66
Merlin, Bella 25, 46, 85, 196
Meyerhold, Vsevolod 1–2, 3, 5, 6, 7, 9, 11–14, 21, 23, 24, 30, 42, 45, 66, 117, 135–70, 171, 174, 178, 179–80, 181, 182, 183, 184, 187, 188, 194, 196, 197, 200, 204, 205–6, 207; *Alinur* 187; Biomechanics 21, 35, 121, 138, 146, 148, 153, 169, 179, 206; *Columbine's Scarf* 147; *Don Juan* 141, 146, 147; *Earth Rampant* 141, 179; grotesque 23, 49, 135, 140–3, 147, 151, 152, 169, 189, 204; *Meyerhold on Theatre* 164; Meyerhold Theatre 154–5, 158, 163; *Mystery-Bouffe* 147; *Roar China!* 154
Mgebrov, Alexander 120, 200
mise-en-scène 11, 12, 35, 40, 51, 84, 118, 129, 142, 164, 179, 186, 197
modern theatre 1–5, 11, 17, 21, 24, 25, 34, 35, 36, 64, 65, 66, 144, 180, 190–2, 194, 203
modernism 2–4, 11, 12, 14, 15, 16–17, 21, 24, 35, 42, 53, 60–1, 63, 64–5, 66, 107, 110, 135, 136, 137, 143, 145, 149, 153, 158, 160, 163, 164, 171, 181, 182, 185, 191, 192, 203, 208; bad modernism 64; High Modernism 136
modernity 2–3, 136
Molière 1, 31, 32, 47, 59
Molotov, Vyacheslav 108
monodrama 7, 175, 176
Montessori, Maria 185
moral dimension of theatre 5, 7–9, 10, 21, 53, 67, 99, 103, 150, 184, 186
Morozov, Savva 104
Moscow 24, 33, 36, 38, 41, 53, 54, 58, 59, 60, 61, 69, 104, 107, 110, 155, 157, 158, 161, 166, 177, 178, 179, 183, 189, 200, 205, 207
Moscow Art Theatre 5, 17, 22, 29, 31, 33, 34, 41, 43, 53, 59, 64, 65, 66, 69, 70, 73, 129, 157, 164, 175, 176, 177, 183, 195, 205, 207, 208
Moskvin, Ivan 51
Mounet, Jean-Sully 32
musical theatre 66
myths 135–9, 181, 203

Napoleonic Wars 8
Narkompros 9, 72
narodnost' 8
nationalism 1
naturalism 10, 42, 127, 135, 142, 178, 195
Nemirovich-Danchenko, Vladimir 6, 15, 31, 33, 41–2, 45, 196
networking 181–2, 208
New Economic Policy 6, 112, 201
New Soviet Woman 173–4
New York Tribune 164
newspapers 24, 36, 69, 98, 134, 139, 155–6, 160–67, 171, 202
Nicholas II 6, 38
Nietzsche, Friedrich 182
non-representational 164

observation 10, 44, 182, 183, 186–7, 188
October Revolution 4, 6, 33, 69, 70, 73, 100, 103, 112, 127, 136, 183
operetta 159, 163
Orel 184, 185, 188
organic development 55, 114
Ostrovsky, Alexander 5, 7, 12, 13, 14, 15, 22, 34, 61, 171, 194; *Artists and Admirers* 22, 34, 47–53, 61, 68, 171, 197; *The Forest* 12, 13, 154, 156, 158, 195; 'Return to Ostrovsky' policy 6, 12
The Ottawa Journal 165
Ozerov, Vladislav 16

Paegle, Leon 189
Panferov, E. 181
pantomime 12, 144, 168–9, 206
People's University (Riga) 188

performance studies 34, 172
periodization 23, 98, 110–12, 129, 196
photography 22, 25, 34, 35–8, 53, 127
physical education 121, 122, 123
physical theatre 141, 149
Picasso, Pablo 177
Pierre Corneille 159
Pinero, Arthur Wing 183
Pink Floyd 90
Piscator, Erwin 53, 182
Pisemsky, Aleksei 8, 10; *A Bitter Fate* 10
Pitches, Jonathan 25, 140, 183, 195, 205
Pitoëff, Georges 157, 206
Plavilshchikov, Pyotr 8
Players' Rest 16
Pletnev, Valerian 66, 105, 110, 113–14, 121
Popova, Liubov 174, 175, 179–80, 207
popular theatre 145, 153
Possard, Ernst 56
post-dramatic theatre 42
Postlewait, Thomas 106, 138, 159, 203
postmodernism 17
Practice as Research 23, 136, 139, 148–54, 205
Prana 56
Pravda 161–62
proletarian culture 4, 13, 18, 66, 77, 103, 109, 114, 115, 118, 124, 185, 200
proletarian theatre 23, 97–8, 106–7, 108, 109, 111, 113, 114–15, 116, 118, 120, 123, 124, 125–30, 130, 132, 171, 200, 201, 202
proletariat 4, 69, 103, 106, 108, 109, 114, 117, 120, 121, 126, 133, 202
Proletkult 4, 9, 22, 23, 64, 69, 73, 77, 98, 100, 101, 103–4, 106, 107, 109–11, 113–15, 119, 120, 124, 126, 200, 202

proscenium 9, 146, 179, 183
Provisional Government 68
psychological realism 157

Radlov, Sergei 152
Raikh, Zinaida 161, 162
Ravel, Maurice 90
realism 5, 9–10, 12, 15, 16, 17, 54, 58, 96, 142, 157, 164, 173, 195, 204
receivers 18, 20, 23, 41, 55, 57, 89, 94, 151, 155, 182, 191, 193
Recher, Johannes B. 182
reconstruction 23, 45, 98, 107, 138, 142, 145, 147, 195, 205
recurrence and difference 58, 139–43, 190
Red Army 99, 115, 119, 130, 141, 147
Redgrave, Michael 55
Rehearsal Transmission 22, 34, 47–53, 171
Reich, Bernhard 182
repertoire 1–2, 44, 45, 46, 59, 71, 99, 100, 106, 116, 119, 132, 157, 184, 189, 194, 195, 196
retrospectivism 7
Richards, Thomas 145
Rouveyre, André 158
Rozanova, Olga 174
Russian theatre tradition 2, 3, 5–17, 21, 22, 23, 29, 61, 99, 179, 191

Sadovsky, Mikhail 140
Sadovsky, Prov 15
Salon des Indépendants 177
Saltykov-Shchedrin, Mikhail 10
Salvini, Tommaso 51
samodeiatel'nost' (do-it-yourself) 105, 189–90, 200
Savina, Maria 175
Scenic Transmission 22, 34, 34–41, 55, 171
Schechner, Richard 116
Schleef, Einar 120–1
School of Performing Arts (University of Malta) 93, 199

Schulz, Vladimir 39
Second Moscow Art Theatre 69, 177
Second Studio 59, 198, 199
Second World War 3, 55
selection/selectivity 10, 21, 57, 139, 142, 144, 145, 147, 191
Selvinsky, Ilya 141, 166
Senelick, Laurence 6, 8, 31, 40, 74, 137, 177
Shakespeare, William 13, 32, 159; *Hamlet* 31, 32, 38, 59, 151, 196, 208; *Othello* 31, 38, 51, 100, 196; *Twelfth Night* 71, 199
Shchepkin, Mikhail 5–6, 7, 10, 11, 14, 15, 61, 194
Sheldon, Edward 165
Silver Age 4, 8, 9, 11, 12, 14, 15, 175
skills 10, 18–19, 23, 25, 27, 77, 104, 122, 123, 124, 125, 133, 185, 187, 188, 191, 192, 198
Smirnova, Alexandra 151, 205
Smyshlaev, Valentin 30, 46, 63–96, 115, 120, 184, 187, 198, 199, 200, 202; feelings of memories 87–8; method of today 84, 128–9; moods 87, 197; score 19, 85–6, 142; second day performance 80
socialist realism 9, 15, 16, 204
Society of Arts and Literature 38, 129
Society of Literature and Art Theatre 16
Sokolovskaya, N. A. 52
Sologub, Fyodor 183
Solovyov, Vladimir 145, 151
South as a State of Mind 180
Spanish theatre 144
spatial dynamics 144, 149, 169–70, 179, 103
St Petersburg Academy of Theatre Arts 142
St Petersburg/Petrograd/Leningrad 16, 24, 68, 104, 110, 120, 142, 167, 169, 182, 187, 195, 200

St. Cloud Times 163
stage movement 40, 152, 178
Stalin, Josef 112, 137, 204
Stanislavsky acting tradition 29, 31, 34, 46, 53–61, 68, 87, 142
Stanislavsky, Konstantin 2, 3, 5–6, 7, 10, 11, 15, 19, 21, 22, 24, 25, 29–62, 64, 65, 68, 70–3, 74–80, 81, 82–3, 85, 87, 89, 100, 126, 128, 129, 136, 142, 154, 163, 164, 171, 175, 178, 187, 194, 195, 197, 199, 208; *An Actor Prepares* 55; *Armoured Train* 14–69, 59; *Days of the Turbins* 59; *The Polish Jew* 37; *A Month in the Country* 51, 74; *A Practical Man* 82; *Tsar Fiodor* 55, 129; *Uriel Acosta* 22, 37–41, 129, 196
Stanislavsky's System 6, 20, 21, 29, 31, 33, 35, 41, 43, 45, 46, 56, 73, 76, 78, 89, 115, 128, 142, 164, 165, 171, 195, 199, 207; Active Analysis 46–7, 80–1, 196, 197; affective memory 87, 199; bits and tasks 75, 79, 81, 84, 85, 87, 128; communication/communion 51, 56, 80, 89, 166; concentration 45, 56, 89, 128; given circumstances 47, 49–50, 81, 82, 199; here, today, now 51, 52; inner images 49; laws of nature 47, 49–50, 81, 82, 199; magic 'if' 56, 148, 149; public solitude 73; relaxation of muscles 56; Round-the-Table 80, 82 tempo-rhythm 56, 85; through-line 49, 51, 84
State Motion Picture of Sovkino 166
Steffin, Margarete 181
Stein, Gertrude 177
Stepanova, Varvara 174, 175, 207
Strasberg, Lee 74
street theatre 66, 102
Strindberg, August 59
stylization 11, 17, 58, 96, 142

Sulerzhitsky, Leopold 43, 45, 46, 59, 71, 76, 123, 175, 196
The Sunday Citizen 161, 163
The Sydney Morning Herald 160
symbolism 15, 21, 135
synthetic theatre 21, 78

tacit knowledge 19–20, 35
Tairov, Alexander 5, 11, 157, 174, 178, 207; *Famira Kifored* 178, 207
Talma, Francois-Joseph 32
Tarasova, Alla 50, 52, 175, 197
Tatlin, Vladimir 3
Theatre Anthropology 144
theatre epidemic 99, 104, 106
theatre studies 108, 172
Theatre Studio 137
theatrical text 79, 125, 126
theatricality 11, 12, 97–195, 143, 144, 167–8, 199
Toller, Ernst 182
Tonal-Plastic Department 115
Toporkov, Vasili 47, 197
touring 23–4, 29, 34, 36, 38, 39–40, 53, 55, 57, 59, 70, 139, 154, 154–60, 157, 158, 162, 166, 171, 176, 196, 197, 205, 206
Trade Unions Theatre 177
tradition building 1–2, 14–17, 24, 29, 31, 33–4, 190
transmitters 18, 20–1, 41, 49, 66, 135, 151, 155, 182, 192, 193
Tretyakov, Sergei 111, 182, 200
Trotsky, Leon 122, 173
Tsvetaeva, Maria 174, 175
tyranny of distance 54, 166

Udaltsova, Nadezhda 174
Unified Studio of the Arts 23, 98, 121–5

Union of Soviet Writers 15
Union of the Youth of the Third International 73
University of Malta 93, 149, 199
Uraneff, Vadim 164–5; *Musk* 164; *The Show Booth* 165
uslovnost' 11

Vakhtangov, Yevgeny 5, 6, 11, 73, 182, 196, 205; *Turandot* 11
Vasiliev, Anatoly 30
vaudeville 142, 163
Verbitsky, V. A. 51, 52
Verhaeren, Émile: *Insurrection* 23, 77, 90, 125–30, 202; *The Dawn* 117, 128, 166
Vilar, Jean 54, 197
Vinogradov, Nikolai 115; Theatrical-Dramaturgical Studio of the Red Army 115
voice 12, 70, 89, 121, 122, 149

Warburg Institute 74
Warden, Claire 183
Weimar Republic 182
Wilde, Oscar 187
Williams, Raymond 113
women issue 171–4
worker-peasant theatre 105
Wreck of the Ship 'Hope' 71, 72
Wysocka, Stanislawa 31

Yale School of Drama 142
yoga 56

Zelinsky, F. F. 144–5, 204
Zhenotdel (Women's Department) 172
Zon, B. V. 49, 51, 197

www.ingramcontent.com/pod-product-compliance
Lightning Source LLC
Chambersburg PA
CBHW072108010526
44111CB00037B/2032